Breaking Broken English

Critical Arab American Studies
Carol W. N. Fadda, *Series Editor*

CRITICAL ARAB AMERICAN STUDIES

Syracuse University Press is pleased to announce the launch of a new series, Critical Arab American Studies, with the publication of *Breaking Broken English: Black-Arab Literary Solidarities and the Politics of Language* by Michelle Hartman. This new series features cutting-edge scholarship that adopts interdisciplinary, intersectional, feminist, transnational, and comparative frameworks of inquiry to develop the study of Arab Americans across various fields of research, including history, gender and sexuality studies, critical race and ethnic studies, anthropology, literature, film and media studies, and sociology, among others.

Breaking Broken English

Black-Arab Literary Solidarities and the Politics of Language

Michelle Hartman

Syracuse University Press

Copyright © 2019 by Syracuse University Press
Syracuse, New York 13244-5290

First Edition 2019

19   20   21   22   23   24   6   5   4   3   2   1

∞ The paper used in this publication meets the minimum requirements
of the American National Standard for Information Sciences—Permanence
of Paper for Printed Library Materials, ANSI Z39.48-1992.

For a listing of books published and distributed by Syracuse University Press,
visit www.SyracuseUniversityPress.syr.edu.

ISBN: 978-0-8156-3620-5 (hardcover)
     978-0-8156-3638-0 (paperback)
     978-0-8156-5466-7 (e-book)

Library of Congress Cataloging-in-Publication Data

Names: Hartman, Michelle, author.
Title: Breaking broken English : Black-Arab literary solidarities and the politics
     of language / Michelle Hartman.
Description: First edition. | Syracuse : Syracuse University Press, 2019. | Series: Critical
     Arab American studies | Includes bibliographical references and index.
Identifiers: LCCN 2018060874 (print) | LCCN 2019004416 (ebook) |
     ISBN 9780815654667 (E-book) | ISBN 9780815636205 (hardcover : alk. paper) |
     ISBN 9780815636380 (pbk. : alk. paper)
Subjects: LCSH: American literature—Arab American authors—History and criticism. |
     American literature—African American authors—History and criticism |
     African Americans—Languages. | Politics in literature. | African Americans
     in literature. | Ethnic relations in literature. | Social movements—United States.
Classification: LCC PS153.A73 (ebook) | LCC PS153.A73 H36 2019 (print) |
     DDC 810.9/8927—dc23
LC record available at https://lccn.loc.gov/2018060874

Manufactured in the United States of America

For a free Palestine

Contents

Preface

Breaking Broken English

Though forty years later, I still recall clearly the words and spirit of one of my elementary school teachers chastising a classroom full of students in 1979. Looking directly at a Black student in class, this white teacher said, if not verbatim, words that I approximate as: "'I aint got none' is not an acceptable answer. It is not correct English. Aint is not a word. If you 'aint got none,' it means you gotta have some. This is called a double negative. In English, it is wrong to use a double negative. When you say a word twice it is redundant. In math, if you use a double negative it makes a positive. We do not say this in English. It is wrong."

This little speech is an invented recollection of a strong childhood memory from 1979. Some of the students in my class, like me, were white and spoke the English he valued and praised at home. Others, mostly Black and poor, did not. I remember this teacher schooling us, repeatedly, on how English does not use the "double negative." Day after day, he drilled into us how it was illogical and also how it was simply wrong. Willfully ignorant of the fact that it is a commonly used grammatical feature of the home language of many of the children in his classroom, this teacher again and again chastised and mocked those who used it, implicitly praising those who did not.[1] As I read the material that would later help form the theoretical backbone of this book, this memory became all the more clear and poignant. One article included a quotation from a Black student from my elementary school, who reported a similar incident, possibly from the same classroom, likely by the same teacher, and most certainly telling a similar story, "That teacher, he too mean. He be hollin at us and stuff."[2]

As a child in the classroom, I was only partly aware that our school—Martin Luther King Jr. Elementary School in Ann Arbor, Michigan—was at the epicenter of the fierce debates over language and cultural politics in the United States in the 1970s. Renowned linguist and advocate for Black Language, Geneva Smitherman, quoted my schoolmate as the epigraph to an essay she wrote recalling and analyzing the events that became the most famous court case defending Black Language rights in the United States: *Martin Luther King Junior Elementary School Children v. Ann Arbor School District Board*. The children won in a decision issued by Charles W. Joiner, which has been cited as the first test of the applicability of 1703(f), the language provision of the 1974 Equal Educational Opportunity Act, to Black English speakers.[3] This case was one of the many moments in the 1970s when Black Americans publicly reclaimed the value of their spoken language and demanded to be heard.

Though I was not aware of the contours of the language debates as a child, I was well aware of the cultural project of Black pride and power. Our elementary school in the 1970s was one that ushered in an era of desegregation, understood by some as an experiment in schooling Black and white children together. Some of my most powerful memories of school are of teachers with Afros singing gospel songs in the gymnasium on Martin Luther King Jr.'s birthday. The entire school day was devoted to studying King and his message; we all marched from our classrooms into the gym singing "We Shall Overcome." I remember student-teacher duets of "Ebony and Ivory" and soulful renditions of "Abraham, Martin and John" that had our teachers in tears. Amid these powerful expressions of Black American culture, we all were taught subtly and more explicitly, that some of our classmates—all of whom were Black—did not speak correctly. A number of the teachers at school regularly punished, chastised, and corrected my classmates until they conformed and spoke in a way that the teachers believed English should sound like.

We all became aware that we were part of something bigger and more controversial as the television cameras descended upon the school in 1979. The school community learned that a number of parents of students in our school had sued and won the right for their children to be taught in "Black English."[4] Reading Geneva Smitherman's account of this case years later, I learned that not only were numerous academic articles written and conferences held about the case, but that the hysteria around it led to more than three hundred newspaper articles being written about it. Many of these made international news, among the camera-toting visitors to our school were crews from the BBC.[5] But I did not need to read her account to remember teachers carrying around books on Black English that they were meant to study. I now know that this was required reading mandated by the court to teach the teachers the value of their students' language and culture.[6]

My interest in language and the politics of language use can, no doubt, be traced back to these experiences and growing up in the contested and loaded political environment of the 1970s United States. Moreover, I am a parent today raising my own child in another environment where the politics of language is equally, but differently, contested and loaded: twenty-first-century Montreal. Raising a Black son between Arabic, English, and French in Quebec, I am faced daily with reminders of what my classmates and so many others faced before us. I find the victory of the parents of my classmates in expressing their anger at profoundly racist and classist mistreatment in school all the more inspiring. The impetus for writing this book was partly an attempt to understand and make sense of the daily, real-life, political struggles we face in our most private and personal expression—our language. It also draws upon the intellectual work and theorization being done in the 1970s by Black American intellectuals, theorists, poets, and writers to think about how language and literary expression engage each other and are linked to politics. *Breaking Broken English* is inspired and informed by this theoretical and political framework and uses it in order to understand literary connections between African and Arab Americans.

A literary study, this book identifies a corpus of literary works by Arab and Arab American poets and writers and explores them in relation to thematic, literary, and linguistic connections to African American language, literature, history, and politics. Believing literary works to be powerful locations of linguistic, creative, and political expression, my project in *Breaking Broken English* is to think about how language on the surface read as "broken English" works in fiction and poetry in creative ways. Drawing on theoretical and intellectual interventions by Black American writers, this book builds a framework for understanding what is sometimes defined as "broken" instead as "breaking." I investigate how such breaking language manifests other kinds of breaks by identifying the linked political and aesthetic possibilities of such breaking in Arab American fiction and reading this with reference to Black American theoretical and literary works.

Informed by the politics of language outlined above, this study seeks out ways to think about how multiple linguistic resources can be a part of new imaginings of our literary and political futures. At the time when I was finishing writing this book in Montreal, North America was continuing to witness urgent and pressing crises: the continued police murder of Black and Indigenous people in Turtle Island (North America), mass incarceration, state repression of dissent, and rising racism against Muslims and Arabs, connected—and at times one and the same—to the targeting of Black and Indigenous people. This is never separate from the ongoing wars and military occupation of Syria and Iraq, the continued, relentless colonization of Palestine and repression of Palestinian people, and new and historical refugee crises that connect powerfully to both of these, feeding off of and powering capitalist exploitation. Part of the project of *Breaking Broken English* is to look back at the politics of the 1970s and the solidarities built between people and communities to reclaim these histories.

The long history of solidarity between Black American and Arab/Arab American—particularly Palestinian—communities is one part of this story. *Breaking Broken English* begins by remembering this solidarity, as part of a retelling of history—a looking back to look forward. Recalling the politics of language in the 1970s, remembering the time when Third World liberation was a vibrant concept, people's struggles were understood as urgent and pressing, and how people imagined ways to make better lives is part of what we can look back upon to think about how we want to move forward.

Acknowledgments

This book was made so easy to publish by the able editorship of the new editor of the Critical Arab American Studies series at Syracuse University Press, Carol W. N. Fadda. Her leadership and hard work has made this possible. Syracuse University Press has been a promoter of works in the field; I would like to thank them for this, and the committed editors for their work that makes our research possible. Suzanne Guiod has been a pleasure to work with once again. Thank you to the able copyeditor, Martha Ash, and to Lisa Kuerbis, Fred Wellner, and others at Syracuse who made this book possible.

Like all books that have been in progress over long periods of time, this one owes many debts of gratitude. I first began thinking on these ideas more than two decades ago, and though the final project looks very different from the initial explorations, many of the very early conversations and engagements I have participated in over the years enriched it and made it stronger. The ideas are born of collective work, collective thought, and collective struggle, and I would like to acknowledge that fact and those many people who I worked, shared, and thought about solidarity, activism, and engagement with for years. A few specific people should be singled out from this group. Rashid El Enany and Rabab Abdulhadi introduced me to Radwa Ashour's work, and I will be forever grateful to them. My colleague Magnus Bernhardsson and I worked together when I began this project; we had many discussions about it, and he made possible my first presentation on the research. In that same period in the 1990s, Alessandro Olsaretti and Jaime Veve were friends, companions, and comrades who enriched my thinking greatly. At a somewhat later period, my thought was enriched by conversation and intellectual exchange on Arab American racialization with Sarah Gualtieri, Nadine Naber, and Stephen Sheehi—thanks to you all.

One of my biggest debts, which dates back to the early 1990s, is both political and intellectual. Thanks to Rabab Abdulhadi, who pushed and continues to push my work and thought and political engagement forward. She has been an inspiration in this project. Other friends, colleagues, and comrades who also have thought about, discussed, and helped this book project advance deserve thanks as well: Samia Botmeh, Dana Olwan, and Dima Ayoub. I would like to especially thank rosalind hampton for working and talking with me about so many of the issues in this book and for "manifesting" together in all senses of the word. Your contributions cannot be replaced, and I am grateful.

Many people have helped with specific elements of the book at times. I thank the organizers and attendees of talks I have given on parts of the book in progress at the American University of Beirut, the Lebanese American University, the University of Toronto, Simon Fraser University, Yale University, and Middlebury College. Particular thanks to Dima Ayoub, Jens Hanssen, Nuwar Diab, Nadya Sbeiti, and Sirène Harb for their efforts in arranging these.

The actual book manuscript benefited immensely from the careful and insightful readings of Carol Fadda, Therí Pickens, rosalind hampton, and the anonymous reviewers. Thanks to people who read specific parts including Ira Dworkin, Ebony Coletu, Ghiwa Abihaidar, and my "Radwa Ashour reading group" at McGill: Ralph Haddad, Sara Sebti, Chantelle Schultz, Niyousha Bastani, Maxine Dannat, and Isabelle Oke. I am grateful to Mourid Barghouti and Tamim Barghouti for generously entrusting me with the translation of Radwa Ashour's memoir. I would like to thank Dima Ayoub, Dana Olwan, Carol Fadda, and Waïl Hassan for reading and commenting on my work on Susan Abulhawa. I would also like to thank Anaïs Salamon, Andrea Miller-Nesbit, the McGill Solidarity for Palestinian Human Rights, and my 2015 class on Arabic Literature as World Literature for thinking about *Mornings in Jenin* with me.

Lena Merhej's artwork graces the cover of the book, and I thank her for her generosity of spirit in providing it and for her committed art practice.

During the time this book was completed Sarah Abdelshamy, Heather Porter Abu Deiab, Peiyu Yang, and Katy Kalemkerian were able and helpful research assistants—thank you all. Zeitun Manjothi assisted with some of the book's final preparation for publication, and I am grateful to her for her smiling support.

This book was largely written and completed when I faced serious and difficult challenges in my workplace. That I managed to finish it is due in part to the incredible solidarity and support of several colleagues, without whom it is difficult to imagine surviving that. For this I extend my heartfelt thanks to Adelle Blackett, Rula Jurdi, and Malek Abisaab.

Personal thanks can never be separate from the intellectual—especially when you are surrounded by engaged, active people who care deeply about the issues you are writing about. For space, time, and inspiration, thanks to Aziz Choudry. For hours of discussion and real grown folk talk, I am indebted to rosalind hampton. Yasmine Nachabe Taan and the whole Nachabe, Taan, Fakih, Merhej family have hosted so much of this book's thought and production—*merci kteer*. Thanks to friend and mentor, Elise Salem. Amanda Hartman and Tameem Hartman may not realize how much they helped in getting this book actually finished, but I hope they see themselves and their thought reflected in its pages.

This book is dedicated to a free Palestine and everyone struggling to get free.

Breaking Broken English

Introduction

Breaking Language, Broken English: The Politics and Aesthetics of Literary Solidarities

Black-Arab political and cultural solidarity in the United States has become visible once again today. African American and Arab American activists and cultural workers have joined together with colleagues in the Arab region, especially in Palestine, to address social justice issues including liberation for the Palestinian people and the specific challenges facing Black communities in the United States, including police violence and murder. Some of today's most vibrant social movements in the United States, including Black Lives Matter and the Movement for Black Lives, openly support Palestine.[1] The group Black4Palestine issued a 2015 solidarity statement with over one thousand signatories and continues to support Black and Palestinian liberation, working on education in Black communities in the United States.[2] While this solidarity may look new—especially in its social media version—its histories are much longer. Black4Palestine affirms this by publishing on the website created to promote its 2015 statement, one of its important precursors, signed by more than fifty Black intellectuals in November 1970 and published in the *New York Times* as "An Appeal by Black Americans against United States Support for the Zionist Government of Israel."[3] Penned by the Committee of Black Americans for Truth about the Middle-East, several of the signatories of that original appeal have joined the 2015 statement. This example of anticolonial solidarity is framed as a struggle for national liberation and reclaiming of stolen land. That it was being recirculated in 2015 is meaningful and demonstrates a conscious awareness of today's struggles as part of a continuous and ongoing movement.

Breaking Broken English: Black-Arab Literary Solidarities and the Politics of Language is rooted in the notion that we must look back at the longer life of this solidarity in order to look forward. Reclaiming histories and seeing history as engaged with the present can allow us to think about new creative and political possibilities in the future. Today these connections are beginning to be understood in greater depth and complexity—not only are these links political, religious, and social, but they also have incorporated a wide range of cultural and artistic activities, including expression in literature and poetry. While people have written about the histories of Black-Arab and Arab American community engagement, connections, and solidarity from a number of angles, very little has been written about creative production, especially literary work. A study of Arab American fiction and poetry, *Breaking Broken English* explores the ways in which Black American art, literature, politics, and language are engaged by Arab and Arab American authors and poets. This is not a comparative study of African American and Arab American literature. Rather, this book reads Arab American literary texts in conversation with African American literary and linguistic theory as well as considers how these texts engage the political, cultural, and intellectual debates that inform them.

The chapters below explore the ways in which a selection of Arab American literary texts express connections, bonds, and solidarities with African America/ns thematically. This book's analysis is not limited to such thematic engagements, however. As its title suggests, *Breaking Broken English* is particularly concerned with language and how the English language can be used to express the ideas embedded in these politics. Therefore, the thematics of Black-Arab solidarity are explored through how they are written into the very fabric of the literary texts, in complex ways. *Breaking Broken English* is thus a literary study that brings language together with politics and isolates this nexus as part of larger political and pedagogical solidarity projects. In what follows, I argue that the language/s of literary works—in particular the creative ways we can think about "breaks" in English and where it is represented as "broken"—is/are crucial to works where aesthetics meet politics in creative and challenging ways.

These breaks contribute to the soundscape of literary texts and produce an experience of hearing a text while reading it. The deep thought and engagement of African American writers, poets, and theorists with questions of language—particularly in how they conceive of orality and vernacular languages—is used in this book to build a framework of inquiry into Arab American literary texts and their literary languages, using the concepts of breaking and the break.

Critical Arab American Studies: Solidarity and Praxis

As a scholarly project therefore, *Breaking Broken English* is above all an intervention in critical Arab American studies. I draw upon African American resources that have not previously been engaged in the study of Arab American literature to read these literary works through a framework of Black American intellectual and creative traditions. In particular I work with Black and women-of-color feminist approaches to highlight moments of solidarity, where struggles of different peoples and communities come together, fighting for liberation and moving toward what Black feminist intellectual Audre Lorde articulated as, "moving toward coalition and effective action."[4] The scholarly, political, and pedagogical project of this book is to draw out some of the histories of these communities that have been occluded and therefore are less understood, especially artistic and creative connections. But this study also investigates how the creative works themselves participate in artistic, political, and pedagogical projects that are writing new histories for our future, presenting creative ways for people and communities to imagine the world, looking forward while also looking back.

Critical Arab American Studies, including literary studies, has increasingly connected itself to theoretical and methodological insights of scholars of color through doing comparative work. Arab American literary scholars have advocated for and indeed practice formulating Arab American literary studies in relation to and in dialogue with other communities of color in different ways. Carol Fadda-Conrey's scholarly work, for example, mirrors the production of a number of Arab American poets and authors themselves. Her reading of Diana Abu Jaber's *Crescent* explores the thematic ways in which people of color engage with each other, through analyzing the novel's white-passing, Iraqi-origin protagonist Sirine.[5] As evidenced by her book *Contemporary Arab-American Literature: Transnational Reconfigurations of Citizenship and Belonging*, Fadda-Conrey's scholarly work more generally seeks to place Arab American literary production and analysis in direct engagement and productive conversation with other writers and communities of color in the United States, as well as to maintain and strengthen its transnational connections outside of the United States. She prioritizes the transnational while identifying Arab Americans as people of color in the United States, not simply to "explore the interethnic and cross-racial connections that tie Arab-Americans to the histories and realities of other US ethnicities and races including Latino/as, African-Americans, Native Americans and Asian-Americans."[6] It is also, as Fadda-Conrey explains, to highlight "the ways in which Arab-Americans' transnational connections to Arab homelands, as expressed through cultural venues, produce anti-imperialist and antihegemonic modalities of Arab-American citizenship and belonging that pave the way for more solid connections among various communities of color."[7]

Fadda-Conrey's vision for critical Arab American studies to build and maintain these solid connections in the North American context resonates with, but is engaged substantially differently in, Steven Salaita's intellectual interventions. Having advocated extensively for critical Arab American studies in literary contexts, Salaita's work is also a model for the ways in which scholarly and political projects can enrich each other. His *Arab American Literary Fictions, Cultures, and Politics*, for example, uses ideas developed in Indigenous Studies as ways to challenge the accepted norms and frameworks in Arab American Studies and to advocate for new ones. In his theorizing and advocacy of ways to push Arab American Studies into new directions, Salaita advances a number of challenges. One is his detailed discussion of Arab American racialization and how he works through and challenges the "replacement paradigm" whereby Arab Americans are labeled the "original sand niggers." In this formulation, Arab Americans "replace" African Americans as the most reviled group in the United States, meriting the modified racial slur.[8] Salaita explores some of the peculiarities of anti-Arab racism while critiquing the notion of replacement. He links this problematic paradigm to his challenge of meaningless, empty notions of multiculturalism in advocating for Arab American Studies. His work continually demonstrates how scholarship can engage politics, literary works, and multiple communities simultaneously.

Using frameworks and methods developed within Indigenous Studies, Salaita engages Arab and Arab American fiction with literary works by Indigenous authors from Turtle Island. This work is particularly important in centering the histories and effects of settler colonialism in North America and Palestine in a comparative context. In *Holy Land in Transit: Colonialism and the Quest for Canaan*, Salaita explores a range of texts to draw incisive comparisons between the narratives and discourses of settler colonialism in Turtle Island (specifically here the United States) and Palestine, and how these are connected to the concrete and material dispossession of Indigenous Peoples. His readings then turn to a comparative look at Palestinian and Anishinaabe texts that mount creative resistance to these discourses and practices. This work is an important study engaging multiple communities, as is his newer study, *Inter/nationalism: Decolonizing Native America and Palestine*, which also draws on literary examples of resistance to make its arguments. Importantly, both works—especially *Inter/nationalism*—lay out a critical method and theoretical framework that rely upon Indigenous theorists as well as others to challenge colonialism and to situate settler colonialism in Palestine and Turtle Island as linked and part of the larger, systemic oppression of capitalism. While making comparisons and drawing links, it also critiques simple and overdetermined assumptions about ideas like solidarity between groups. This latter work thus pushes Salaita's comparative paradigm further, nuancing it while advancing the larger political and scholarly project of his work which advocates social change, linking today's urgent political issues—for example, support for the Boycott, Divestment, and Sanctions movement as an Indigenous response to colonialism—to the theoretical questions he engages.

In his focus on Indigenous Studies and literary production, Steven Salaita engages literary and intellectual communities that have rarely been centered in American Studies more broadly or Arab American studies more specifically. *Breaking Broken English* seeks to engage in a similar project, in direct conversation with the only full-length study to date that addresses Arab American-African American literary connections explicitly: Therí Pickens's *New Body Politics: Narrating Arab and Black Identity in the Contemporary United States*. In this insightful monograph, Pickens argues for opening and sustaining a conversation between Arab and African American literatures. Part of her study's stated project is to pair Arab American and African American narratives to construct what she calls "a new cultural history of the two groups in conversation with each other."[9] This is partly a corrective to the ways in which these groups' relationship/s with each other have been represented in the past. Like Salaita, she critiques the replacement paradigm, whereby Arab Americans simply become, as she puts it, "the new Black."[10]

New Body Politics also pushes forward conversations in both fields to reshape what American Studies is and can be. Pickens asks what might happen if Arab American Studies engaged more with African American texts and if African American Studies engaged more with Arab American texts. Her own book, which uses phenomenological methods and concepts like embodiment and disability to put a series of works by Arab and African Americans in conversation, offers suggestions of ways to deepen the understanding of these relationships beyond the clichés and limitations of how they have been looked at previously. *Breaking Broken English* responds to and engages with some of the issues that Pickens lays out incisively in her study. One example of this is how Arab American and African American perspectives and texts can shed light upon each other in ways that enhance the understandings of both—where they are in conflict and where they are not. The Arab American texts I explore in this book invoke and engage African American figures, literature, and language in multiple ways, but this is not always neat, clear, or conflict free. Reading these engagements together with a historical contextualization of individual and community connections lends depth to the analysis.

Responding to Pickens's warning in *New Body Politics*, I would like to emphasize from the outset that *Breaking Broken English* is similarly not an exhaustive list or chronicle of all of these relationships or texts that mention them. I follow the lead here of Pickens, who draws upon the rich scholarly traditions of Black and woman-of-color thinkers to emphasize working together from within difference, rather than from a point of sep-arate identitarian politics.[11] This means my study is not about isolating these two groups or constituting them as different or opposed. Neither study refers to every single work by an Arab American that evinces a con-nection to African Americans or Black America more generally. Many Arab American literary works use characters, themes, and histories that connect to Black American communities and their vast and important creative and literary contributions to American society. Indeed many Arab American works pay homage to histories of political work, aesthetic work, and literary engagement by Black Americans.[12] Nor can or does this book engage all of the very interesting experimentations with language by Arab American writers. Unlike Pickens's *New Body Politics*, moreover, *Breaking Broken English* is not a comparative study. It works with a limited cor-pus of texts by Arab and Arab American poets and writers, each of which engages with themes, issues, and figures in Black America that also offer compelling examples of extensive experimentations with language. It is underpinned by the idea that productively discussing mutual engagement without subsuming difference creates a dialectic. To draw once again on the work of Audre Lorde, we must work together across difference to find the shared creativity that will give us power.[13]

The chapters that follow analyze a number of texts in some detail: poetry by Suheir Hammad, D. H. Melhem, Saladin Ahmed, and Naomi Shihab Nye; Susan Abulhawa's historical novel, *Mornings in Jenin*; Randa Jarrar's novel, *A Map of Home* and short story collection, *Him, Me and Muhammad Ali*; and finally, Radwa Ashour's memoir, *The Journey*. Because my focus is on solidarity and positive connections between com-munities—as well as engaging the question of language, literature, and politics—I have chosen texts that work with these ideas specifically and directly; all of them in one way or another are linked to solidarity and/or activism on behalf of the liberation of Palestine. The works chosen there-fore are analyzed both in relation to their thematic connections to Black America and also the way they use linguistic and literary techniques to "break" the English language, manifesting many other kinds of breaks. All deal with elements of shared and different struggles. Before moving to the chapters that analyze these works, the rest of this introduction is devoted first to outlining solidarity histories between these communities, including a discussion of race and racialization as well as how they have linked struggles, and second, to an exploration of literary solidarities, including a brief overview of their representation in Arab American literary production.

Solidarity Histories: From Ferguson to Palestine Occupation Is a Crime

The year 2014 stands out in the contemporary articulation of Black-Arab solidarity as the "Ferguson-Gaza moment." People beyond radical activist communities and those dedicated to Palestine solidarity work saw Palestinians under siege in Gaza tweeting practical messages to residents of Ferguson, Missouri, about how best to deal with tear gas, while proclaiming their support for an uprising against a militarized police force, which had killed an unarmed member of their community, Michael Brown. The news of these messages and the reciprocal messages sent from African Americans during Israel's relentless war on an already besieged and embargoed Gaza reached mainstream news in the United States and were spread widely over social media.[14] As Kristian Davis Bailey, who has both written on and participated in many of these events, states, "no one could have predicted the actions that pushed Black-Palestinian solidarity into mainstream focus," as chants rang out, declaring the connections between struggles "from Ferguson to Palestine, occupation is a crime."[15]

Drawing from the words of Palestinian scholar and activist Rabab Abdulhadi, herself long implicated in and dedicated to coalition building, Davis Bailey is quick to remind us that such solidarity is possible because of the longer history of connecting anticolonial, antiracist, and anticapitalist revolutionary politics. In an important contribution to a roundtable on Anti-Blackness and Palestinian Solidarity sponsored by the online platform Jadaliyya, Abdulhadi articulates this clearly:

> Black-Palestinian solidarity has had a long and rich history that we can
> trace back to much earlier times than the recent expressions in Ferguson,

Baltimore, Gaza or Nazareth. This includes by Malcolm X, Robert Williams, Black Panthers Party, SNCC, Patrice Lumumba Coalition, the African and Caribbean Resource Center, the December 12th Coalition, and the 1968 Student Strikers at San Francisco State University, to name a few. The same applies to Palestinian solidarity with Black Power movement, including support for Mohammad Ali in his defiance of the US military orders to fight in Vietnam and the letter sent by Palestinian freedom fighters who were incarcerated in Israeli jails to Angela Davis, who was imprisoned at the time in US jails.[16]

I cite from Abdulhadi's contribution at length here because she mentions specific events, groups, and individuals who are not only symbols of this solidarity but who also concretely demonstrated the principles it was based on and what this meant practically. In the same roundtable discussion Robin D. G. Kelley, scholar of the Black radical tradition and supporter of Palestine solidarity work, echoes Abdulhadi and reminds us about some of the pitfalls of thinking in terms of reciprocity rather than resisting injustice as a basis for political action:

> Let us not forget the LONG history of Black radical solidarity with Palestinian liberation going back at least to 1967, with traces emerging as early as 1948, and with Malcolm X in the early 1960s. These examples of solidarity and identification were not based on an expectation of reciprocity—we support your struggle so long as you support ours. Rather, it was based on the principle of resisting injustice everywhere and recognizing that Zionist logic undergirding the founding and management of the state of Israel was based on racialization and colonial domination.[17]

Reflecting on these histories and identifications that were LONG—Kelley capitalizes this to make a point—is important not merely because they are long but also because of what they meant to people. Some of the points underlined by Abdulhadi and Kelley are crucial to the underlying principles of this solidarity, in particular the resistance to colonial domination and oppression of the Black and Palestinian and other Arab peoples.

One key location to see how this solidarity was expressed in two very different historical moments is located in two parallel statements, mentioned in the opening paragraph to this chapter. The first is the 1970 letter by the Committee of Black Americans for Truth about the Middle-East[18] published in the *New York Times*, which was then reprised by the second, the 2015 Black Solidarity with Palestine Statement issued by Black4Palestine. Looking at the two statements together, the continuity in their support for Palestine and profound connections between communities shine through. Their common message is clear. That common message, however, is very much articulated in the language and rhetoric of the time when each was written. Juxtaposing sentences reveals this clearly. Take an example from 1970: "WE STATE that the exploitation experienced by Afro-Americans, Native Americans (Indians), Puerto Ricans, and Chicanos (Mexican-Americans) is similar to the exploitation of Palestinian Arabs and Oriental Jews by the Zionist State of Israel."[19] In 2015, a similar line reads, "While we acknowledge that the apartheid configuration in Israel/Palestine is unique from the United States (and South Africa), we continue to see connections between the situation of Palestinians and Black people."[20] The work being done in these two lines is shared, but it is focused somewhat differently. In 1970, the letter names exploitation directly. This is in line with the tenor and language of the statement more generally, which is concentrated on challenges to oppression, imperialism, and colonialism, with self-determination and revolution offered as the solution. The focus has shifted in 2015. The language of apartheid appears here, but with an immediate qualifier of difference. Though what is shared between Black people and Palestinians can still be rightly called exploitation, the language here is one of "connections" between the communities. The later letter is also more squarely focused on Black people and Palestinians, and though larger, broad-based coalition work is still important in the twenty-first century, it does not appear as prominently in this statement as it did in 1970.

In 1970, the statement in the *New York Times* closes with a paragraph of two sentences, in capital letters and with a demand: "WE DEMAND THAT ALL MILITARY AID OR ASSISTANCE OF ANY KIND TO ISRAEL MUST STOP. IMPERIALISM AND ZIONISM MUST AND WILL GET OUT OF THE MIDDLE EAST. WE CALL FOR AFRO-AMERICAN SOLIDARITY WITH THE PALESTINIAN PEOPLE'S

STRUGGLE FOR NATIONAL LIBERATION AND TO REGAIN ALL OF THEIR STO-
LEN LAND."[21]

This message of solidarity is shared in 2015, where the somewhat longer statement is urgent and pressing, focused on Palestinian resistance and
shared struggle:

> We offer this statement first and foremost to Palestinians, whose suf-
> fering does not go unnoticed and whose resistance and resilience
> under racism and colonialism inspires us. It is to Palestinians, as well
> as the Israeli and US governments, that we declare our commitment
> to working through cultural, economic, and political means to ensure
> Palestinian liberation at the same time as we work towards our own.
> We encourage activists to use this statement to advance solidarity with
> Palestine and we also pressure our own Black political figures to finally
> take action on this issue. As we continue these transnational conversa-
> tions and interactions, we aim to sharpen our practice of joint struggle
> against capitalism, colonialism, imperialism, and the various racisms
> embedded in and around our societies.[22]

Rather than a demand, it offers a commitment. And the commitment is made to people, but in an important shift, also to the "Israeli
and US governments." This is an unmistakable political difference with
the 1970s, which refers clearly to stolen land and the illegitimacy of colonial governing structures. Just as resilience is added to resistance in the
2015 statement, doing very different political work (and different work in
English than *sumoud* does in Arabic), the normalization of the roles of
governments, as well as calling on "Black political figures" to take action,
represents a major shift not only in language but also in politics. The
political language/s of the 1970s, in particular that used in Black American intellectual and political thought as represented here by the statement
of the Committee of Black Americans for Truth about the Middle-East, is
significantly different from what we use in the twenty-first century. I point
to this here to emphasize both continuities and ruptures in the solidarity
work between these two communities and also to point ahead toward my
analysis of similar dynamics in the 2018 translation of Radwa Ashour's *The
Journey*, her memoir of the 1970s, in chapter 5 below.

This comparison of two solidarity statements is just one small example of how language, politics, strategy, and other things shift and change with time, even if many of the larger shared principles do not. Understanding the differences and nuances between earlier work and expressions of Black-Arab/Palestinian solidarity and what is being done today allows us to think about what the longer-term social and political visions being espoused were and are. A number of other historians and activists have excavated the meanings of these bonds of solidarity and connection to people and movements at the time they were active. American historians have actively participated in this project by chronicling some of the complexities of the political and historical links between African Americans and Arabs, dating back into the late nineteenth and early twentieth centuries. For example, Alex Lubin's *Geographies of Liberation: The Making of an Afro-Arab Political Imaginary* traces these histories through different moments in time to propose a genealogy of connections between Arabs and African Americans. This book includes chapters on the Afro-Orient, Black Marxism and Binationalism, the Black Panthers and the Palestine Liberation Organization (PLO), and what he calls the Afro-Arab International. He proposes we look at political and historical events, episodes, and meetings as a way to think about unified political imaginary, which draws together members of these different communities.

One example he gives that is particularly relevant to this study is a discussion of Black American poet June Jordan's travel to Lebanon in 1996, which she has documented in a number of essays and poems. Lubin shows how different this visit was to earlier contexts in which Jordan had visited and written about the region, such as in 1982. Lubin uses Jordan's work as a demonstration of the concept of the political imaginary, which is the centerpiece of his history. He then proposes that her identification with Arabs and Arab causes was "constituted by Jordan's recognition of a shared structure of feeling uniting African Americans and Arabs."[23] Therese Saliba has also drawn attention to this visit to Lebanon in her discussion of June Jordan, placing emphasis on her reaction to the Israeli massacre in Qana, calling its filming, "the Rodney King video of the Middle East."[24] She presents Jordan's visit and her analysis and writing after it as a strong show of solidarity. Lubin also underlines Jordan's solidarity with Arabs, and Palestinians in particular, and connects this work to her earlier poetry and essays.

Lubin ends his study by drawing on June Jordan and several poems that Suheir Hammad wrote in homage to her in order to elucidate the development of this political imaginary into the 1990s and 2000s. He opens the only discussion in his book that uses literary examples, however, with a very different work by Jordan. His epigraph to this final chapter, which focuses on the changes in the Arab-Black shared political imaginary, draws on a line from Jordan's poem that has become iconic for Arab Americans, "Moving towards Home." Dedicated to the victims of the 1982 Sabra and Shatila massacre, Jordan announces: "I was born a Black woman, and now, I am become a Palestinian."[25] On the one hand, bringing these texts together allows Lubin to show continuities in the shared political imaginary that he endeavours to draw out throughout the course of the book. Part of his focus here is on how "Jordan's acts of solidarity with Arabs and Arab Americans emerged in a different context than the one that shaped the 1970s third world leftist solidarity movements forged by the Black Panther Party and the PLO."[26] What follows in the rest of this section draws out some of those differences much as the examples of the solidarity statements by Black American groups with Palestine above show them in language. In the chapters that follow, *Breaking Broken English* attempts to fill in some of what is missing in relation to thinking through literary connections and solidarities, and how different contexts come together in literary works in ways that do not necessarily match—but of course still do engage—historical and political moments.

Similarly to Lubin's study, Keith Feldman's *Shadow over Palestine: The Imperial Life of Race in America* also draws upon literary texts in order to illuminate and deepen his historical analysis. His prologue frames the book with a discussion of the visit of another iconic African American thinker, James Baldwin, to the region. This was not June Jordan in Lebanon in solidarity with the Palestinians, however, but rather an Israeli-sponsored trip beginning in Tel Aviv.[27] Feldman unpacks some of the complications of Baldwin's views: his appreciation of Zionism in creating a homeland for Jewish people and his awareness of the contradictions between this and the dispossession and policing of Arabs in their own land. He also traces the development of Baldwin's thought in this opening sketch, particularly after 1967, of feeling he was himself "an Arab at hands of the Jews" as a Black American. Though this statement was understood at the time by some to be anti-Semitic, Feldman's study uses the development of Baldwin's thought as a lens into some of the ways in which his "imperfect analogy" revealed a useful relational analytic for thinking through race, racism, and American empire.

Unlike Lubin's longer historical span, Feldman's study is limited to the period between the 1960s and 1980s. He investigates what he calls the post–civil rights United States and Israel's post-1967 occupation of Palestinian lands in order to examine how "struggles over hegemony in the United States became entangled with transformed relations of rule in Israel and Palestine, that is when US civil rights and anti-war struggles, Zionist settler colonization and Israeli military and administrative occupation, and Palestinian narratives of dispossession, dispersion, and resistance, were forged, felt, and thought together."[28] The epigraph to Feldman's last substantive chapter draws from the same poem by June Jordan cited by Lubin, "Moving towards Home." His longer citation from the poem is mirrored by a longer discussion of it, and his final chapter is devoted to exploring woman-of-color feminisms in the United States and their engagement with Palestine, race in the United States, and American imperial projects. Some of the projects he highlights include anthologies of writing such as the now classic *This Bridge Called My Back*, its follow-up volume *This Bridge We Call Home*, and the Arab American anthology of feminist writings, *Food for Our Grandmothers*.[29] These are several among many other sites which he uses to explore the ways in which anti-Jewish and anti-Arab racism were expressed and challenged within the feminist movement in the United States and the ways in which white women's racism was mobilized, in particular against Arab and Muslim women. Importantly, Feldman not only focuses on how women-of-color feminists developed bonds of solidarity and gives sustained attention to June Jordan's poetic and political projects, but also how anti-Arab sentiment was linked to support for Zionism and dehumanization of Palestinians in racialized terms. His focus on race and racialization in tracing the contours of the US relationship with Palestine in these two decades is instructive for thinking through some of the complexities of African American-Arab/Arab American literary solidarities into the twenty-first century.

Race and Racialization in the United States

As Lubin's interventions point out, echoing Baldwin's visit, the relations between Arabs/Arab Americans and African Americans are complicated and at times even contradictory. That Lubin and Feldman both emphasize Black and other women of color is not an accident. The solidarity work highlighted in their studies is heavily informed by Black and women-of-color theorists, some mentioned in the paragraph above. The theorizing on solidarity in these feminist circles is among the most important, influential, and nuanced. Keeping an eye on the complex dynamics of inner- and inter-group relations, Audre Lorde's theorization of sisterhood is crucial here. She extensively explores how we must work in roles as women, men, Black people, other people, and that we cannot limit our politics to exclusive categories we identify with. As she puts it on many occasions, we must know the "other sister." One of the contributions and interventions of *Breaking Broken English* is to see difference and solidarity not through the lens of identity politics, but through shared struggle that enriches differences that are generative and not focused on single issues but fight for the liberation of all.[30] This reminds us that we must not look for simple relationships either of uncomplicated solidarity or merely competing for resources when understanding the dynamics of Arab/Arab American and African American relations. These two groups are and have related to each other in a variety of ways, which are neither solely negative and destructive nor solely positive and productive.[31] I have made a conscious decision in developing *Breaking Broken English* to explore and focus on areas of these relationships that are and have been positive and generative. This focus is contextualized within the complications of histories in the US context, as well as how they have been written. For example, Blacks and Arabs/Arab Americans were and are often played against each other in a racist society. Within the racial hierarchy of the United States, they therefore often competed against each other for resources and recognition. In a study of literary solidarities between Arabs/Arab Americans and African Americans, it is crucial to think about their relations in the context of race and racialization in the United States and to consider some of the ways these played out over time and continue to play out today. Drawing upon insights of Audre Lorde and others will help this study point to locations where we can identify sites of shared struggle.

Relationality in the racialized United States context is crucial to understanding the larger conversations about interactions between Blacks/African Americans and Arabs/Arab Americans. Because these two particular groups have in different times and places been pitted against each other, they have frequently been defined against each other relationally in racialized ways. Therí Pickens highlights this pointedly in *New Body Politics*: "As scholars seek to explore race within the United States, they cannot ignore the tension between how Arabs and Blacks have been mutually constituted, at times in opposition to one another."[32] The histories of Arab Americans in the United States, particularly those that focus on early immigrant communities and how they were racialized, is one location in which these tensions have been explored. Over time, the changing US immigration policies and laws, as well as the changing nature of race politics in the United States, meant that Arabs and Arab Americans over time fit differently within the Black-white model of the United States.[33] There is an active and engaged scholarship around race and racialization of Arabs and Arab Americans that has produced important understandings of these dynamics. A study like Sarah Gualtieri's foundational history, *Between Arab and White: Race and Ethnicity in the Early Syrian American Diaspora*, looks closely at relations between Arab American and Black American people and communities in order to think through processes of racialization.[34]

Pickens has usefully summarized and deconstructed the large trends in the ways Arabs/Arab Americans and Africans Americans have been discussed in scholarly work and offered critiques of this. She notes that scholarship looking at these communities in relation to and against each other falls into three historically based, but limited, options: competition, hierarchies of whiteness, or replacement paradigms. In a brief sketch, she outlines the intertwined histories of Arab and African Americans that demonstrate how, during the twentieth century, "the two groups navigated the American racial, cultural, and economic landscape seemingly pitted against each other for resources."[35] Pickens makes an important contribution to the larger field of scholarship on race and racialization of Arab Americans,[36] particularly challenging scholarship that focuses on hierarchies of whiteness as normalized. She states that this focus with "whiteness as a standard and arbiter of national identity deposes both Arab and African Americans from citizenship and repositions them as subordinate to whites within the national narrative."[37] Her critique of the replacement paradigm—the statement that "Arab is the new Black"—is also trenchant, especially in pointing out the flaws in logic that thereby assert Blacks as having progressed within this narrative and pointing out its capitalist underpinnings. Her newer analyses also delve into the ways the racialization of these groups is mutually constitutive and complex across time and contexts.[38]

These are important dynamics that inform my decision in *Breaking Broken English* to try to think about community connections with a different focus and approach. This study consciously examines and engages with the links and bonds that are and have been generative rather than negative and/or destructive. Part of the reason for this shift is to rework the ways in which we study, write, and think about links between the communities. As the scholarship discussed above demonstrates, the difficulties in relationships between Arab and African American communities have been documented and emphasized over time. Sources of conflict—for example, the Arab entrepreneur/Black customer relationship in a number of communities in the United States—are one area of focus.[39] The choice to center this study differently does not mean idealizing or glorifying certain historical moments, events, people, or connections, but rather begins with textual and historical moments where people in these communities have been in contact, worked together, and built together. When there are problems with difference, inequality, and power imbalances, this will be identified and analyzed. The kinds of critiques advanced by Stan West's article, "An Afrocentric Look at the Arab Community," published in *Mizna*, are crucial to consider here. West explores the tensions between communities in the US and Arab world, voicing a particularly strong condemnation of Arab anti-Black racism. West concludes his article with optimism where he states, "there is some progress, some movement, some hope despite many lingering problems between the two communities."[40] West's optimism is reflected here in my decision to highlight and work with generative connections. The focus here on solidarity demands a different starting point than competition, hierarchy, and/or replacement and a focus that is critically engaged, but shifts the emphasis.

Reciprocity, Antiracism, and Linking Struggles

Because of this focus on what I am calling generative links, it is also crucial to discuss cultural borrowing, appropriation, and the notion of reciprocity. As the quotation from Robin D. G. Kelley above asserts, solidarity is not based on reciprocity but on the notion that we must fight all injustice as a shared problem. This recalls the very powerful statement by Audre Lorde about not contributing to your sister's oppression, even if you don't fully understand it, or it is different from your own.[41] But as is the case in many relations between communities, using examples from one group to prop up or justify another group's claims is common, and histories are often complex. The Jadaliyya roundtable cited above, from which I quoted Rabab Abdulhadi as well as Kelley, was devoted to the question of anti-Blackness and Palestine Solidarity work for a reason—the pervasiveness of anti-Black racism in organizing, including radical political organizing. This conversation centers anti-Black racism and thinks more thoroughly about the particular and specific place of African Americans in the United States, as a community carrying the legacies of chattel slavery, ongoing systemic racist violence, and a long history of resistance. This is one reason it is important to give space to thinking about which struggles are centered at which moments and credence to charges of appropriation and upstaging when necessary. Kristian Davis Bailey discusses this in his analysis of the "Ferguson-Gaza moment" in 2014 when he points to two Palestinian American women who were among a group of about a dozen people slated to speak at a civil rights meeting. These women then gave up their own space to allow youth from Ferguson more time to express their "rage at establishment civil rights organizations for avoiding Ferguson during the heat of the repression."[42]

What was behind this rage in being excluded is talked about in some detail in *From #BlackLivesMatter to Black Liberation*, where Keeanga-Yamahtta Taylor details some of the ways in which younger activists felt sidelined by older, establishment civil rights leaders like Al Sharpton.[43] In her discussion of organizing by the younger generation and how they navigated changing relationships with leaders they admired, she also notes that in Ferguson, "the young activists were beginning to politically generalize from the multiple cases of police brutality and develop a systemic analysis of policing. Many began to articulate much broader critique that situated policing within a matrix of racism and inequality within the United States and beyond."[44] To demonstrate this focus on building up the broader critique, she cites the words of one young activist making the connection to Palestine: "[Johnetta] Elzie also observed, 'Thanks to Twitter, I had been able to see photos of Gaza weeks before, and feel connected to the people there on an emotional level. I never thought the small county of Ferguson, this little part of Greater St. Louis, would become Gaza.'"[45] Taylor's discussion of this coalition work also brings out some of the complications that the Black Lives Matter group faced, for example in relation to the #MuslimLivesMatter hashtag borrowing from theirs that was circulated after the racist murders of three young Muslims in North Carolina, Deah Barakat, Razan Abu-Salha, and Yusor Abu-Salha. Taylor points to how quickly this led to the charges of appropriation of the struggle by using the hashtag and also the dangers for a movement of claiming itself as different. Taylor's analysis focuses on the solidarity principle, urging people not to "miss how we are connected through oppression—and how these connections should form the basis of solidarity—not a celebration of our lives on the margins."[46] In this section on building solidarity, indeed, Taylor argues for an examination of recent histories—such as how African Americans began advocating for racial profiling after 9/11, even though they had been targets of this destructive and ineffective policing and security policy. Her argument in *From #BlackLivesMatter to Black Liberation* advocates building stronger and stronger coalitions against racism of all forms to challenge the policing state and make the transition from protest to movement in bringing about Black liberation.

Like most other histories, Keeanga-Yamahatta Taylor's looks back in time to draw links to the past—in her case to illuminate how #BlackLives Matter was born from what came before it. Recovering the histories of Black-Arab/Arab American solidarities in the United States from the 1960s and giving them space on the page honors the work done in the past and helps us understand what went into making what is happening today. Kristian Davis Bailey's references to earlier work that went into making the "Ferguson-Gaza moment" of 2014 able to be so generative testifies to this. He looks to the work of Black radicals in supporting Palestinian liberation and draws in particular on scholarship by Alex Lubin and Rabab Abdulhadi. His work shares with Abdulhadi's a focus on ethnographic study as a scholar and activist himself, engaged in the work of Black4Palestine and documenting the achievements and challenges of their work.

Davis Bailey's analysis of the more recent Ferguson-Gaza connections echoes in many ways Abdulhadi's ethnographic work, in which she documents and explores some of the ways that Palestinian organizing in the 1980s is connected to that of the early 2000s. Her article, "Activism and Exile: Palestinianness and the Politics of Solidarity," for example, opens and closes with an event in New York held in solidarity with Bir Zeit University in Palestine, organized primarily by a Black American graduate student in Africana and American Studies who worked transnationally with Palestinian activists as well as the local chapter of Students for Justice in Palestine. Abdulhadi uses this particular event to frame her deeper discussion of activism throughout the 1980s and beyond. Her extensive activist ethnography charts and analyzes the deep and lasting organizational links that grew out of this solidarity work and continue to build it. Some of the deep and rich histories of organizing in the 1980s that she examines include Palestinian American support for the Rainbow Coalition, including Jesse Jackson's bid for the presidency, when he became the first major candidate to call for a Palestinian state, and their organizing especially in Chicago through Arab community centers as well as individual efforts.[47] She points to how Palestinian youth in New York at the time were organizing "coalitions with other international students and students of color to celebrate Black History Month and International Women's Day; to honor Malcolm X and to protest CUNY tuition increases"[48] and how Palestinian youth-based organizing epitomized "1980s-era Palestine centered activism, where asserting Palestinianness meant identifying with the struggle of other nationally and racially marginalized groups."[49]

Abdulhadi's documentation brings together examples of many different moments as well as groups and individuals who forged bonds of solidarity. One of these took place in 1981 when there was an eight-thousand-person demonstration at the United Nations building in New York, called by the November 29 Coalition for Palestine (named for the International Day of Solidarity with the Palestinian People). In documenting and analyzing this event, she gives the example of the wide range of endorsements received from international groups throughout Africa, Asia, and Latin America as well as groups of color in the United States, naming "Patrice Lumumba Coalition, the Caribbean People's Alliance, *Haiti Progress*, Black United Front, and the National Conference of Black Lawyers" in addition to Puerto Rican and other Latin American groups, Indigenous groups, and anti-Zionist Jews.[50] The date November 29 is invoked in another solidarity action, this one organized by Black Americans, as a way to tie together a campaign against racist police attacks. She describes the demonstration at the time of what is now known as the First Intifada:

> Palestinian identification with activism in antiracist struggles in particular seemed only "natural," given the unwavering solidarity African Americans expressed with the Palestinian Intifada. For example, African American activists organized the Days of Rage campaign to protest escalating police racist attacks in the New York area to coincide with November 29, the international day of solidarity with the Palestinian people. On that cold evening hundreds of African Americans, wearing *kafiyyahs* (Palestinian scarves), linked hands across the United Nations demanding justice for both peoples.[51]

Abdulhadi here emphasizes the solidarity of linking hands to demand justice for both peoples and the organization of the Days of Rage campaign to coincide with November 29 and the International Day of Solidarity with the Palestinian People. She also highlights antiracism as a framework for support for the Intifada, consistent with the first example above.

She draws our attention to the notion of identification between some groups being seen as natural through her use of quotation marks around the word. By highlighting this word, Abdulhadi underlines reciprocity, as Robin D. G. Kelley does in the quotation cited above, and refocuses our attention onto the concept of solidarity and the articulation of the indivisibility of justice in the struggle for the liberation of Palestine.[52]

Another important Arab American feminist scholar, Nadine Naber, has also documented Black-Arab solidarity work, explicitly connecting earlier and later moments together, through an auto-ethnographic study of her involvement with the Arab Women's Solidarity Association–San Francisco, a leftist, feminist, diasporic Arab collective. She writes about how while involved in this group, she and other members connected to the Women of Color Resource Center (WCRC) because of their aligned interests in antiracist organizing. In discussing her involvement in this work, she delves into the histories of bonds built between Arab and Black feminisms in the United States and excavates some of the ways in which the organizational work done in the 1960s continues with younger generations of feminists. In her essay "Arab and Black Feminisms: Joint Struggle and Anti-Imperialist Activism," Naber centers the narrative of the women who founded and organized the WCRC to draw out their histories of internationalism, coalition building, and solidarity with Arab and Arab American women. She presents the narrative of Linda Burnham, who traces the group's lineage back through the Black Women's Liberation Committee of the Student Non-Violent Coordinating Committee (SNCC) to forming the Black Women's Alliance, and then the Third World Women's Alliance, before founding the WCRC with Miriam Ching Louie. Naber's intervention not only does the important work of recording these women's histories, it also underlines their commitment to educating themselves and others about Zionism and anti-Zionism in the US context. Further it explains how the WCRC came to adopt a strong politics of Palestinian liberation as tied to other antiracist and anti-imperialist struggles. Naber also highlights the work of the Z Collective in Detroit as an Arab American group working closely with African American activists supporting struggles for peace.[53] Naber clarifies that her aim is "making these and other connections visible" to "enrich the activist landscape" and "envision further the more inclusive world feminism aims to build."[54] Naber's discussion of these examples points to much broader and diffuse locations of feminist and women-of-color organizing all over the United States and their international connections. Local and national organizing and community building efforts are widespread, even if they are not all well documented or well known.

Another specific example where African Americans and Arabs/Arab Americans have come together to link struggles and analysis is in delegations to Palestine. As Davis Bailey states in his account of the development of Black4Palestine organizing, the Dream Defenders and other groups that went on delegations to Palestine returned to work on shared ideas and struggles in Black communities in the United States. Another documented example of such a delegation is one led by Rabab Abdulhadi with ten other Indigenous and women-of-color activists to Palestine in 2011, that produced a strong statement of support for the Boycott, Divestment, and Sanctions movement upon their return to the United States: "Justice for Palestine: A Call to Action by Indigenous and Women of Color Activists."[55] It was on this delegation that Indigenous and women of color from different communities spoke to women in Palestine about their struggles. As Abdulhadi recounts, Black Panther and former American political prisoner Angela Davis movingly spoke as a member of this delegation about how touched she had been to receive letters of solidarity from Palestinian prisoners held in Israeli jails when she was a political prisoner in the United States.[56] Davis has written about this and the evolution of her political consciousness around Palestine in many locations including her recent collection of essays published as *Freedom Is a Constant Struggle*. Like June Jordan did in the 1980s, Angela Davis traveled to the region years later to learn and meet people in order to share ideas and work together.[57]

A delegation to Palestine is also one of the focal points around which Sa'ed Atshan and Darnell L. Moore worked to build their own friendship, as well as their theorizing and political work as queer activists, one Palestinian, one Black American. They met on a LGBTQ solidarity delegation to Palestine in 2012 and have been working together ever since to deepen their shared understanding and building on what they have done.[58] In their article "Reciprocal Solidarity: Where the Black and Palestinian Queer Struggles Meet," they have written about their work together in queer movements; they not only document their own work, but also link together examples of what they call "reciprocal solidarity." The notion they are working with is somewhat different than what Kelley was referring to in his critique of "reciprocity," in which sharing and working together is based solely or primarily on the notion of doing things for each other being contingent on reciprocity rather than justice. Here Atshan and Moore work through the notion of "deep participation" borrowed from Wenshun Lee.[59] They also draw on Audre Lorde among others to build an analysis of erotics, love, and friendship as a way to develop queer solidarity work in Black and Arab/Palestinian communities. Their naming of locations in which this is being done are varied and diverse including freedom rides to Ferguson and within Palestine—hearkening back to the 1960s in the United States—as well as support for the family of Trayvon Martin, among many other projects.

Solidarity histories are complex, even messy, and at times contradictory. This section has revealed some of these dynamics, with a focus on solidarities that are generative. It has emphasized the dialectic sparked by creativity, when you see others' struggles as a part of your own not because you or they are the same but from a recognition that your liberation as *different* people is bound up in the liberation of others.[60] Though not all of the stories we tell and histories we unravel are positive, this book looks primarily at the ways in which Black and Arab American communities and individuals have interacted in ways that were and are positive, nourishing, and mutually beneficial. This is not the full history of interactions between communities and individuals; both have been complicit in harming each other in different moments. Keeping in mind the larger contexts, *Breaking Broken English* looks at stories, narratives, and poems as a way to think through relationships and solidarities, using its focus on language to unpack some of these complexities. In thinking about building analyses and identities in the United States, Therí Pickens observes that "Arab American and African American women writers find common ground in their explorations of intersectional identity. Andrea Shalal-Esa notes that Arab American writers 'deriv[e] strength from feminists, black theorists, and post-colonial thinkers . . . to chronicle decades of racism, oppression, and marginalization in the United States.'"[61] Pickens opens

her study invoking these connections. She closes it citing Moustafa Bayoumi's book, which tells stories of Arab American youth, framed around
W. E. B. DuBois's famous question, *How Does It Feel to Be a Problem?
Being Young and Arab in America*. She shows why we must bring together
and tell the stories of Arab Americans and African Americans. Pickens's
moving closing lines allude to another now iconic contribution of Audre
Lorde: "It is precisely because projects of domination are sophisticated
and intertwined that the stories we tell need be also. Complex stories create an alternative cosmology that permits both possibility and praxis. To
see them, find them, create them, and tell them, is not a luxury but an
obligation."[62] For Lorde, poetry is not a luxury. Similarly, then telling complex stories is not. Emphasizing Black women's contributions to theory,
Pickens asserts that we must meet this obligation and so in addition to
telling and creating stories, we must also find them and see them. This
section has told a brief story of Arab-African American solidarities over
time; the next section will continue developing this story, with a focus on
literary solidarities.

Literary Solidarities

African American and Arab/Arab American, and more specifically Palestinian, histories of solidarity outlined only briefly above are long, rich,
and deep. This is particularly true of Black and women-of-color feminist theorizing and scholarship. As the examples I brought together in
the previous section demonstrate, the scholarship and other writing on
these connections is growing and expanding in a number of directions. I
agree with scholars like Therí Pickens that few studies engage deeply with
these questions on a literary and linguistic level. Both Alex Lubin and
Keith Feldman work with literary texts to engage in historical analysis.
They draw attention to cultural and literary works in this context; they
use them in conjunction with other materials to propose arguments about
shared political imaginaries and race and imperialism, respectively. In
contrast, *Breaking Broken English* centers literary works as literary. This
section focuses briefly on putting literary works—poetry, short stories, and
novels—in dialogue with each other and draws out some of the ways that

creative works exemplify, thematize, and talk about these kinds of connections, both centrally and more marginally.

The first—and often only—text critics turn to as evidence of Arab American engagement and connection with African America/ns is *Born Palestinian, Born Black*, Suheir Hammad's poetic homage to June Jordan. Jordan is an important Black American poet and iconic figure who, as noted above, has been much studied and cited in relation to her naming of herself as a Palestinian in the wake of the Sabra and Shatila massacres in 1982. Jordan's poem continues to influence Arabs and Arab Americans, and Hammad's poetic work in her honor does as well.[63] Of all of the Arab American writers and poets with connections to African Americans, Hammad is the best known and most explicit in her politics and deep connection to this community. Scholarship on her poetry—both deep and superficial—points to these connections.[64] In her opening to this collection of poetry, which went out of print and was later reissued, Hammad defines what Black means to her in a number of ways, which are worth noting in order to think about positive and literary connections. For example, by defining Black as a color and concept—"Black like the genius of Stevie, Zora and Abel-Haleem"—she is going beyond a superficial linking of Black and Arab creative artists and forging a new kind of literary, artistic, and musical bond between communities.[65]

While Hammad is the best-known Arab American literary figure today whose creative work invokes and explores these solidarities, she is not the first or only poet and writer to express them. Much less known is the Arabic-language novelist, scholar, feminist, and activist Radwa Ashour, who traveled to the United States as a student in the 1970s to complete a PhD in Afro-American Studies at the University of Massachusetts–Amherst. Her Arabic language memoir, *The Journey*, extensively details her connections to African American activists, professors, students, and others and pays homage to specific literary figures and works, such as those of Langston Hughes and Frederick Douglass. This text is discussed in more detail in chapter 5 below. Though her work is much more deeply engaged in these relationships than that of most other Arabic-language authors, Arab literary production is not devoid of more symbolic use of iconic African American figures and symbols. Syrian poet Adonis, for example, invokes Harlem frequently in his representations of the United States in contrast with white America and the Statue of Liberty.[66]

Dating back to the early 1960s and 1970s, and contemporaneous with Radwa Ashour, other kinds of invocations of Black America are also inscribed within Arab American poetry and writing, and this becomes more frequent and prominent in later writing, prose and poetry. As discussed in chapter 2 below, D. H. Melhem's connection to African American literary communities and figures, like Suheir Hammad's later ones, are long, extensive, and deep. To contextualize Melhem's poetry, which evinces direct solidarity with and affiliation to Black America, a starting place might be Lawrence Joseph's "Sand Nigger," taken as one of the earliest expressions of Arab American identity in a racially stratified United States. The provocative naming of the poem is one location to begin to work through the larger contexts of Arab American writing and connections to African American communities. Itself using the replacement paradigm right in its title, the poem is a long meditation on being an Arab in the twentieth-century United States. And Joseph is not simply from the United States, but hails from Detroit—the American city with the largest concentration of Arab Americans and one of its oldest and most organized communities. In the twentieth century, it was also in the process of rapidly becoming the quintessential Northern Black city, a focal point for racial tension and also radical politics in the 1960s and 1970s. This city's Arab American community has produced a number of other poets and writers including Saladin Ahmed (discussed in chapter 2), Alise Alousi, and Hayan Charara, among others.[67]

Joseph's poem is often pointed to as a landmark of Arab American literature for its complex articulation of what and where "home" is for Arab Americans.[68] Carol Fadda-Conrey's reading of the poem in this context focuses on his construction of home and homeland, and how he produces what she calls "more informed and critical versions of national belongings and allegiances."[69] Fadda-Conrey links this to an awareness of racialization and suggests that he draws upon the racial slur to meditate on his identity within a Black-white binary in the United States. Joseph's use of the derogatory term is articulated and repeated in the poem in the following lines:

> "Sand nigger," I'm called,
> and the name fits: I am
> the light-skinned nigger
> with black eyes and the look
> difficult to figure—a look
> of indifference, a look to kill—
> a Levantine nigger
> in the city on the straight
> between the great lakes Erie and St. Clair
> which has a reputation
> for violence.[70]

Fadda-Conrey reads these lines as challenging "the equally harmful effects of assimilation on the one hand and stigmatizing racialization on the other hand, the two primary options available to most Arab-Americans in public enactments of their individual and communal identities."[71] This reading rhymes with Steven Salaita's meditation on the increasing use of this term and the marking of Arab Americans and Muslim Americans adopting this devastating slur as their own, as "the new niggers."[72] Importantly, Salaita strongly urges a move away from using what Pickens identifies as the "replacement model" (Arabs are the new Black), so as better to understand and contextualize the meaning and specificities of anti-Arab racism. As Pickens rightly argues, it is important to maintain recognition and acknowledgement of Black presence and that Blacks are still subjected to this derogatory label, as well as the racist thought, feelings, and actions that inform it.[73] The replacement model obscures this, and in centering other experiences, displaces Black experience and presence.

Moves toward such recognition can be read in Hayan Charara's reworking of Joseph's poem. As Fadda-Conrey points out, Charara adds layers to this analysis and shows a different engagement with a term and concept loaded with so much meaning to African Americans.[74] She points out how he cites Joseph by writing, "I am a slightly lighter-skinned nigger from the city on the straight,"[75] but reformulates the second part as, "I am an Arab and from Detroit."[76] This important shift moves away from a poem that could be read to mobilize the replacement model toward a deeper understanding of self. This in turn could potentially result in a deeper connection to other communities, particularly Black communities—as other examples of literary solidarity explored in this chapter will show. Joseph's poem, Charara's link to it, and the fictional works I discuss in the section below all set up the ambivalent and complicated context of Arab American-African American literary connections, reflecting the at times fraught and difficult relationships between these communities.

The shorter and more fleeting links evinced in poetry—a title, a line, a concept—are developed further in fiction. In what follows, I discuss several works of fiction in which there are visible thematic links to Black America in order to sketch out the larger background within which literary solidarities can be explored. This relatively brief discussion is meant to provide a context in which to situate the in-depth close readings of solidarity projects that are the focus of *Breaking Broken English* in the five chapters that follow. Chapters 3–5 are all devoted to the study of fiction and memoir. As I noted above, this book does not catalog or cover all of the links, themes, or creative uses of language that Arab American fictional and poetic works employ to engage African America. I do not claim or attempt to be exhaustive in this study. In fact, placing Arab American fiction and poetry in the context of US literary production more generally, it comes as no surprise that Black American characters, figures, references, and themes recur in a number of different ways, in multiple and diverse locations. A wide variety of Arab American literary works evince literary engagements with Black America within this context. This can be in more or less deep or superficial ways, and not all texts can be understood to operate in a solidarity perspective or one that is antiracist. In line with my objectives in this book, I will discuss several well-known and well-studied fictional texts that can help to paint a broader picture of the kinds of works here that can help to set up a larger political and literary framework in which generative ties and solidarity with African America/ns can be read. This broader context informs the framework for studying creative uses of breaking language in a series of texts in the chapters that follow.

Many Arab American literary texts include minor African American figures—usually in order to represent resistance to white supremacy and racism in the United States. Often these characters are drawn sympathetically and discuss and/or advance plot lines to do both with racism more generally and anti-Black racism specifically, such as the transatlantic slave trade and other markers of US history in which Arab Americans are linked sympathetically to Black Americans. Laila Lalami's *The Moor's Account*, for example, is a retelling of the history of the slave trade in the Americas that centers a Black Moroccan character. The title reflects the position of the work's narrator—the "Moor" in question, Mustafa ibn Muhammad ibn Abdussalam al-Zamori—who is stripped of his name and becomes known as Estebanico. This novel's premise is that Mustafa is recounting his life after selling himself into slavery to a Spaniard who then brought him to what becomes Florida. As a self-identified Black slave, Mustafa is a Muslim of Moroccan origin who is educated, can read and write Arabic, and therefore upends typical representations of Black people who were enslaved in the Americas. This novel is important in how it forces a rethinking of African American heritage, connects it powerfully to the Arab world and Islam, and also reimagines positive and complex relationships with the Indigenous Peoples of Turtle Island.

Another example of an African American character used to advance a discussion of slavery is Aunt Khadija in Mohja Kahf's *The Girl in the Tangerine Scarf*. This powerful elder figure in the mosque community at the center of the novel explains to a young Syrian-American woman, Khadra Shamy, how the headscarf is powerful for a people whose history involved being stripped naked and sold on an auction block. The protagonist, Khadra Shamy, experiences her coming of age as an Arab American, Muslim woman in Indiana, partly in relation to Aunt Khadija and other African American characters, including her friends Hanifa and Hakim. Kahf's focus on Islam within the novel and reimagining an *ummah* to which all Muslims belong and have equal access means that the place of African American Muslims in the United States is probed in some detail. This includes Khadra's feeling that she cannot escape being a Muslim whereas Hanifa can, as she has a non-Muslim African American community to escape to and take refuge in should she want to do so. Hanifa and Hakim's African American background causes Khadra to question their authenticity as Muslims,[77] and they are used as a way for the Arab community's subtle racism to be exposed in other locations.[78] The two women have many discussions that highlight racism in the Muslim American community, naming and confronting its own anti-Black racism. An important plot line in the text also deals with the murder of Kenyan American university student Zuhura, who is herself a member of the mosque community; the question of how her death is treated is raised in terms of her being a Muslim and also being Black.[79]

That Khadra returns in her later life to Indiana to find herself romantically interested in her old friend's brother, Hakim, draws upon another familiar character—the Arab American female character's Black American boyfriend. This is a fairly frequently evoked figure that appears in other novels that use Black American characters as foils to advance the plot and bring the question of racism into play. An example of this is Alicia Erian's *Towelhead*.[80] As chapter 4 below discusses, this figure appears in different ways in Randa Jarrar's work, both in *A Map of Home* and in several short stories in *Him, Me, Muhammad Ali*. With a slightly different focus, this is somewhat reminiscent of Rabih Alameddine's novel, *Koolaids: The Art of War*, in which the AIDS epidemic among gay men in the 1980s is paralleled by the devastation wrought by the Lebanese Civil War. In this novel, one of the protagonist Mohammad's closest friends, James, is Black. That Mohammad, a gay Lebanese man far from home during the civil war, strikes up a friendship with James becomes important in the text because they share things that their white gay friends do not. Diana Abu Jaber's *Arabian Jazz* focuses on the character of Jemorah Ramoud and her Indigenous boyfriend. In this novel, it is Jemorah who herself is considered racially ambiguous and whose confrontation with her boss leads her to explicitly identify with Black Americans.[81] This novel also draws on African American music and symbolism in the title and elsewhere, with "jazz" playing an important symbolic role for the Ramoud family, particularly Jemorah's father, who is referred to as "no better than a Negro."[82] Though these are not the only Arab American works of fiction that depict Black American characters or use symbols, motifs, and images with particular resonance within African America, I have provided these brief sketches to give a sense of the broader context in which the texts I discuss in the chapters below operate. The following section offers a brief glimpse into the specific focus of each of the chapters that follow.

Breaking Broken English: Chapter Outlines

In each of the next five chapters, one or more literary texts are discussed in detail in relation to the ways in which they express thematic links with African America. I explore Arab American authors' and poets' use of heavily coded African American symbolism and imagery, literary intertextuality, references and homage to real and symbolic, ordinary and iconic Black American figures, images, and characters, as well as plot lines and themes that reflect these. The project of drawing out these more thematic connections in each chapter is woven together with a detailed reading of the creative use of language within the text/s studied. More specifically, I draw together an understanding of the thematic, artistic, political, and other connections to Black America with an analysis of the particular ways in which the English language is represented as "broken." In order to develop a framework for understanding this, I reformulate this use of "broken language" through the concept of the break and breaking language. The framework, developed further in the sections below, is informed and developed through drawing upon work from Black American theoretical, aesthetic, and political traditions, linking in particular to Black and other women-of-color feminist theorizing of these. *Breaking Broken English*, therefore, does examine representations of African American and Arab American communities and individuals in conversation with each other, but not simply to chart or document them. Rather, thematic and other depictions of these relationships are examined dialectally with language and linguistic strategies.

Chapter 1 builds the book's framework of analysis through a deeper discussion of creative language use in literature, as the blending of politics and poetics, ideas and sound. It does this in two parts. The first is to explore in some depth how language builds literature and literary works build their own creative languages. The chapter explores how language has been theorized by Black American intellectuals, poets, and writers.

The basis for these discussions in particular includes the following: the ways in which the language/s spoken by African Americans were historically stigmatized and reclaimed, the links between spoken language and writing, and the connections between racism, oppression, and literary languages—using language as resistance and a way to literarily inscribe social justice messages. These theoretical and historical insights into African American language and literary expression work to build an analytical framework around the notion of "breaking language." I propose this concept as a way to understand creative responses to languages that are marginalized, othered, and demonized in the United States. Such a use of language has been central to the creative power and genius of African American culture. Though Arab American poetry and fiction have a different history and practice of language use, they draw upon similar creativity in language/s. I argue that we can use the concept of the break to analyze the power of creative language in Arab American literary texts by drawing on African American critical resources on language. In order to build this framework more robustly, the second section of this chapter is devoted to a detailed analysis of Suheir Hammad's *breaking poems*. In an approach different from the analyses of literary texts in chapters 2–5, I propose that Hammad's collection be read as informing my method, as it is entirely devoted to the concept of breaking and its power. My reading of Hammad here contributes to the conceptual framework of breaking so as to use it analytically in the rest of the book. Chapter 1 establishes the framework that is used in the four chapters that follow it, all of which present readings of how literary works by Arabs and Arab Americans offer unique insights into race, oppression, and potential for liberation through breaking language.

Chapter 2 builds on the analyses of breaking language by presenting an in-depth, comparative analysis of Arab American poetry by D. H. Melhem, Saladin Ahmed, and Naomi Shihab Nye. Thematically, the chapter is framed by the notion of the poetry of homage as solidarity and coalition building. The works by these poets honor a diverse group of Black American figures. The chapter opens with an analysis of the work of Melhem, who was active from the 1970s on and wrote many poems to honor Black American figures, including Amiri Baraka, Jayne Cortez, Angela

Davis, Jennette Washington, Richard Wright, and the Black Panthers. I then focus on one poem each by Saladin Ahmed and Naomi Shihab Nye. Ahmed and Nye belong to a later generation of writers, producing most of their work in the 1990s and 2000s. I analyze Ahmed's 1999 poem, dedicated to Harlem Renaissance poet, Countee Cullen, putting it in conversation with a poem he wrote for his great-grandmother, Aliyah Hassan, "Things Important to an Eight Year Old." Active somewhat earlier than Ahmed and Hammad, Naomi Shihab Nye began publishing in the 1980s. Her poem analyzed in this chapter, however, is more recent, written in the aftermath of the Ferguson uprisings in 2014, in homage to nine-year-old Jamyla Bolden, killed by a stray bullet. The focus of the readings of poetry in chapter 2 is not merely their homage to these figures but the ways in which they develop them through language. Hammad's poetry and conceptualization of breaking help us to see how the poems by Melhem, Ahmed, and Nye all use techniques that can be read through the concept of breaking language. I explore this in relation to their formal use of poetic features like line breaks and also in the ways their specific techniques include breaks in meaning, rhythm, and sound. The creation of soundscapes in the poems is dwelt upon in some detail.

Chapter 3 then moves from poetry to the novel, investigating how thematic and formal experimentation are intertwined in language. In this chapter, I argue that Susan Abulhawa's *Mornings in Jenin* uses language represented as "broken English" as a technique that is breaking language, particularly in its manipulation of sound. *Mornings in Jenin* is a long epic novel charting Palestinian history from before the Nakba until the early 2000s. This third chapter examines closely how Arabic is layered into the English language of the text and the two are used to interanimate each other to create a Palestinian soundscape. The notion that language might be presented as broken in order to "break with something" is important to Susan Abulhawa's project in *Mornings in Jenin*, as is her use of language to create home. The novel's thematic engagements with African America are crucial in relation to this central idea. Though the novel does not engage with Black American culture or literary figures like the poems in chapter 2, African American/s are central to how *Mornings in Jenin*'s protagonist is able to conceptualize home in the United States. African American theories of breaking language offer particular insight into how *Mornings in Jenin* trains its sights on language as home. Abulhawa's extensive use of vernacular language, some of which read initially as "broken," are part of her project of breaking language to create a soundscape of home.

The fourth chapter focuses on Randa Jarrar's novel *A Map of Home* and two stories from her more recent collection of short stories, *Him, Me, Muhammad Ali*. Jarrar's uses of language are complementary to those of Susan Abulhawa but also rather different. She similarly draws upon the vernacular English of Arab Americans and represents Arabic extensively. The chapter therefore looks in detail at Jarrar's explorations of ways in which the English language is and can be broken, through extensive experimentations with dialogue and weaving Arabic words into the text. Like *Mornings in Jenin*, these texts are all centrally concerned with home and using language to create a soundscape of home. Jarrar's thematization of this home as connected to African Americans is similar, but more significant, than Abulhawa's in *Mornings in Jenin*. In addition to incorporating a general discussion of connection and solidarity with Black Americans, Jarrar also mobilizes iconic literary and cultural figures like Toni Morrison and Muhammad Ali to layer more meaning into her texts in the US context.

The final chapter then shifts the focus on how language is used in its exploration of feminist activist, novelist, and academic Radwa Ashour's "translation" of Black America into Arabic in her memoir. Originally published as *Al-Rihla* in Arabic in 1982, it appeared in English translation as *The Journey* in 2018. *The Journey* relates Ashour's experiences studying African American literature as an Egyptian PhD student in the United States in the 1970s. The focus on language in this chapter examines Arabic in relation to English and thinks through how in the twenty-first century we can develop an English language around race and liberation that does justice both to the Arabic text and ideas of the 1970s. It asks how different languages and times can and cannot express concepts like race and the shared struggles of Arabs and Black Americans in the United States and abroad. This text is centrally concerned with African American and

Arab realities as connected in the solidarity context of its era. It is therefore a text used to look backward in order to look forward. Ashour's memoir, like all of the chapters before it, highlights how creative languages manifest the break, and breaking language, to link their poetic, literary, and aesthetic projects to larger projects of literary and political solidarity.

1 Building a Theory of Language, Poetics, and Politics in the Break

The 2017 release of *I Am Not Your Negro* brought the words of African American writer and theorist James Baldwin to the big screen. The film is a compelling portrait of Baldwin's contribution to the urgent political and intellectual conversations in the United States in the 1960s and 1970s, with a focus on race, racial inequality, and African American struggles for justice. Throughout the ninety-three minutes of the film, we hear only words he wrote or spoke; the beauty and power of his language are unmistakable. These words are part of the film's aesthetic and political relevance. The political point is unmistakably underscored by the use of images from the time he wrote, juxtaposed and interspersed with more recent images, those captured during the Black youth uprisings against police murder in the United States from 2014 and onward, as well as other powerful imagery from the periods in-between. I invoke Baldwin's film here—in particular the connections it makes between the politics and aesthetic languages of the 1960s, 1970s, and the twenty-first century—because Baldwin joins Geneva Smitherman, June Jordan, and other Black American intellectuals and writers as my starting point for a discussion here of Black American languages and poetics.

The discussion of Black American politics and solidarity movements in the 1970s gives a context for the intense debates in the period over African American language and literature. Leading to what became known in the United States as the "culture wars," the vibrant political atmosphere, which gave rise to Black Power, the Black Panthers, and radical conceptions of how to challenge authority, centered language in a number of ways. The preface to this book documents my own encounter with this as a schoolgirl. The vigorous defense of Black Language—also called African American Vernacular English, Black English, Ebonics, Spoken Soul, and Black Talk among other things—was undertaken by a number of important writers and thinkers, including June Jordan and James Baldwin, as well as many others. Debates about language and its importance were a crucial part of the debates over race and racism, culture and its place within social life, and how the shape of society is determined by language/s of expression. The focus on language as a flashpoint has arisen several more times around Black Language in the United States. The so-called Ebonics Debate of 1996 in Oakland, California, is one of these, and a number of scholars working in the field today have produced excellent scholarship on this moment with a view to challenging ongoing and new misconceptions about language.[1] Now, as in the 1970s, discussions about language have always been about the role and form of aesthetics and literary production. This was centrally important to the flourishing Black Arts Movement in the 1970s.[2] Though discussions today look different, many of the same tropes recur, whether in relation to the speeches and rhetorical impact of Barack Obama or Kendrick Lamar winning the Pulitzer Prize in 2018.[3]

This chapter delves more deeply into these discussions around language and literature in order to continue building a framework for reading and analyzing literary texts in the following chapters. The conceptual tools emerging from this conversation are framed as breaking and operating "in the break" as a way to rethink and reformulate what is seen as and labeled "broken," especially "broken English." To do this, I will first examine the contours of the debates over Black Language with a focus on the 1970s and explore how they engage questions of language, power, and values. The next part of this chapter outlines the ways in which African American literary criticism and poetics can inform a study of Arab American literature. Suheir Hammad's collection, *breaking poems*, formulates a theory and practice of breaking through poetry; this chapter therefore concludes with an exploration of how her poetry can be used as methodology to help build a stronger notion of breaking and the break.

Language, Power, and Values

To set up the context of Black intellectual production around questions of language, I would like here to recall the scene set in the preface to *Breaking Broken English*—the students of Martin Luther King Jr. Elementary School in Ann Arbor, Michigan, who sued for and won the right to have their own home language acknowledged and valued in school. These children and their parents fought for the right to be treated and addressed with respect, to be valued in the same way as their non-Black classmates were. Analysis of the court case links together how race and class factored in mounting this challenge—and winning it—more specifically, how language was the *only* factor allowed to be considered as an unfair burden as opposed to the students' poverty and the economic discrimination they faced, which was not.[4] The debate was tightly controlled by the judge in the case, who required that arguments be made only in relation to language. In what follows, I briefly sketch out some of what is at stake in the struggles over Black English/African American Vernacular English/Black Talk/Black Language/Ebonics/Spoken Soul. Though the repression and belittling of this language within and outside of the community was and still often is widespread and commonly accepted, the theorization, discussion, and defense of it was and is sophisticated and politically astute.[5] As the discussion below demonstrates, people who engaged vigorously in the debate over language, weighing in to promote and give value to Black English, were clear about it being an issue of power. Where the power is held and who wields it in society is central to any analysis of language. June Jordan simply and eloquently poses this as a question and answers it herself, "Then what is the difficulty? The problem is we are saying *language* but really dealing with power."[6]

The scholarship of linguist Geneva Smitherman is a testimony to the depth and richness of what she calls Black Talk or Black Language (and at other times Black English or Ebonics). A teacher and linguist by training,

Smitherman was a key figure in advocating for children's rights to have their home language/mother tongue honored in school and was called as an expert witness in the King case. Her scholarly project of charting, documenting, and deeply analyzing Black American English gives a detailed sense of how language maps onto the political landscape of African America before and after the 1970s and up through the late 1990s, including the 1996 Ebonics furor in Oakland, California. One of Smitherman's linguistic projects was to record and transcribe Black English, documenting and analyzing syntax, linguistic form, vocabulary, and lexical items as well as grammar. She is one of a number of scholars who worked to prove the language's West African origins and has also provided a rich resource for scholars of language and linguistics, while always maintaining a sharp eye on the politics of language and how power defines it.[7] Smitherman's scholarship is so important here because she politicizes her own findings and analyzes them in light of school battles, but also literary debates, and other current discussions important to African Americans.[8]

As a linguist, Smitherman's discussion of the terms and terminology used to discuss the language in question is full of nuance, and she provides ample historical material to put the question of names and naming into context. She opens her reissued collection of essays, *Talkin That Talk: Language, Culture and Education in African America*, for example, with a discussion of the term Ebonics. Because of the popular attention it received when the Oakland School Board passed its resolution in favor of Ebonics in December 1996, people often think this is a recently coined term.[9] Its use, however, has been documented as originating with Robert L. Williams and a group of African American scholars at a conference on "Language and the Urban Child" in 1973.[10] He published the conference proceedings two years later in a volume titled *Ebonics: The Language of Black Folks*. Therefore, though many treat it as a new invention of the late 1990s, the term Ebonics was developed about twenty-four years prior to the case in Oakland. As Smitherman points out, however, this concept of a "linguistic continuum from Africa to the 'New World,' and the terminology to express that concept, as created by these Black scholars, never caught on in the academic world, nor the educational establishment."[11] In the same essay, Smitherman discusses her own shifting between terms, finally preferring Black Talk or Black Language, and it is noticeable that in mainstream writing and publishing from the period—June Jordan's and James Baldwin's writing cited below for example—Black English remains the most commonly used term. John Russell Rickford and Russell John Rickford's study of this language cites Claude Brown as coining another evocative term, "Spoken Soul," and indeed they title their book on the subject by invoking it: *Spoken Soul: The Story of Black English.*

As the quotation above demonstrates, the conceptual power behind "Ebonics" goes beyond mere terminology: it is a continued connection with life in Africa and an expression of culture. Smitherman's concise definition of Ebonics draws out a number of important points:

> The Ebonics spoken in the US is rooted in the Black American Oral Tradition, reflecting the combination of African languages (Niger-Congo) and Euro American English. It is a language forged in the crucible of enslavement, US-style apartheid and the struggle to survive and thrive in the face of domination. Ebonics *is* emphatically *not* "broken" English, nor "sloppy" speech. Nor is it merely "slang." Nor is it some bizarre form of language spoken by baggy-pants-wearing Black youth. Ebonics *is* a set of communication patterns and practices resulting from Africans' appropriation and transformation of a foreign tongue during the African Holocaust.[12]

I cite here at length because of the complexity with which Smitherman breaks down the language she is defining: both in working against stereotypes and assumptions and also for conceptualizing the struggle against oppression, the resulting creative production, and how this affirms life. In the discussion below, other thinkers reprise a number of these themes in different contexts. Her emphatic insistence on Ebonics not being "broken" English or "sloppy" speech is one I will return to in building a framework for understanding the language/s of Arab American poetry and fiction. It is also crucial to point out here the notion of transforming and appropriating language while subject to oppression and domination by the mainstream society in which it is being spoken.

For Smitherman, therefore, as for others participating in these debates, language is not primarily or necessarily solely about communication or expression. Like June Jordan above, and as expressed by so many others, she also points to language as being deeply invested in power: "There is a fundamental, dialectical relationship between language and power, between language and oppression, and between language and liberation. Surely it is only the unwise who consider language a 'mere' instrument of communication."[13] This is so important in the case of Black Americans because of their particular position in the United States. The dialectic she points to has a much bigger impact on Black people because language is tied to thinking, tied to culture, and tied to being. This recalls the dialectic pointed to in the introduction to *Breaking Broken English*, as articulated by Audre Lorde—the creativity in difference that sparks a dialectic through which Black women can find power.[14] In an essay that is a powerful defense of the right to study, learn, and live in one's own home language—the language closest to you—Smitherman asserts in conclusion, "As black people go moving on up toward separation and cultural nationalism, the question of the moment is not which dialect, but which culture, not whose vocabulary but whose values, not *I am* vs. *I be*, but WHO DO I BE?"[15] She uses a vernacular expression in order to underline her point: the self is deeply tied to language. The questioning of yourself within your own cultural framework and language allows you to define who you are on your own terms, literally and metaphorically. A strong definition of self can again lead to power as it can work together with others, across differences. I develop in greater detail below that the use of language and representations of that language are deeply connected to culture, values, and who you are. Languages shape and are shaped by literary expressions of these issues and are crucial to investigating and understanding these dynamics. This is of central importance to the literary texts analyzed below.

The use of and attention paid to language is something Smitherman has also studied and come to important conclusions about. Her definition of Ebonics above cites enslavement, apartheid, and the struggle of the dominated to survive and thrive as its foundation as a language. She has also identified periods in which this language becomes more important, more commonly used, and stronger. She asserts: "The Black Experience is a narrative of resistance, of an on-going struggle to be free, perhaps the motive force in African American history. Since language is inextricably interwoven with a group's culture and history, US Ebonics would have been affected/continues to be affected by the concrete historical conditions of Africans in America. Stated more succinctly if somewhat oversimplified: in historical moments of racial progress, the language is less Ebonified; in times of racial suppression, the language is more Ebonified."[16] This observation of Black Language has important implications for Arab American language and the use and expression of different kinds of englishes in Arab American writing. If Smitherman's pronouncement about the increased use of Ebonics in times of greater suppression is correct, then even if the contexts are different, it is no surprise that Arab Americans have used and experimented with language in creative ways in the twentieth and twenty-first centuries. This particular moment in history, particularly after 2001, not only demonized Arabs and Arab Americans, but also focused on their language in particular. Recalling Baldwin's essays published in newspapers, Sinan Antoon phrases his question as a statement in his essay title, "Why Speaking Arabic in America Feels Like a Crime." This short article in *The Guardian* denounces a phenomenon experienced by so many Arabs in America, where language is demonized as a racialized expression of otherness. The chapters that follow examine and analyze different ways in which languages are formed and shaped between Arabic and English, reading them through some of the principles developed by theorists and defenders of Black Language. Certainly the late twentieth and early twenty-first centuries were times in which there was much more "racial suppression" than "racial progress" for Arabs and Arab Americans in the United States.[17] Smitherman's observation here is an important focal point for developing a relevant framework of analysis for the building of creative Arab American literary languages, in the twenty-first century particularly.

The development of a "more Ebonified" language identified by Smitherman might also be called "creolization" in more commonly used linguistic terms. She discusses the push for decreolization, or standardization, in other essays. Because she is an advocate of language preservation and the value of spoken languages, her scholarship is invested in locating moments when what she calls the "whitening" of Black speech is slowed and halted. One such moment she locates was during the Black American Freedom Struggle, particularly throughout the 1960s and 1970s, when so many African Americans were working on reclaiming languages: in everyday speech, in schools, and in literary projects. Smitherman connects language and literary production and emphasizes the role of the movement in advancing the significance of language in community building and liberation: "Black Power intellectuals and activists sought to speak the language of the people, tapping into the Black Oral Tradition, using its metaphors, images and rhetorical stances. Black Arts/Black Power writers sought to capture the idioms, nuances, and speaking styles of the people and represented Ebonics in their work, seeking to make the medium the message."[18] Giving value to language with a phrase like "making the medium the message" is another way of underlining the generative ability of creative languages. Smitherman here picks up on some of the well-known techniques writers who were part of the Black Arts Movement used in their works and identifies this as connected to the broader project of language preservation and advancement. She cites numerous examples of experimentations with Black Language in literary works, dating all the way back to the origins of African American literary history.

June Jordan's Language, Power, and Pedagogy

Scholar, intellectual, activist, and poet June Jordan's work could hardly be more aligned with the projects that Smitherman identifies here. She is not only a writer but also a wordsmith; in addition to writing pieces advocating for Black English, and teaching it,[19] she also experiments with the language herself, publishing a novel written entirely in this language in 1970, *His Own Where*.[20] Jordan, like Smitherman, was a fierce advocate for children. As an educator she worked to promote respect for children in schools through respect for their language.[21] Many of her essays written in the 1970s firmly echo stances and ideas advanced by Smitherman at the same time.[22] In her well-known article, "Nobody Mean More to Me than You and the Future of Willie Jordan," Jordan discusses the pedagogical techniques she used to promote Black Language by teaching texts that use it. For example, she talks about how she taught Alice Walker's *The Color*

Purple, despite the resistance of her students who were fluent speakers of its language. This essay shows how Jordan identifies sources of pride, value, and power in Black English and how she overcame her students' resistance, connecting her classroom activity to the very real issues facing the community. While she was teaching the class, the brother of one of her students was murdered by the police. The students mobilized to write statements to the police that they tried—unsuccessfully—to publish. Jordan discusses how she was privy in this class to a discussion "with so much heart at the dead heat of it. I will never forget the eloquence, the sudden haltings of speech, the fierce struggle against tears, the furious throwaway, and useless explosions that this question elicited."[23] The question was: Should their group statement be written in Black English or Standard English? Jordan describes how she knew at that moment that they had doomed the beautifully eloquent statement they then crafted to never being published, because they chose to write it in Black English. And she was right. Her analysis here at once illuminates language and politics and is devastating. As she points out in the article, the student's brother is still—after all their learning and work together—dead.[24]

Just as this article chronicles her students' rejection of Black English and the disrespect with which the language is treated in the United States, Jordan's discussion of her own novel *His Own Where*'s reception is also important to unpacking the dynamics of this issue. The example of how Jordan's novel was received in Black communities is one lens into the issue of languages of literature and culture; her discussions and analysis of it are also important to seeing the political context/s of this time. Jordan asserts that she wrote *His Own Where* to prove that "this language despised as ghetto/gutter dialect punctuated by unprintable epithets, could carry narration and dialogue describing an urban, teen romance of genuine pathos and hope."[25] She continues on by saying that she wanted to prove that "the verbal components of their consciousness pointed to a complexity of character and thought equal to their way-earlier Elizabethan counterparts."[26] She also echoes Smitherman's observations that in some way the medium is also the message. Some people, however, did not appreciate the message being inscribed in this medium. She writes about how she was expecting that the young characters' decision to make a baby would lead to controversy, but not that Black parents would organize against the book because they felt its language of expression meant that it would be an educational disaster—exactly what Jordan herself was working against.[27] This was eventually the grounds on which some schools banned the book. Jordan's brilliantly incisive 1972 essay, "White English/Black English: The Politics of Translation," is partly a response to this move to prohibit the reading of her book. It is a spirited defense of both the project and also Black English.

Jordan's discussion of *His Own Where* does not remain focused within the Black community but ventures more largely into white American society and the interest it maintains in depriving Black people of their creativity, culture, and genius—as she calls it, "the futures we dream and desire."[28] She juxtaposes Shakespearean English with passages from her novel to compare "nonstandard" English of different types, mobilizing her own use of Black English to comment upon a scene from Romeo and Juliet: "Now that ain hardly standard English. But just about every kid forced into school has to grapple with that particular rap."[29] What is so important in Jordan's analysis is that it is not narrowly limited—her critique of white American power is international, anti-imperial, and uses language and analysis derived from the Black radical tradition, as discussed above. Her rejection of white English identifies it as an imperial language that supports the war in Vietnam; her defense of her own language is one that also rejects "pacification" and the euphemistic vocabulary of then-President Nixon and others that serve to justify perpetuating an imperial war in the Third World.

Beginning a series of sentences with the words, "As a Black poet and writer," Jordan discusses her complex relationship with the English language and with words, stating that "I hate words that cancel my name and my history and the freedom of my future: I hate the words that condemn and refuse the language of my people in America; I am talking about a language deriving from the Niger-Congo congeries of language."[30] As she continues this discussion, the parallels between her views and Smitherman's become all the more clear: "I am proud of our Black, verbally bonding system born of our struggle to avoid annihilation—as Afro-American self, Afro-American marriage, community, and Afro-American culture. I am proud of this language that our continuing battle just *to be* has brought into currency. And so I hate the arrogant, prevailing rejection of this, our Afro-American language. And so I work, as a poet and writer, against the eradication of this system, this language, this carrier of Black-survivor consciousness."[31]

James Baldwin: Language and Humanity

June Jordan's righteous anger is found also in her contemporary James Baldwin's pair of scathing articles defending and promoting Black English. His best-known interventions into the debates about Black English are two op-ed pieces in mainstream newspapers. In 1979, the *Los Angeles Times* published "On Language, Race and the Black Writer," while "If Black English Isn't a Language Then Tell Me What Is" appeared in the *New York Times*. Unlike Smitherman and Jordan, Baldwin does not mobilize the language about which he is writing to make his point. He instead writes in an elevated register in which he documents Black American contributions to American English, and therefore culture, giving examples such as "jazz," as in "jazz me, baby," "sock it to me," and "funk."[32] These examples demonstrate something of Black genius and also showcase Baldwin's wit and humor. His message is clear and powerful: "The brutal truth is that the bulk of white people in America never had any interest in educating black people, except as this could serve white purposes. It is not the black child's language that is in question, it is not his language that is despised: It is his experience."[33]

  As his words demonstrate, Baldwin's interventions into the debates around language align with those of Smitherman and Jordan as a powerful defense of Black language, how crucial it is to children and their ability to learn in a respectful schoolroom atmosphere, and its importance to communities, as well as literature and creative art. It is remarkable how much some of his most searing lines of prose speak to these larger analyses, as in one of his most frequently cited lines, *"A language comes into existence by means of brutal necessity, and the rules of the language are dictated by what the language must convey."*[34] This of course underlines both the point made by Smitherman of how Black Language was initially forged, and also her assertion about its resurgence in times of community repression. Like Smitherman and Jordan, Baldwin has a strong analysis of power and language: "It goes without saying, then, that language is also a political instrument, means, and proof of power. It is the most vivid and crucial key to identity: It reveals the private identity, and connects one with, or divorces one from, the larger, public, or communal identity."[35] Like Jordan, Baldwin advocates for Black Americans to identify the power that oppresses them and rejects it, not only in the name of this community but for all those facing injustice.

To Baldwin, it is necessary for both literary and political purposes to define language, identify your oppressor and enemy, and challenge what does not allow for your freedom and liberation. Like Jordan, he is clear that white language is a problem for Black Americans: "Writers are obliged, at some point, to realize that they are involved in a language which they must change. And for a Black writer in this country to be born into the English language is to realize that the assumptions on which the language operates are his enemy."[36] Language here, as in Smitherman's analysis, is not only a system of communication but also structures thought and action: both the language produced and its underlying assumptions are a problem. Other thinkers echo Baldwin's message that the English language should be identified as the enemy and challenged. Audre Lorde, for example, agrees: "we share a commitment to language and to the power of language, and to the reclaiming of that language that has been made to work against us."[37] Baldwin's message here is radical in how it ties language use and literary expression to advocating for a better society for all people in which everyone's humanity is recognized. It is not just about communication or expression, but about worldview, theories of knowledge, and existence as human. Smitherman's "who do I be" is recalled by Baldwin's intense identification of the language as profoundly constructing the self.[38]

Language and Speakerly Texts: Hurston, Walker, and Morrison

Filling in the outlines of this debate over language use and literature with some discussions of literary texts gives them more shape. Black American literary production is so vast and rich, even a discussion of only recent works cannot be adequately sketched in a few paragraphs. Several concrete examples, however, can help illuminate some of the literary expressions of how these debates played out. Early examples of using Black English in literature are often dated back to the work of major African American literary figures like Paul Laurence Dunbar[39] and Langston Hughes.[40] In his now classic work on and of African American cultural practice, *The Signifying Monkey: A Theory of African American Literary Criticism*, Henry Louis Gates Jr. identifies Zora Neale Hurston specifically as the first true genius of Black American linguistic experimentation, who wrote entire texts in a language of spoken expression. Hurston's use of language is now celebrated, and she has entered the canon of African American writers to be reckoned with. But through the 1970s, before the publication of Alice Walker's essay, "Looking for Zora,"[41] she still was relatively unknown and uncelebrated outside of certain, limited, rarefied circles—despite her prolific and important production.

Gates details the use of language in Hurston's work and argues for how her thematic and formal use of Black language inscribes important layers into her work, with his main focus on *Their Eyes Were Watching God*. He identifies the voice of Black oral traditions in direct speech, though for him what is more important is also how she uses it in both indirect discourse and free indirect discourse. These uses of language are all central to Hurston's literary projects, and Gates demonstrates how her texts become "speakerly" in powerful ways. Just as Baldwin asserts, Gates locates within Hurston's work a quest for a Black consciousness through the use of language and the ability to become a speaking Black subject. Though he traces the origins of this back much further into the late nineteenth century within the work of Dunbar, he credits Hurston with setting up the ground that would lead to the eventual reclaiming of language in different ways throughout time, including the Black Arts Movement.

Other writers who have been celebrated for their use and defense of Black language in literary works include Toni Morrison and Alice Walker. Both in the United States and beyond it, Walker and Morrison have won major literary prizes for their fiction including Morrison's Nobel Prize (1993). *The Color Purple* by Alice Walker has been singled out for particular attention in this regard, including by theorists of language and liberation. This is the text that June Jordan's students so resisted reading. Jordan points out how their comments devalue their own language of expression and how she struggled to make them see this without embarrassing or shaming them. It is the character of Celie's own challenges in learning to read in which some of Walker's most poignant and sophisticated analyses of language come through: "Look like to me only a fool would want you to talk in a way that feel peculiar to your mind."[42]

Toni Morrison has also used and advocated Black English; Baldwin famously cited her definition of the language as "sheer intelligence" in his *New York Times* article cited above. Novels like *The Bluest Eye* and *Beloved* have become classics of American fiction, and both make ample use of spoken language to convey complex worlds and worldviews often marginal to literary production in the United States. These few works give just a glimpse into some of the ways in which the language of literature is informed and built through Black English. The world views and positions of these authors, I would underline, are also informed—as in the case of June Jordan and James Baldwin—by strong analyses of US imperialism and solidarity with international social justice issues. All four of these Black American intellectuals have evinced strong stances in relation to Palestine: Jordan and Walker have made this central to their political work. Using creative language in speakerly ways to advance a message of social justice is one way in which African American poetics connects to other literary and linguistic traditions.

Language between African American Poetics
and Arab American Literature

Toni Morrison's iconic role as an African American writer whose texts poignantly move people, particularly young marginalized women, is highlighted by Randa Jarrar's short story, "Lost in Freakin' Yonkers." The story's Arab American teenage protagonist, Aida, is pregnant and alone, searching for solace in her university library. Finding not a single book by an Arab woman author there, she retreats to the women's room weeping as she says, "Defeated, I read *Beloved*."[43] It is no mistake that *Beloved*, the

Toni Morrison novel Jarrar alludes to, is known for its extensive use of Black language and how it creatively integrates language as part of the story. Jarrar's own short story itself is full of spoken language that could be identified as slang, dialect, or "broken English." Randa Jarrar represents the characters partly through their use of language, in relation to literary allusions, examples, and mixing Arabic with English. Chapter 4 below discusses "Lost in Freakin' Yonkers" as an example of how using "broken" English can exemplify breaks with a number of linguistic, literary, and other conventions. This analysis of Jarrar's texts, those of Hammad's poetry later in this chapter, and those of the chapters that follow explore the representation of spoken language—including "mixing" Arabic and English languages, the use of multiple languages together, and incorporating "broken English" into narrative and poetry.

These readings are particularly important because few analyses of Arab American writing study language use in any depth or engage language as a primary site of investigation.[44] Indeed, within the literary studies that investigate language use, particularly postcolonial literary study, Arab and Arab American writers are glaringly absent.[45] An investigation of language use is not only a productive way to understand Arabic and/or Arab American literature, but the close reading and exploration of language use in poetry and creative fiction, which melds, mixes, and experiments with language, can also help us think more about English, the multiple englishes that exist and can exist, and American writing more generally. Moreover, the study of language is never about language alone. As Geneva Smitherman notes, language is not just about communication, but also about power: "There is a fundamental, dialectical relationship between language and power, between language and oppression, and between language and liberation. Surely it is only the unwise who consider language a 'mere' instrument of communication."[46] In the twentieth and twenty-first centuries, literary works by Arab Americans offer unique insights into how language is connected to race, oppression, and the potential for liberation. Below I detail how *Breaking Broken English* develops a study of language through the concept of the break, and breaking language, to think through how the languages of Arab American literary production help to further such projects through the soundscapes they produce.

Theorizing the Break: From Broken English
to Breaking Language

Just as the debate over Ebonics in 1996 was not new, building a concept of breaking English out of broken English is not new. The history of reclaiming and reconceptualizing languages is long and storied, building on older literary, linguistic, and other histories. The concept of the break has a particular and powerful genealogy in African American traditions, especially in music, avant-garde artistic production, and Black radical traditions, as Fred Moten elaborates in detail in *In the Break: The Aesthetics of the Black Radical Tradition*. His work builds a theorization of the break from slave narratives, through fiction, poetry, and music, especially improvisation. Part of what interests Moten are the sounds between words, the spaces that are unfilled. He works with soundscapes of literary texts to value those things that cannot always be articulated, what is occluded by language, what exists only in the break. Important to Moten are breaks as spaces of multiple generative possibilities. Moten's theorizations are dense and complex, but some of the notions I have drawn from his study are how breaks that might on the surface appear to be "grammatical insufficiency" instead can be read as spaces of "lyrical surplus."[47] Moten works with the notion of breaking down language within poetry and how sound can be a location within which generative breaks reside: "these organizational principles break down; their breakdown disallows reading, improvises idiom(atic) difference, and gestures toward an anarchic and generative meditation on phrasing that occurs in what has become, for reading, the occluded of language: sound."[48] The location of the sound of poetry, how this is transposed into prose narrative, and the sounds generated by breaks are crucial to my conceptualization of the break. My analyses that follow show that reading texts as using breaking language is a way in which spoken languages and their sounds can be recovered; breaking languages create soundscapes that carry different kinds of meaning within the texts.

This break identified by Moten, and other kinds of breaks in, with, and from language all allow for spaces of thought and action that other theoretical models of language and literature do not. This is why the analysis of the use of vernacular, spoken, or "broken" English as breaking is so important here. When we think of language as broken, it is by definition passive, weakened, and thus can be defeated. Calling language "broken" implies that it needs to be fixed. Even if the challenge posed by "broken English" is to Standard English as an imperial language, an oppressive language, or one that "should be changed" according to Baldwin's intervention, something broken does not have the same potential to do positive work as something that is participating in the more active process of "breaking." Breaking language and creative soundscapes can be used as a framing device for the study of literature, therefore, that locates and taps into the power and creativity of language that other frameworks do not. To follow Baldwin, Jordan, and Smitherman and integrating their insights with Moten's suggestion about how lyrical surplus exists in grammatical "insufficiency," breaks allow the identification of where power resides in language and the potential of working to harness it.

My use of the concept of the break in this study focuses on generative possibilities—it allows us to "break into" the texts and let them "break things down." Writing and language that may on the surface look "broken"—according to mainstream conceptualizations of what the English language should be—are reconceived here as strategically engaged in "breaking" to open up critical and creative spaces to develop new and challenging soundscapes in texts. When Arabic is layered into English, when language represents Arabic but looks like English, whether or not this is representing speech, we are offered this kind of break. Breaking language draws on spoken languages or vernaculars, slangs, mixing languages, language play, accents—whether Ebonics, English inflected by Arabic, or otherwise—and rejects conceptualizing these creative and non-standard languages as "broken." Here instead, I place value on them as breaks: positive, generative sources for manifesting other kinds of breaks that reimagine society, liberation, and freedom. The break can therefore open up spaces for us that something "broken" does not. The words associated with breaking demonstrate this: to break something up—to separate something that does not need to be together anymore; to break something down—to explain something needing more explanation, or make something into a smaller size; to break in—to enter a space you are not meant to be in; to break free—to escape something oppressive and find liberation.

There are many other kinds of breaks and breaking: taking a break, a wave breaking, break dancing, using poetic line breaks. All of these metaphors help to bolster a framework for reading the break and in the break. They also work with the analyses below that see manifestations of other kinds of breaks within the linguistic breaks and what the potential of these are.

Breaking might, on the surface, seem conceptually distant from one of the other major organizing concepts of *Breaking Broken English*—solidarity. The notion of coming together, standing together, and fighting together in shared struggles can seem opposed to concepts of breaking with or breaking from. The metaphor of breaking is in a dialectic relationship with solidarity, however, even if they seem to be opposed. Here, Black feminist and other feminist work is once again helpful in unpacking the critical discourses around solidarity, sameness, and difference. The solidarity called for by Black and other women-of-color feminists does not require us to be the same, to seek universals, or to ground struggles in narrow politics. Rather it asks us to learn from others in understanding where struggle is located. This is a solidarity for fighting for someone else's liberation even when it is not the "same" as our own, even when this is difficult. It recognizes that forging meaningful coalitions is tedious and difficult work across many types of differences.[49] When Audre Lorde reminds us of these difficulties, for example, she also underlines how this joint struggle enriches us all.[50] The break as a metaphor and concept then is not at all opposed to solidarity work, but rather helps amplify it by reminding us how difference is something not to be "tolerated" as liberal discourse would have it, but can be generative in and of itself.[51]

In what follows, I read how texts inscribe breaking language—how they break up language, break into language, break from language, break free from language. All of the works advocate for justice for oppressed people; in most cases this focuses on freedom from racism and occupation, but often this is tied to other kinds of liberation as well. As an example above, I singled out Randa Jarrar's "Lost in Freakin' Yonkers" as exemplary of how a text makes extensive use of vernacular English—different kinds of spoken and broken English—while also thematizing an Arab American literary identity in solidarity with African Americans, and exploring these generative connections. It is an important example because it tackles racism directly and argues for less conventional expressions of Arab American identity, particularly as these are expressed in gender and sexuality.

Randa Jarrar's text is feminist and also allows for us to think about how breaking works in conversation with feminist theories of difference, discussed above. Her short story is a good example of how breaks in conventions of language can work together with breaking conventions conceptually to argue for social change. This story, like other texts examined below, is analyzed within the framework of breaking language. Reading breaks in language in these texts is joined to an analysis of their thematic and political representations of Black America(ns). These are then linked to how they use language to engage ideas about justice and liberation. The literary works analyzed here nearly all treat social justice as related to the liberation of Palestine—and this liberation is directly connected to fighting racism in the United States. In most of the texts, there is a clear message that Arabs are an integral part of the United States, are American, and that as Americans and Arabs they stand in solidarity with Blacks/African Americans. The arguments developed below deeply connect thematic, historical, and political links to the use of language: neither one is solely privileged here. *Breaking Broken English* is an attempt to put value on these different elements all at once and highlight their connections.

"never this broken": Suheir Hammad, *breaking poems*, and the Politics of Language

Suheir Hammad's collection *breaking poems* invites us to explore the concept of the break and breaking by theorizing it within her poetic practice. This next section of the chapter focuses in some detail on this collection in order to draw out methodological principles to help build a stronger notion of "breaking" to use in the four chapters following this one. *breaking poems* contains thirty-eight poems, each of which is titled with the word "break," suggesting that there is more than one way to understand the concept of breaking. *breaking poems* has been lauded as making an important linguistic intervention in poetry, particularly because of its use of Arabic and English.[32] Even more than in her previous poetic output, which uses multiple ways to express spoken languages, this collection's experimentation breaks new ground in integrating language/s. Hammad's extensive use of creative language in the project is part of what makes the poems "break" and gives meaning to the title *breaking poems*. They break with poetic and linguistic conventions by using language that is not translated or explained, exploring implicitly meanings that reside in the interstices between the languages and relying on sounds to create meaning, as much as the words on the page. As is her hallmark style, Hammad uses line breaks in suggestive ways, complicating her poems' meanings. At the same time that the poems actively break standard language/s, they also suggest double meanings based in experimenting with sound. The soundscapes created by Hammad are complex and full of what Moten calls "lyrical surplus" in their richly evocative play. The linguistic interventions in *breaking poems* are overcoded by the title, but in their substance also manifest multiple ways of thinking about breaking and what working in the break means. The readings that follow explore a number of examples in detail in order to delve more fully into how Hammad's *breaking poems* theorize the concept of the break and demonstrate elements of the framework being built in this chapter to analyze breaking language in other texts.

Before moving on to the analysis of *breaking poems*, I begin by discussing specific elements drawn from Hammad's considerable poetic oeuvre that lays the ground for her creative experimentation with the break in this collection. *breaking poems*' later interventions in language debates are prefigured in many locations in her earlier poetry. It is also important to remember that her linguistic experimentation with vernacular languages and "the way people speak" is infused by what might be identified as Black Language; this is an even more prominent feature of her earlier work. She continues to make use of elements of Black Language throughout the *breaking poems*, even as she increases the impact of Arabic on the English. This collection allows multiple experiments with language to coexist and suggest multiple breaks with, and ways of breaking, Standard English. At the same time a particular line might be read as "broken English" because it uses Arabic grammatical structures, it also might be read as African American vernacular English. An example of this, discussed below, is the line, "This beat nar yo." This and other examples demonstrate Hammad's extensive linguistic and cultural range and the broad resources she draws upon to craft her poetry and develop soundscapes.

Cultural and linguistic resources from Black American art, music, language, and literature are prominent in all of Suheir Hammad's poetry. Hammad's poetry is clearly influenced by and reflects not only the rhymes and rhythms but also the break beats of hip-hop. This is an appreciated, frequently mentioned, and integral part of her poetic production.[53] She also is and has been deeply involved in Black American poetic and artistic production, including in the hip-hop scene in New York City. Her first books were published by Harlem River Press, she regularly performed at slam nights including at the Nuyorican Poets Café in the 1990s, she forged connections with poets and artists of an earlier generation of the Black Arts Movement, and also linked up with new, fresh voices who would become known as the poets of the hip-hop generation, or as some have called them the BreakBeat poets.[54] This new kind of poetry emerges from the particular way that the early MCs experimented with the breakdown of records as a way to challenge and rework musical norms. MCs created the sounds that rappers began to rhyme over. Coval defines this school of poetry as the BreakBeats in introducing the anthology he coedited: "They extended those couplets to make verses and choruses and began to slant rhyme and extend the line and line break in odd, thrilling places. A break in time. A rupture in narrative. A signifying of something new. Fresh, Dope. Ill."[55] He defines this new poetry as an explicit extension of the Black Arts Movement and cites this as one of many influences. He also underlines the ways in which it is a rupture with the past, with ideas about high and low art, what is academic and what is popular, what is rap and what is poetry—as he puts it, "page and stage."[56] Coval's coedited anthology in fact includes three of Hammad's *breaking poems*, all of which exemplify his definition. Some of these poems will be discussed in more detail in the section below and all use techniques of language—particularly rhythm and rhyme—together with the break to create their effects.

Even before the *breaking poems*, however, Suheir Hammad was engaging the idea of what it means to be "broken" and what it means to "break." These concepts arise repeatedly in her poetry and deserve attention here, before moving on to her more specific and sustained theoretical and poetic intervention into "breaking." There are a number of places to locate Hammad's work on these ideas. One location to begin with is what is now probably Hammad's most famous poem, "first writing since." Hammad wrote and circulated this poem by email before it was published or even performed and it "went viral" in 2001, long before this expression came into common usage. The "since" in this poem refers to the morning of September 11, 2001; the poem was the first thing she wrote after the destruction of the World Trade Center and the tragedy that unfolded in her city that day. The poem openly declares, "there is no poetry in this," but goes on to become a powerful and moving testament to that event and what followed. The poem's renown grew, and Hammad was then invited to perform it on Russell Simmons Def Poetry Jam in late 2001. She subsequently joined the cast of the Def Poetry Jam on Broadway as the first and only Arab American performer. The poem's content and language, its reception by the largely Black audience of Def Poetry Jam, as well as her performance of it is a good example of how she has connected herself and her work to African American artistic forms, genres, and spaces.[57]

In "first writing since," Hammad characteristically makes many connections—political, historical, and otherwise—between the United States and the rest of the world, especially but not limited to Palestine. In her grief and anger, she explores what it might mean to be "broken"—invoking and ultimately rejecting this. She uses the rhythms of English to state,

> i do not know how bad a life has to break in order to kill
> i have never been so hungry that i willed hunger
> i have never been so angry as to want to control a gun over a pen
> not really.
> even as a woman, as a Palestinian, as a broken human being
> never this broken.[58]

Her statement is clear and stark. She can understand pain, anger, hunger, but not enough to will it upon someone else. She may be broken, but never "this broken." The idea of being broken is something that leads to hatred and murder. The other use of the word "broken" in the poem comes near the end in section seven. Here she states, "I have not cried at all while writing this. i cried when i saw those buildings collapse on themselves like a broken heart." The comparison of falling buildings to a broken heart humanizes the tragedy of this event and personifies the metal and steel, as she says several lines earlier, "skyline brought back to human size." Hammad conceptualizes being broken as something she relates to and something she even is, "as a woman" and "as a Palestinian." But it is also something that she refuses. This poem, which implores its reader/listener to "affirm life," is one of many poems by Hammad that makes connections between individuals and communities all around the world in an attempt to strive for positive futures.

Hammad's use of language in "first writing since" is less experimental and challenging, particularly on the level of integrating spoken language, than in her earlier works. Many of her poems, written before the *breaking poems*, experiment more extensively with Black language and other forms of English deemed to be nonstandard, including Arabic-inflected, "broken" English. Her creative and challenging uses of language in poems from her collection *Born Palestinian, Born Black* like "Taxi," Mariposa," "Yo Baby Yo," "99 cent Lipstick," and others prefigure her interest in breaking language in poems and/or breaking language through poems. Language that might be described as "broken" is shown to be productive and generative, speaking to, for, and about vibrant living communities and people. In this way breaking is the opposite of being broken for Hammad.

It is relevant in this context to situate Hammad's poetic oeuvre in conversation with her extensive and explicit engagement with African American poets and poetry, in particular June Jordan. Hammad's connections to June Jordan's poetry and politics have been documented and written about at some length, so I will not dwell extensively upon excavating these genealogies here.[59] It is important, however, that it is June Jordan who so inspired Hammad, given not only her political solidarity with Arabs and Palestinians but also her advocacy of Black Language and spoken languages more generally. Hammad clearly admires her political convictions and draws on this in her work that pays homage to Jordan, but she also honors her other literary and poetic innovations including using the language and speech of everyday people in her work.[60] Hammad takes up some of the tasks set out by Jordan in working on both solidarity and education through poetry, while also innovating on the level of language and form.

The most notable and frequently cited location of the homage Hammad pays to Jordan, as well as her way of signaling this, is in the title of her first full collection of poetry. *Born Palestinian, Born Black* reverses the terms of June Jordan's poem—mentioned in the introduction above— "Moving towards Home" in which she names herself a Palestinian:

> I was born a Black woman
> and now
> I am become a Palestinian

As a Black woman, she could not stay silent in the horrific aftermath of the massacres at the Sabra and Shatila refugee camp in Beirut, and her poem openly and directly expresses this identification with the victims as well as solidarity with them.[61] Hammad does not simply let her title signal this connection, however, she also includes an author's note to *Born Palestinian, Born Black* which uses this stanza from Jordan's poem as an epigraph. Inscribing herself within a poetic lineage descended from Jordan, she discusses what it means to be Palestinian, what Black means in a number of contexts, and closes the note talking about how this stanza "changed her life."[62] She also dwells on the question of language, in another gesture to and echo of June Jordan's life work, "Language is power, politics."[63]

This author's note is a rich source of insight into Hammad's thought and the ideas behind the poetry presented in the pages that follow. Her definitions of what she calls the "many usages of the word 'Black'" are particularly important in unpacking how she lays out a conceptual theoretical framework of Black-Arab/Palestinian solidarity in *Born Palestinian, Born Black*, together with and also beyond her affiliation to Jordan. One technique she uses here is to align herself and the concept of "Blackness" or "being Black" with people of Arab and African American backgrounds, in her definitions: "Black like the genius of Stevie, Zora and Abdel-Haleem."[64] In this line, Hammad names three important musical and literary figures—Stevie Wonder, Zora Neale Hurston, and Abdel-Haleem Hafez. These are only three of many figures who Hammad invokes repeatedly and in different ways in her poetry. To give just a few other examples, she also regularly names Fairuz, John Coltrane, Umm Kulthum, Bob Marley, Public Enemy, and Mahmoud Darwish in poems. Hammad uses other techniques in her author's note to build connections between Arab/Palestinian and African American identities and communities. Here, I have chosen to focus on the invocation of iconic figures. One reason for this is that I will explore the poetry of homage in more detail in Chapter 2, particularly ways in which Arab American poets pay homage to African American literary, cultural, and other kinds of figures. Moreover, by juxtaposing such figures, Hammad builds a notion of shared expertise, culture, art, and language. Experimentations with language, form, and style are all a part of the genius not only of June Jordan, but also Stevie, Zora, and Abdel-Haleem.

Hammad invokes Jordan indirectly in her author's note when she announces, "Language is power, politics."[65] It therefore is productive to take seriously how Hammad uses language in her poems in connection with Jordan's extensive theorizations of language and power in the Black American context. Though June Jordan perhaps may be a more visible influence on Hammad in her first collection because it is cited in the title, her ideas and politics run deeply throughout Hammad's poetic oeuvre. I am suggesting in fact, though less visible on the surface, this becomes increasingly important as Hammad's poetic oeuvre develops, from her first collection *Born Palestinian, Born Black*, through *Zaatar Diva*, and on to the more linguistically experimental *breaking poems*. The homage Hammad pays to Jordan, and also the other named and unnamed figures upon whose creativity she draws poetic energy, tie her political commitments to her linguistic and literary experimentations. For example, Sirène Harb has shown how Jordan's insistence on "naming oppressions" is crucial to Hammad's poetic project. Harb's article with the same title reads Hammad's work as emphasizing bonds and connections between women of color who themselves rewrite anti-colonial and anti-racist literary histories.[66]

The feminisms embraced by Hammad and Jordan work in the ways discussed above in relation to Audre Lorde and others who see interlocking oppressions as crucial to understanding how to build shared struggle. As Lorde put it, "There is no such thing as a single-issue struggle because we do not live single-issue lives."[67] *This Bridge Called my Back*, the classic collection edited by Cherríe Moraga and Gloria Anzaldúa, is another location to see how women of color articulate interlocking oppressions while not negating difference/s. Here I would underline that the fights against racism, poverty, and violence—especially war and military occupation—are deeply imbricated in feminism. This is a feminism that holds all oppressions together and sees them as working together. I am building here on this part of Harb's argument and connecting all of these thematic and political bonds between Hammad and Jordan to read how they are tied to their praxis of language. I argue that Hammad's insistence on language play, especially in working with spoken language/s that are called "broken" but in fact break the conventions of Standard English, can also thus be linked to Jordan.

To give another concrete example of how Hammad manifests this in her work, the author's note to *Born Palestinian, Born Black* once again recalls Jordan's mix of Black and white English in her own essays. In talking about her poems, Hammad states that "some of them were mad cool to write,"[68] among other lines and turns of phrase. Because she is now so well-known and her poetry is so widely circulated, it is perhaps possible to lose sight of the fact that Hammad—like Jordan in her time, especially in the early 1980s—was not universally praised or admired.[69] Indeed Hammad was not immediately embraced within Arab American circles when her work first circulated in print in the mid-1990s, partly because of the community's politics of respectability including around language use. Suheir Hammad is the only Arab American writer/poet who extensively uses and masters Black English in multiple ways in her poetry and other writing. Other Arab American writers and poets experiment with spoken language/s in different ways, including expressions or representations of dialect, but she is the only one who expresses herself in this language and who has identified herself *as* Black, explicitly, repeatedly, and without reservation.[70]

In fact, like Jordan, Hammad was criticized by Arab American communities for her use of language identified with the Black community. The poems in *Born Palestinian, Born Black* are full of the kind of Black

Language Smitherman documents, inflected at times by the Palestinian Arabic spoken by Hammad. They also use profanity, the language of the "ghetto," and a rougher-edged street language, not merely the sounds and rhythms of hip-hop for which Hammad has been so praised. Hammad does not shy away from the language that has been systematically reviled in mainstream culture despite being an important language of expression and culture, remaining so to this day.[71] This criticism of Hammad is reflected in Marco Villalobos's introduction to the reissued volume: "Some readers may have to take a few extra steps in accepting the validity of the younger Hammad's perspective. Her use of a black vernacular may still challenge readers whose categorization of ethnicity divides one slang from another according to pre Hip Hop notions of legacy and cultural property."[72] Hammad and Jordan's shared marginalization because of language use is important to recall here. First, it is a reminder that language is politics. Writing and creating in spoken language/s is a powerful tool and one often rejected by both the white mainstream and those invested in "minority respectability" as it relates to this mainstream in the United States. Hammad and Jordan share the experience of being criticized and rejected for their language use. They also continue/d throughout their careers working with language in creative ways, as well as resisting co-optation by a mainstream that once rejected them, Jordan until her death and Hammad to this day.

Suheir Hammad from Broken to Breaking

Drawing together Hammad's and Jordan's poetry further are the ways in which they fuse aesthetics and politics through language. The examples above demonstrate how Hammad works with language in different ways in her earlier poetry, beginning to theorize the difference between broken language and breaking language from her first collection, *Born Palestinian, Born Black*. In this section, I will analyze selections of her *breaking poems* to probe more deeply how she develops these concepts. I propose that Hammad's latest collection makes use of the break, particularly through language, as an integral part of her politics of solidarity.

Further, her use of breaking language both reflects and inscribes artistic, social, and community bonds between Black and Arab communities. In Hammad's earlier poems, spoken languages break with the conventions of Standard English. The breaks inscribed through different formal and linguistic experimentations work on the level of language and also conceptually. This is largely accomplished by using Black Language in her poems, though also at times by using Arabic words and expressions.

Similarly to her earlier output, politics and aesthetics in language cannot be separated in *breaking poems*. The language that is created is at once visibly marked as inflected by Arabic and English and invisibly read as more than just these through the soundscape created when read aloud. As critic Marwa Helal points out, for example, these poems do not identify words in Arabic or other languages with italics or in any other obvious way, allowing words that would be normally marked and understood as Arabic to meld into English and create a new poetic language.[73] Helal notes two frequently used examples: ana (I/me) and wa (and). In her brief article on *breaking poems*, Helal quotes Hammad as saying, "I wanted to write more like how I think and speak"[74] and proposes that this use of what she calls this "hybrid half English, half Arabic" will appeal to many Arab Americans because they will relate to bilingual thought processes and natural code switching. She also warns that it may alienate others, much as Villalobos remarked that some readers might find it difficult to accept the validity of her language. In her thoughtful analysis, Sirène Harb proposes that we understand Hammad's use of language in *breaking poems* by using theories of interlingualism and hybridity, particularly the notions of abrogation and appropriation suggested as postcolonial literary devices by Ashcroft, Griffith, and Tiffin.[75]

Harb's suggestions are helpful because they seek to understand how multiple linguistic techniques work together to create new languages as resistance to dominant or hegemonic languages, like English. I suggest here that it is productive to maintain a focus on multilingualism and resistance, but shift away from seeing the creation of new languages as an experimentation between two stable entities, English and Arabic. Hammad challenges us in *breaking poems* to look beyond Arabic as simply breaking Standard English. We must unpack what Helal calls English-Arabic bilingualism and look at the many languages layered into both the English and Arabic sides of this binary equation. Hammad's creative language works to bond and fuse languages, but not just as "Arabic" and "English." Her language also bonds Black and Arab American language/s, within and between English and Arabic. Below I show some examples of how this sort of bilingualism or multilingualism functions in examples of breaking language, and in the break between languages. I also examine how Hammad reclaims the space of the break and its beats within the soundscape she creates in the individual poems, arguing that this can be generalized to the collection as a whole. All of Hammad's poetry is sound play; it is as—if not more—suited to being performed and read aloud. *breaking poems* is a continuation of the kinds of language Hammad worked with in her earlier collections, *Born Palestinian, Born Black, ZaatarDiva*, and other works. Hammad's larger political and poetic project, like that developed by her role model June Jordan, involves language as politics as much as the politics of language.

The *breaking poems* use many overlapping and layered techniques of language to achieve their effects, particularly of breaking. A close study of the poetry shows that its bilingualism (or better, multilingualism) may reflect the use of spoken Arabic and English—how people think and speak—but importantly many registers of arabics and englishes, including Black Language. This close analysis also reveals that Hammad's poetic techniques are indeed much more complex than simply reflecting or demonstrating how people speak. As a poet, Hammad uses real, lived, experiential, and everyday language to create something new and challenging in poetic form. To do this, Hammad plays extensively with sound/s, double and triple meanings, allusions and alliteration, and assonance between words in many languages including words that shift and have multiple meanings. As in her earlier collections she also makes full use of the potential of line breaks to challenge, distort, and create meaning. This use of linguistic and grammatical innovation immediately recalls Moten's notion of lyrical surplus, discussed above. In his theorization, one of the locations of the break that offers creative potential is precisely where there is what he calls "grammatical insufficiency." I am suggesting that we read Hammad's poetry through Moten's lens, which proposes these locations where words, grammars, and meanings on the surface seem insufficient or "broken" to be the very breaks that are generative. They are where lyrical surplus—and sound—is born; this is the location in which meaning, power, and transformation are embedded.

Moten's conceptualization of how alleged grammatical insufficiency exists in the break to reveal lyrical surplus is a productive way to understand Hammad's theorization and practice of breaking. Hammad often juxtaposes words to achieve their full sound impact and also manipulates grammar/s in order to achieve particular effects of sound and meaning. One specific grammatical example that Hammad plays with for effect in multiple ways is the elimination of the present copula, or zero copula—that is, no verb "to be" is used in the present tense. This is a grammatical feature shared by formal Arabic and all Arabic dialects as well as Black English. Geneva Smitherman has written extensively on this feature of Black Language, tracing its genealogy in African American communities to West African origins.[76] June Jordan also notes that this is something Black English has in common with other languages, like Arabic, as well as Russian and Hungarian.[77] She defines the present copula as "a verb interjected between subject and predicate. Or, to break that down a bit: I am talking about a language where I will tell you simply that, '*They mine.*' (And, incidentally, if I tell you '*they mine,*' you don't have no kind of trouble understanding exactly what I mean, do you?)"[78] There are many examples of locations in which Hammad leaves out the present-tense verb "is" or "are" in *breaking poems*. This can be read in multiple ways—as spoken language, Black Language, Arabic, a mixed Arabic-English, a sentence not needing a verb, and so on. In poetry, these multiple, multiplying readings offer Hammad opportunities to layer additional meanings into her work and offer us a sort of lyrical surplus that plays with sound, suggesting ways to expand our thought and action.

"yo this beat nar yo"

In the poem "break (bayou)," Hammad invokes Black dance and music in a three-line stanza, recalling the bayou itself, named in the poem's title:

check how we crunk
check how we dip
check how we slide.[79]

Here Hammad not only uses vocabulary from contemporary Black Language (crunk, dip, slide) but also the expression that is used with them, "check" as the verbal command with no preposition rather than the slang expression, "check out." Two lines follow that are not paired, but stand alone as separate stanzas, "we loud and muted" and then "you hear me."[80] "We loud and muted" eliminates the present copula and the reader must supply it. If we follow some of the multilingual possibilities of the poem and its grammar that exists in the break, this poem is more easily read, on the page and aloud, as Black Language than Arabic. Titled after a geographical feature of the Southern United States, specifically Louisiana, "break (bayou)" does not invoke or supply any other surrounding words, ideas, or contextual clues connected to Arabic.

In the sentences in which this grammatical feature is prominent, sound is invoked contextually. The first is through the level of sound—the words "loud" and "muted" are not exact antonyms but express opposite ideas. This demonstrates the diversity of the people being referred to in the poem and the complexity of their situation. Here they are shown dancing, but in the rest of the poem we understand that they are facing dire circumstances in the aftermath of the devastating Hurricane Katrina and the US government's subsequent ignoring of the Black population of New Orleans in its aftermath. The line that then follows "you hear me" is also connected to sound. It not only recalls the line before it, but also reads either as a question or a declaration depending on the form of grammar and register through which you read it. "You hear me?" as a question reflects Black Language; it is as much an imprecation and command to hear as it is asking, and meant to reaffirm the need for the listener to hear. "You hear me," especially written on the page, can read also as a simple declarative statement. The power in these multiple levels of language use resides in subtle techniques of poetic bonding of ideas, themes, communities, and people through the poems. This is cumulative in the collection

of thirty-eight poems. Because the poems all make use of similar techniques but in different ways with different allusions, the reader/listener
experiences this effect increasingly toward the end, and can then fully
appreciate the unity of the overall poetic project.

Hammad uses this same construction once again in the poem "break
(vitalogy)" to make full use of a grammatical moment as a break. This
poem makes its statements and then leaves them ambiguous for the reader
to interpret their meanings. "break (vitalogy)" does not locate itself geographically or draw upon obvious symbols, except in relation to Gaza,
in Palestine. It opens with a pair of lines, "all matter related / we connected."[81] Even before we know anything of what the poem is about, this
is a move that sets up a perspective that ties people together from the
very beginning. The use of the word "matter" here at first likely reads as
the stuff of life, what we are all made of. The present-tense verb is eliminated, but implied: "all matter is related / we are connected." Leaving out
these verbs not only allows the poem to be read in vernaculars evoking
both Black English and Arabic, but also connects these two languages to
each other. Just as all matter is connected in the meanings of the lines,
a further meaning—a surplus—is created by allowing people who use or
are familiar with these spoken languages to be bonded together through
their understanding of the words in this way. The break here in grammar
creates something larger, through the sound of a spoken language and
through the increase in meaning/s created.

Additional meanings can be read into these lines as well. "Matter"
can also be read as "matters"—issues, ideas, causes—rather than matter
only being the stuff of life. The poem continues on with a set-apart line
serving as stanza three, "gaze me," followed by stanza four, also a pair
of lines, "ana gaza / you can't see me."[82] These lines powerfully connect to the first in that they both command the reader to see, using an
unexpected and unidiomatic expression, "gaze me," but then use a sound
play with "ana gaza" (translated into English: I am Gaza) that evokes the
sound of the word "gaze" in the word "Gaza." She uses a short Arabic
sentence that exemplifies the same grammatical rules about the verb "to
be," used in the lines discussed above, further reinforcing them. The
soundscape created here through her use of language and grammar is

interesting as well, in that it functions more readily as English sounds, even while infusing it with Arabic words and grammar. For example, the place name that is pronounced "Gaza" is not the same in Arabic, where it is pronounced "gh" (in linguistic terms, a voiced velar frictive, like a French "r"). The resonance with the word "gaze," therefore, is only produced with the anglicized pronunciation of the place. This is once again why I argue that we cannot read the *breaking poems* only as working with Arabic to break the hegemony of English, but must recognize that the ways Hammad uses language are multidirectional and complex. She then immediately follows the command to gaze at Gaza with a rebuke, or observation: you can't see me. This may be a metaphorical statement about how we do not see Gaza—despite the desperation of a people living under siege and occupation; the world has ignored this place. These are powerful messages inscribed within few words. The examples I have given here show how this poem makes use of line breaks, "broken" sounding English, and multiple meanings between languages, as well as grammatical structures that represent and also question languages. All of these are examples of Hammad's bringing theory and practice of breaking language together.

There are too many examples of this and similar techniques to catalog them all. "break (rebirth)," however, deserves attention here as another poem that mobilizes Black Language and Arabic together in order to add layers of meaning to it, while fusing imagery, ideas, and connections between communities. The third independent line, which is also the third stanza of this poem, reads, "math a myth wa language a lie."[83] This is another example of the zero copula, discussed in the poems above. In this case, the two short sentences missing the verb "to be" (is) in Standard English are placed side by side and joined by the Arabic connecting particle "wa." Hammad does not use the word "and" here, the English equivalent of "wa." She instead privileges the Arabic word, giving the sentence a different sound composition. Once again the zero copula can be read as drawing a solidarity link between Arabic and Black Language. Within each of the two short sentences, alliteration makes the sounds stronger, foreshadowing the ideas presented within the poem about the difficulties of life and people struggling across spaces. The poem's first two longer stanzas also eliminate the copula in the first line, echoing this earlier use in the first line.

The argument that the zero copula links Arabic and Black language is further reinforced by vocabulary items, imagery, and thematic links that connect communities that speak and/or know these languages:

> yo this beat nar yo
> nod head right off blow up spot wa kill crowd wa
> bomb walls break dance wa break off grilled face
> iced teeth wa break me sick ill music sickle
> self amnesia
>
> ana gathering selves into new
> city under construction gaza eyes pitted zeitoun spit meat taqasim
> brooklyn broken english wa exiled arabs sampled.[84]

The first line uses the familiar "yo" and the Arabic word "nar" to represent youthful ways of talking about music, an English translation would be "this beat is fire." Hammad chooses words that very clearly play off of others with sounds. Another example is "grilled face / iced teeth." Iced teeth uses a wordplay that sounds like iced tea, the drink, while referring to actual teeth with the word "grill," jewelry worn over the teeth and associated with the face, referred to popularly as bling or ice. "Sickle self amnesia" recalls the illness sickle cell anemia, a disease that disproportionally affects African Americans in the United States. Hammad plays with this to comment on "self amnesia"—forgetting the self—to lead into the following stanza, which talks about gathering selves. She compares these to being sick and ill; both terms conjure up the illness but also are used in opposite fashion to mean things that are good and desirable.[85] The gathering of self and selves that Hammad points to in the second stanza here is defined with a city under construction. It seems this could be any city, but is identified as Gaza. Eyes here are "pitted zeitoun," using an olive metaphor typical of Palestine positively, but she also plays with the double meaning of pit as hole, therefore something full of holes. It/they could be being spit out, and/or the spit could be to cook the meat referred to.

The connector between this line and the one that follows it is the word "taqasim." The last word mentioned here, it ties together Gaza and Brooklyn. "Taqasim," the plural of "taqsim," is an untranslated Arabic word that does not appear in the list of Arabic words with translations at the back of the book.[86] The function of the word is matched by its meaning, which itself invokes musicality and sound. Taqasim are musical improvisations that can be performed at different moments in a composition. The word here could be standing in for the sort of musical interlude, which is a taqsim, marking that moment with the word in Arabic. But the way it is used between lines could also suggest that she is referring to taqasim from Brooklyn, and/or that the Brooklyn taqasim are broken. Here, if the words are read through the lens of Arabic grammar, but with English words, this makes sense. The way in which this reads in English, however, once again sounds "broken." Moreover, the word "broken" itself could be the end of one phrase or the beginning of the text. This can be understood as a commentary on the language represented in this, and other, breaking poem/s and also the very idea of being broken that Hammad is challenging by writing her poems.

"jordan black / june in jerusalem"

Each breaking poem in Hammad's collection has many meanings; these are illuminated and expanded when they are read aloud not only as a collection of sounds that are connected to meanings and not merely as printed words. The soundscape more largely is a crucial part of Hammad's contribution to the philosophy and practice of breaking and what is created in the break. My final example here returns us to the figure of June Jordan. None of the *breaking poems* are dedicated to any individual, and unlike previous collections of Hammad's poetry, they do not make frequent reference to important poets, artists, and musical figures directly or by name, though there are some.[87] Hammad does however inscribe these poems within multiple literary, cultural, and political traditions—particularly Black American ones—in often less direct ways. The second poem in the collection, for example, indirectly highlights June Jordan. The subtlety of how this and other uses of language play out in "(wind) break (her)."[88] From the very title, for example, wordplay and double meanings add layers to the poem, which must be deciphered through sound, not just by the way the words look printed on the page. "Wind break her" read literally leads us to believe that the wind might harm the female person, the poet perhaps. But the sound implies that the poem is telling us something opposite: it invokes clothing used to protect against the weather and suggests her resilience as a wind breaker. This poem, like many others in the collection, juxtaposes many words which, when read together in different combinations, give different meanings, drawing a wide range of allusions. The first stanza reads:

> fairuz turquoise dawn ears ring
> voice diwan detroit divine
> smoke full lips fall on back baalbek
> museum mezze sabra jordan black
> june in jerusalem.[89]

The placement of these at first seemingly unconnected words is the key to analyzing this poem. There is a way to read the poem as operating outside of English grammar, in that there are no verbs. Taking into account the zero copula, Arabic and Black Language both have grammatically correct sentences that do not use verbs. Moreover, though it is possible to read the poem as having no verbs at all, a number of the words here can be used as either nouns or verbs—"dawn," "ring," "voice," "smoke," and so on. The first line immediately draws attention to this wordplay and its double meanings, at the same time alerting the reader to the importance of sound. It is through sound and reading aloud that it is possible to decide if "ring" should be understood as a noun or a verb: "ears ring," invokes earrings, as much as the sound reverberating in your ear. Hammad's language thus might be called grammatical multiplicity rather than insufficiency, as Moten would have it. It is important to underline, however, that Moten is actually playing off the notion of insufficiency and rather referring to how such grammars are viewed and understood. For him, of course, this is lyrical surplus, the very location of sounds that can become home.

Hammad's theorization of the break is productively read with Moten's. This can be seen particularly well in "(wind) break (her)" in the kinds of grammatical and word play explored in the examples above, which are connected to other kinds of play like that in line breaks. Her work creates undeniably distinct soundscapes to hold its lyrical surplus. The line breaks are meant to be where a line stops and meanings stop, but in poetry each line can also be read as spilling into the next, depending on how they are constructed, a technique poetry critics call enjambment. Hammad uses line breaks to challenge and inscribe meaning, to play with grammar, and to create sounds. Words that seem unconnected then can be connected, and other words connect differently than they might otherwise. In "(wind) break (her)," for example, "Fairuz" and "turquoise" are placed next to each other. The juxtaposition of these two words can read as a translation, which it is—as the two words mean the same thing in Arabic and English—but no indication is given of this. If the two words are read as a sentence with a zero copula, they would become "Fairuz is turquoise" in Standard English. No indication is given that these words mean the same thing; Fairuz is absent from the glossary at the back. You must supply this knowledge yourself in order for this level of meaning and wordplay to become clear. Fairuz is not just the precious stone, after which a color is named, but also an iconic singer, whose songs for Palestine are particularly well known and appreciated throughout the world.

Hammad connects Fairuz, and thereby also turquoise, to the ears ringing in the same line, which leads to the word "voice" opening the following line. This reinforces the meanings connected to the iconic singing voice. The word "voice" then introduces the words that follow, "diwan detroit divine," an alliterative trio that makes use of an almost identical sound pattern with the two words on the ends. A *diwan* in Arabic can mean a place to sit or a gathering, and is the origin of the word divan or sofa in English. This is close to the godly, heavenly, or wonderful meaning of the word divine. In Arabic this word has another meaning as well: a collection of poetry is also a *diwan*. These two words are separated by Detroit, a city known today for both its majority Black population and important musical history, as well as large and well-established Arab American communities. The three words create sound together that infuses a positive meaning to Detroit, and connects this both to poetry and to a place of gathering. The concept and word "divine" is one also often associated specifically with the singing voice of Fairuz, tying the first and second lines together in meaning, as well as sound and grammar.

Poetry, gathering, and positive meaning, as well as sounds and divinity, are then echoed and reinforced further in the last line of the stanza. The surface meaning of the word "June" is of course the month, and this has meaning in the context of Palestine and Lebanon—associated with Fairuz—for being the month of the Six Day War of 1967, also referred to as the June War, particularly in Arabic. This meaning is then reinforced by the word "black" preceding it; "jordan / black june" can be read as an allusion to the Black September massacres of Palestinians, which took place in Jordan, the word preceding "black" in this stanza. The word "sabra" reinforces this implied meaning, being the location of a different massacre, at the Sabra and Shatila refugee camp in September 1982. This placement of the words, however, adds another layer of meaning and can be read as Hammad calling the name of June Jordan. "jordan / black june" could be a way of naming the poet and then referring to her proudly as Black. June Jordan's famous poem "Moving towards Home" is dedicated to the children of Atlanta and Lebanon, in the aftermath of the massacre at Sabra and Shatila, further shoring up this suggestion. Inverting her name and using the line break to add in the adjective reverses grammar and challenges the reader/listener to think in more depth about layers of meaning. Another link drawing this all together is the *diwan* of poetry, and the sounds of the divine voice of Fairuz ringing out and singing for Jerusalem to June Jordan who wrote of the massacres at Sabra.[90]

"i miss my people"

All of the examples above demonstrate how Suheir Hammad's poetry works with the concept of the break, and breaking language. Her theorization and practice of breaking are fused together in one of the collection's shortest, last poems, "break (me)." The title of the poem can be read as a reworking of the idea discussed above in relation to "first writing since," of how Hammad thinks about herself as a "broken" person. "break (me)" suggests multiple ways of thinking about this idea—if the "me" is the poet, then is the poem breaking her? Or is she breaking the poem? Will the poem express things that might break her? Or is the poem an expression of how she exists in the break?

This poem explicitly works through what it might mean to break and be broken in a number of ways, deeply embedding her theorization of the concept using similar poetic techniques of language to those analyzed above:

> ana my language always broken all
> ways lost ana my language wa
> i miss my people.[91]

One similar technique that is evident from the first word of the poem, and recurs three times, is the use of Arabic words. Here she uses "ana" meaning "I" or "me" and "wa" meaning "and." The use of "ana" as the first word, untranslated (unlike other words appearing in the book's glossary), reinforces both the sound of Arabic from the beginning and strengthens the concept of self in the poem by recalling the (me) of the title and following with the second word, "my." In Arabic, it would be a normal sentence construction to repeat these words, whereas in English it is not, once again infusing a Standard English reading with Arabic sounds and grammar. The same grammatical structure in which the verb "to be" is omitted occurs here; one way to read the first line as a grammatical sentence in Standard English would be "my language is always broken." Omitting the "is" once again inscribes levels of grammatical questioning and allows the poem to have more meanings, while still being understandable to readers of Standard English. We can read this as lyrical surplus, as Moten suggests, and also understand the poem's content as reinforcing conceptually what she is doing poetically. When she says her language is always broken, we see it demonstrated in a sentence that reads as "broken" English. This is suggested as what might break her, but also what she might break. She moves on to say that she is "all / ways lost." The words "all / ways" sound exactly the same as the single word "always," adding additional possible meanings to the poem in hearing it or reading it aloud. But the difference here means that there are more ways to be lost. Being lost is therefore not just a matter of frequency, but also direction here—she is lost in all the directions she moves.

The "ways" of the poem is thus crucial in the poem as it indicates direction at the same time as echoing frequency. Hammad *wa* her language are lost—frequently and in multiple directions—as well as broken. These concepts then come together in the poem's short final line, "i miss my people." It is important that she uses the Arabic connecting particle "wa" here and not the English word "and," reinforcing Arabic sounds and underlining her commitment to repeating them. She implies through word order that not only is she lost, but her language is lost too. Being broken is connected here to this loss. The poem itself, however, is a reclaiming of this loss/brokenness by writing Arabic within it and breaking language. It is important in this regard that she does not claim her people as lost and/or broken. She simply reminds us that she misses them. We do not know in this short poem who "her people" are. This expression could indicate her family, her fellow Palestinians, fellow people of color, fellow poets, fellow travelers. The short poem is a crucial contribution to the overall collection of *breaking poems* because Hammad claims that she is lost and has lost her language, impeding her connection to her people, but also because through the poem itself, she uses Arabic and English words to break each other and break through these ideas reinforced by the soundscape she creates in these breaks.

Conclusions

The three-line poem "break (me)" demonstrates how Hammad develops "breaking" as a methodology and theoretical intervention that is manifest in her poems. The entire collection *breaking poems* allows her to work through this in some depth. The section above has analyzed the poems in detail in order to suggest how this method is also a theory, and one built out of, in connection to, and in solidarity with African American poetry, intellectual work, and particularly theorizations of language. The soundscapes that Hammad creates allow her to propose ways to exist in the sounds of poetry, not only in its words or concepts. This theoretical intervention strongly recalls the work of Fred Moten. This is true of the ideas worked with in the readings above, such as how grammatical insufficiency leads to lyrical surplus, and how the break is a way to conceptualize some of the spaces in which this can occur. The break for Moten is more complex than this, however. Another feature he theorizes about the break is how spaces between sounds can offer a kind of possibility for a home, particularly for those who have been dispossessed. Those spaces can be a refuge, a place to exist, or following June Jordan might be called "living room," to recall her eponymous poetry collection. When Hammad states that she misses her people she is articulating her search for home within language and also her resistance to simply assimilating and using languages as they have been passed on to her. This is deeply connected to her homage to June Jordan and crediting her as an inspiration for developing this praxis of language. This resonates with the work of Moten and carries forth the work of Black intellectual and creative work, within a Palestinian/Arab American context. Hammad's connections to Jordan are neither isolated nor unique, moreover, and should not be read as a curiosity. The work being done to locate home and "living room" is also part of a solidarity project. Therí Pickens has argued that "subtending *breaking poems* and, for that matter, all of Hammad's work, is the idea that systems of oppression are related, the corollary of which is that people under those systems must seek solidarity and cross-cultural coalition."[92] Harb concurs with this in her tracing of June Jordan's thought in Hammad's work. Above, I tied this to larger Black and other women-of-color feminist projects, linking them to theories of language. My analysis here builds on Harb and Pickens, in this way, by showing how Hammad draws on these feminist resources and uses language to conceptualize the break, theorizing and putting into practice breaking language in her poems. Using her poetry to resist being broken is an embrace of solidarity and shared political purpose. This is expressed powerfully through languages that use breaking to achieve unity.

The following chapter picks up on these themes and focuses on mentorship, homage, and building solidarity through the analysis of poems honoring prominent and well-known, as well as less-known, African American figures. Chapter 2 and the three chapters that follow it all analyze literary works by Arab Americans within the broader framework built through the concepts of breaking language and the break, plus the soundscape they create, each from a different angle and engaging different texts. The next chapter opens with analyses of several poems by D. H. Melhem. Active beginning in the 1970s, Melhem herself inspired Suheir Hammad and was deeply involved in the world of Black art and poetry from this period until her death in 2012. Melhem wrote many poems, including a series of kwansabas for African American literary and political figures. The chapter then moves on to discuss Saladin Ahmed's poem for Harlem Renaissance poet Countee Cullen and Naomi Shihab Nye's poem in memory of Jamyla Bolden, killed in the aftermath of the uprisings against anti-Black police violence in Ferguson, Missouri.

2 Homage as a Politics of Solidarity

Coalition Building and Arab American Poetry

Poetry uses language in ways other literary genres do not. It distinguishes itself from prose through its use of rhythm, rhyme, meter, form, and other techniques, all of which are bound up in language. Poems also work with sound differently than other literary forms; meanings are created through these sounds and within these sounds themselves. The previous chapter showed how theory and practice are fused in Hammad's poetry, especially her *breaking poems*. I suggest there that the collection uses breaking as a methodology and praxis. Hammad's theorization of the break, which she puts into poetic practice in her poems, builds on the work of Black intellectuals and poets like Audre Lorde, Geneva Smitherman, James Baldwin, Fred Moten, and most prominently June Jordan. All of these poets and thinkers engage explicitly and directly with theories of language and connect these to politics and action. They all talk about the radical possibilities of challenging accepted notions of language. Moten and Hammad are specifically concerned with producing and understanding soundscapes as part of larger projects to locate home/s for the dispossessed and make positive social change.

Continuing this analysis, chapter 2 explores ways to further analyze breaking language and its potential in Arab American poetic production in the work of three poets—D. H. Melhem, Saladin Ahmed, and Naomi Shihab Nye. The readings below focus on how political messages are inscribed within the poems, specifically analyzing the ways in which the power of language/s is harnessed through "the break" in the poems and how this breaking inscribes lyrical surplus. All of the poems are written in Standard English, and these analyses identify breaks in this language, how language might be breaking things, and how the poems challenge, reuse, and/or shape language and its power. These poems use the concept and practice of "the break" in ways resonant with Suheir Hammad's theorization through poetry as discussed in chapter 1. The readings below offer similar kinds of readings, including analyzing linguistic and grammatical techniques used to create soundscapes through the break. These breaks in language will be read in relation to conceptual breaks. The detailed investigation of language in this chapter is tied to a thematic focus on poems written in homage to Black American figures. The breaking language in the poems is understood as part of the larger project of constructing a soundscape. Sounds can express things differently than words on the page alone. The larger ideas suggested by these soundscapes are honoring the languages of Black America through honoring certain figures, building a shared poetic space through them. I argue that this homage can be read as a strategy to express solidarity as a form of coalition building.

The analysis of poetry in this chapter begins with works created in the mid-1970s and closes with a poem from 2014. This spectrum of time is one in which Arab American poetry began to be defined as such, and advanced as a tradition. Criticism and anthologies highlighting work by Arab American poets flourished at the end of the twentieth century. This includes works devoted primarily to poetry,[1] to poetry along with other kinds of creative writing,[2] and other kinds of anthologies in which poetry plays a prominent role.[3] As this poetic tradition was forming, gelling, and being documented, it began to solidify a unique identity, at times linked and connected to other US traditions, increasingly those produced by other communities of color. Feminist projects have been instrumental in working in this direction, especially in criticism.[4]

This chapter builds on and extends the kind of critical work being done by Arab and Arab American feminists by prioritizing connections to African American cultural and literary contexts, poetry, and figures, with an analysis of language and politics. This means not only works by and/or about women but also works with a critical race-feminist perspective tying an analysis of gender to other crucial issues like racism, poverty, violence, and war. Thus the inclusion of two poets who are women and one who is a man, who wrote poems for both men and women, which are in line with such feminist projects. It is important to recall Audre Lorde, once again, on how feminism—even lesbian feminism as she defines and explores it in her now classic *Sister Outsider*—does not and should not exclude men. Just as solidarity and breaking exist in a dialectic, feminism interacts and interlocks with many kinds of struggles and helps to produce change. This is one interesting way to work through and think through the complex gender dynamics of poetry written by men and women. Poetry of homage is one fruitful location to probe the contours of this.

The focus on the poetry of homage in this chapter might imply, on one level, connections between traditions rather than breaks with them. But as Hammad's poetry above shows us, building coalitions and solidarity through poetic projects can be a sort of positive and generative break—particularly with hegemonic and oppressive languages, politics, and systems. This analysis in fact underlines and solidifies community connections. In what follows, I suggest that solidarity is expressed and encouraged through these poems, but I also demonstrate how the poems highlight the work and struggles of the people honored as their own as well. This underlines the meaning of taking up struggles as your own, even as you exist within and inhabit difference.[5] Honoring African Americans in poetry is an important statement by Arab American poets. Putting African American figures at the center of poetry and the analysis of poetry is part of the kind of coalition building a poet like Hammad is engaged in, as noted by Pickens and cited above as when Lorde calls this work "unromantic and tedious."[6] Analyzing the poetry of homage thus excavates these connections, but also teaches us as readers about community struggles, artistic achievement, and the brilliance of language. It also demonstrates how these are connected. The argument developed in the chapter below underlines the ways in which this is produced by language and poetic soundscapes, offering breaking language as a conceptual tool to push forward in imagining justice and liberation for Arab Americans. I will begin with the poetry of D. H. Melhem before discussing two poems by Saladin Ahmed and closing with an analysis of one poem by Naomi Shihab Nye.

D. H. Melhem: Speak the Truth to the People!

In contrast to the fairly large amount of criticism on the poetry of Suheir Hammad, relatively little has been written about one of her literary fore-mothers and fellow New Yorker, D. H. Melhem. Like Hammad, Melhem was raised in Brooklyn to displaced Arab immigrant parents, hers hailing from Syria and Lebanon. Also like Hammad, her ties to Black communi-ties in New York City—African American literary, poetic, and political communities in particular—were strong and deep. Hammad has referred to D. H. Melhem as a role model and inspiration, and it is not difficult to see why when examining her poetry, her political commitments, and how she links these together. Melhem's fierce defense of the poor and marginalized, her antiwar advocacy, and her commitment to Black causes in particular mark her work as similar to that of Hammad in many ways, even as her poetic production is clearly that of an earlier generation, with a different language and style.

Melhem is cited in nearly every anthology or collection of works on Arab American writers, and while her contribution to scholarship and literary work by African Americans is not ignored, it is not highlighted. Throughout her life, she was an activist with connections to radical poli-tics, particularly on the Upper West Side of New York City: her opposition to the Vietnam War and involvement in the antiwar movement is usually noted, as are her contributions to women's organizing, antipoverty, and tenants' rights activism. Her work on Black American literature and her book on, and ongoing lifelong relationship with, Gwendolyn Brooks are mentioned, but usually as a footnote, literally or figuratively. Her antholo-gized poems are most often those written for her mother or as antiwar poetry; for example, her best-known work is *Rest in Love*, a book-length poem written to her mother after her death, focused on women's relation-ships and her Arab American heritage and identity. Perhaps unsurpris-ingly, this is the work Carol Fadda-Conrey analyzes in some depth in her study of Arab American literature. Her discussion of this work connects Melhem to other American poets, and in a footnote mentions her study of Gwendolyn Brooks and her other poetic collections.[7] Described as a moving elegy, *Rest in Love* is contrasted even on its back cover to her more challenging work depicting the life of New York City. As Olga Cabral writes, "Instead of the honed down language and social anger of *Notes on 94th Street*, she has given us this delicate, sorrowing and lyrical outcry against death."[8] The next section of this chapter focuses on this "honed down language," and how Melhem uses it to pay homage to Black American figures in *Notes on 94th Street* (1972).[9] This is followed by a discussion of four additional poems from her later collection, *Art and Politics/ Politics and Art* (2010). The poems discussed here are all written to honor Black American personalities, figures, and symbols: a local welfare rights activist in New York (Jennette Washington), the panther (referring to the Black Panther Party), three Black American literary giants (Amiri Baraka, Richard Wright, and Jayne Cortez), and finally, activist, intellectual, and former political prisoner, Angela Davis.

Crucial to situating these poems in relation to Melhem's longer standing and deeper ties to African American literary communities is her close relationship to poet Gwendolyn Brooks. Melhem's book, *Gwendolyn Brooks: Poetry and the Heroic Voice*, was published in 1988 and they worked collaboratively to complete it. Brooks was also the subject of Melhem's doctoral dissertation completed in 1976 at City University of New York. In his introduction to Arab American poetry for the *American Book Review* in 2012, Philip Metres uses Melhem's scholarship on Brooks to point to her paving the way for later generations of Arab American writers who would assert proud identities and politics as Arabs. Metres writes, "It's emblematic, I think, that Arab-American poet D. H. Melhem focused her scholarship on Gwendolyn Brooks, whose career moved from the witty and empathic formalist portraits of Bronzeville residents to increasingly sympathetic poetic dialogues with Black Nationalism."[10] Like most criticism on Arab American writers and poets, the focus here is more on Melhem's development as an Arab/Arab American and for that community rather than on what she might contribute to or learn from Black America. Melhem's own statement about her connection to Brooks in her project is therefore revealing: "My respect for Black culture began long ago with an awareness of the political realities of Black life, realities that engaged my own experience with a multicultural family background. I learned early that, as with people themselves, a literature of beauty or nobility could be ignored or deprecated because it diverged from prevailing norms."[11] Melhem's own understanding of how she became engaged with Brooks and what she chooses to emphasize in her prefatory note to the book is her respect for Black culture. She also takes the time to underline the political realities of Black life. She draws the parallels with her family background without naming her own communities.

As June Jordan had on Suheir Hammad, Gwendolyn Brooks is clearly the artist who made a formative and lasting impact on Melhem. She states that she was inspired to write her book after sitting in a poetry workshop offered by Brooks at the City College of New York in 1971, and the book is dedicated to her.[12] But also like Hammad, Melhem's connections and engagements do not end there. Her next book, which won an American Book Award in 1991, is *Heroism in the New Black Poetry: Introductions and Interviews*. Moreover, Melhem's interviews and discussions of Black poets are published in a range of other locations as well including the *MELUS Journal* (Multi-Ethnic Literatures of the United States Journal) and the *Black American Literature Forum*.[13] People she talked to whose works she engaged include Amiri Baraka, Jane Cortez, Dudley Randall, and Sonia Sanchez. Her interest in the Black Arts Movement and literary participation in projects in the community continued through her life. She attended events throughout the twenty-first century until her health declined; one of her last public events was a tribute to Amiri Baraka, at which she and Suheir Hammad both offered tributes.[14]

"for jennette washington" and "the panther": Notes on 94th Street

The sharp and short language of *Notes on 94th Street* reflects its gritty realism. There is a poem in this collection about cockroaches, another about a doorman, and one devoted to SROs (single room occupancy, subsidized housing projects for low-income people in New York). These poems, like all those in the collection, reveal and contest the poverty and inequality of New York City in the 1970s. They are joined by a number of others that have more manifestly "political" content in a section labeled "Heroines and Heroes." This naming of the section signals Melhem's desire to recognize and pay homage to a series of individuals and symbolic individuals engaged in important resistance work. For example, two poems clearly protest the war in Vietnam: "CORRECTION PLEASE" and "incident at st. gregory's, april 21, 1970."[15] The first attacks media misrepresentation of the war; the second is a lyrical rendition of what happened at the protest in St. Gregory's Church on that day, leading to the case of the Catonsville Nine—including priest Daniel Berrigan.[16] Other antiwar poems are two dedicated to Max and Isabel Manes,[17] and the poem dedicated to Kay Leslie praises her for marching for voter registration in Mississippi.[18] Within this collection, among the heroines and heroes, are two more powerful poems, written in homage to one real and one symbolic Black figure—"for jennette washington" and "panther."

Melhem's short, three-stanza, twenty-four-line poem, "for jennette washington," is followed by an asterisk, leading to a note which reads, "formerly eastern regional director, national welfare rights organization."[19] Melhem is careful to give attention to Washington's official title, and not leave her name undefined as in the case of other figures she writes poems for in the collection (Max and Isabel Manes or Kay Leslie, for example). Washington worked in a number of other capacities and also was a local activist and organizer in New York City throughout the 1950s and 1960s, and by publicly acknowledging her title and role, Melhem is highlighting her official position. This may partly be to assure her status and stature but no doubt is also because the work she did—as evidenced by her biography and also the words of this poem—was often undervalued.

Washington was herself a welfare recipient who, acutely aware of the stigmas about and difficulties in accessing welfare, particularly for poor Black women,[20] cofounded the Westside Welfare Recipients League. Both her biographers' and her own accounts credit her rebellious personality with helping her become an effective community organizer in New York in the 1950s and 1960s, where she also worked in a number of other organizations on urban renewal and housing rights, in parent-teacher associations, and eventually the National Welfare Rights Organization.[21] She is recognized in the literature on welfare rights as an important activist and organizer.[22] Melhem's poem honors her and her work in these roles and sets her up as someone whose commitment and contributions she wishes to support and sustain.

The poem "for jennette washington" is offered within the collection as homage, and she is included among other heroines. The tone of the poem at first seems to be offering advice; but it is more of a call to action than the words of someone telling someone else what to do. It acknowledges the rage of a Black woman community organizer working on poverty in New York and uses strong imagery and ideas to encourage and support her. After opening the poem with one line consisting of Jennette's first name (in lowercase letters as in all of her poems in this collection), she then writes:

you're mad as hell
at almost everyone
stay mad
keep that hard rage.[23]

We do not know what the hard rage is related to, but in the context of the poem—how Washington is identified by Melhem and general knowledge of the struggles of poor, Black, working-class women in the 1970s in New York—we imagine that is has to do with her struggles in advocating for a decent life. Melhem not only encourages Washington to keep her "hard rage" but also to "give none of it / away" in the last lines of the first stanza. These words are echoed in the third and final stanza of the poem as well, in its final lines, "give none of it / away," as is her name, when Melhem urges her "so / on guard, jennette / keep that hard rage."[24] The second stanza of the poem contains Melhem's most direct and severe social commentary, in counseling Washington to defend herself because the street is not safe and warning her she will be "raped / with promises / vote stolen / no redress" and follows this with the observation "they'll say it's just / the local / high crime rate."[25] Melhem's words here are pointed: the streets are not safe for women, Black women in particular, and there will be no way to get justice (redress). The issue of unsafe streets and having no recourse or protection is one of great concern to African American urban communities—women in particular—and is an example of Melhem's involvement with the issues of the communities she is engaged in. Her ironic commentary on how such a complaint might be managed makes reference to the notion that "high crime rates" in New York are blamed abstractly for the very real social problems arising out of situations of extreme poverty and deprivation.

Melhem's poem "for jennette washington" thus blends a social critique of the problems in New York that Washington fought her entire life to improve with a respect for her work. In encouraging her to keep "her hard rage," Melhem is sending a powerful message to her readership. Her repetition of several crucial words and lines in the characteristically spare language of poems in this collection should be noted in an analysis of this poem's soundscape. The sounds Melhem creates thus resonate with Hammad's breaking poems in their brevity and succinct use of words, though she does not employ spoken language, or "broken language," like Hammad does. Her poetic language in *Notes on 94th Street* manages to say a great deal through the strategic use of carefully chosen words and repetitions. The sound effects of the repetition of jennette's name, for example, as well as lines like "keep that hard rage / dry" and "give none of it / away" perform sound work that conveys messages to the reader. The messages here are of hardening one's stance, making a fist, and challenging official narratives that harm people and the community. The breaks in English in the poem parallel breaking with oppressive social structures and conventions, and this is continued in other poems in this same section, "Heroes and Heroines," as the poem "panther" demonstrates.

The poem "panther" uses similarly sparse language to honor a figure in the Black community, if not one specific person.[26] The panther as hero pays homage to the symbol of the Black Panther Party for Self Defense, which was an important force in the United States in the late 1960s and early 1970s and one which built extensive intercommunity solidarity between African Americans and other radical political groups, both in the United States and internationally. Some of these links were discussed in the introduction above, and as Alex Lubin points out in *Geographies of Liberation*, the party was one of the single most important locations in Black political life in the United States for building Black-Arab solidarity, at home and abroad.[27] As Lubin argues, "the Panthers' intercommunal political imaginary formed a community" that worked to connect groups with the United States, as well as to link the Black Freedom Movement with the Palestinian national movement abroad."[28] This became increasingly important in Arab contexts when Eldridge and Katherine Cleaver went into exile in Algeria (1968) and also to building strong links with the PLO and Yasser Arafat.

The internationalist outlook was important to the work being done in the United States by rank and file members of the Black Panther Party as well. As Jeffrey O. G. Ogbar recalled, "Although inextricably tied to the impulse of Black Power, the Panthers were also intimately familiar with other, nonblack radicalism. They were open to coalition-building from inception."[29] This coalition building was not limited to particular communities, as another party member, Elder Freedman, recalled in a recent interview: "It was a matter not only of addressing the problems that we had in the black community but also of aligning ourselves with the brown community, the Native American community, the Asian community, the Palestinian community, the indigenous Australian community, people in India and people in various parts of South America. They identified with the Black Panthers as a symbol for social change."[30] These connections to communities built upon the symbolic and practical commitment to social change and empowerment of the dispossessed more generally. The Black Panther Party's dedication to Palestine solidarity work was also powerful and not limited to the 1960s context. Some members have maintained a life-long commitment to the struggle for a free Palestine; one of the most prominent examples is Angela Davis, to whom Melhem dedicated a poem, which I will return to below.

The early 1970s was the height of the Black Panther Party's activist power, and it had already begun to fragment and split at the time D. H. Melhem's poem, "panther," was published in 1972. The series of raids, attacks, murders, and intense pressure by the FBI's COINTELPRO program eventually undermined the party's organization and cohesion, though it remained, and even today remains, a powerful symbolic force and inspiration for generations of Black and non-Black activists and organizers. The symbolism of the party, represented in its Black Panther image, remains strong in popular memory and cultural representation.[31] Melhem's poem therefore is part of a larger context of poetry, art, and cultural production that honors and pays homage to the party and what it stood for.

Melhem's poem "panther" is substantially longer than "for jennette washington" and consists of seven short stanzas, the last of which is only one line long. The imagery in the poem, perhaps predictably, hinges on the color black. It begins by associating black with four naturally occurring phenomena: the sun, the earth, the stars, and ice.[32] These four words work to valorize the word "black" and the concept of Blackness, which in turn is strongly linked to the panther. Blackness in the poem is used as a bridging device, true to the spirit of the time and the context in which D. H. Melhem was composing this poem.[33] The poem is written from the perspective of the panther, who is black, as black as the other life forces—the sun, earth, stars, and ice—and who moves both through the jungle and through offices. In the second stanza, the panther in the jungle "wears a white suit" and in offices, "crawl[s] / through glass doors."[34] This reversal of what is expected—the suit in the jungle and crawling in offices—sets up the way in which the panther moves in the rest of the poem, where some of its important challenges are mounted. The use of language in Melhem's poem is once again spare; here she also uses line breaks in ways similar to Hammad, where meanings are challenged depending on how lines are read. This, in addition to reversals of meaning, allows the poem to inscribe challenges to the reader through its language as well as its message.

The important lines in this regard are in stanza four:

I will claw
suckle
strike monuments
and men
with paradoxes
learned
by the terrors and furies
of my wounds
I must be animal
toward man
a man
among animals.[35]

This stanza has no punctuation and uses a breaking strategy prefiguring Hammad's more extensive experimentations, which runs ideas and words into each other. Melhem develops this technique further in her kwansabas, discussed below. Here we can see how the extremely short lines of at most five words can be read as one long run-on sentence or many, depending on where the break is located. The paradoxes are learned by "terrors and furies." Are the furies, however, furies and terrors "of" the panther's wounds? Or do these terrors and furies coming from the wounds then make the panther an animal? The stanza can be read as all one line or in pieces, slightly changing the meaning with each different grouping of words and lines, but leading to an unequivocal message at the end about the connection between animal and man. This play with grammar is like Hammad's but uses briefer and starker language and sounds, expressing Melhem's more direct and pointed commentary.

Here Melhem is playing with the classic imagery from the Black Freedom Struggle whereby people protested with signs, placards, and sandwich boards proclaiming "I am a man." In a struggle to assert humanity, the use of animal imagery can be both powerful and dangerous. The Black Panther Party for Self Defense in fact chose this animal as its symbol because it is powerful, but lashes out only in defense.[36] Thus needing to be "animal toward man" can be the need to claim this figure and this power, and also the need to respond when attacked. The final line shows, however, that those attacking are themselves animals and that the narrative voice itself claims to be "a man." This stanza powerfully questions who is the animal and who is the man in both positive and negative senses in both cases. It is crucial to remember that the notion of being a "civilized man" was unavailable to Black people, and thus the choice of the panther is also a refusal to appeal to this identity through a politics of respectability.

The fifth stanza also reinforces the panther's perspective, showing the poet's solidarity with their struggle. Though it does not directly name prison, the line "I number my days" certainly evokes imprisonment and the limited lifespan of Black liberationists—a major challenge members of the party were facing in the 1970s, under intense attack and disintegration. She follows this by waking to "dim mornings," which again could refer to low prison lights or simply days that do not seem bright, literally and metaphorically. This imagery is contrasted with the shining "white lies" evoked in the final lines of the stanza, where the panther wakes: "my story revised in newspapers / white lies for others."[37] Here Melhem uses a wordplay on the term "white lies," directly invoking and criticizing the sustained attack on the Black Panther Party by the white US media. As the panther is Black, the lies are white, and thus lies that are contained within newspapers spread misinformation.

The end of the poem also manipulates whiteness in different ways to makes its point, visually. In the final line of the poem, which is set apart as a separate stanza, she uses a large white space. Parallel to Hammad's use of line breaks, Melhem's use of white space employs a literal break between words to represent breaking language, visually, and in sound, manifesting moreover a conceptual break. This is preceded by three lines setting up the scene of the panther facing its attackers:

and a storm coming
now is my time to receive
every hunter who seeks me

I am here in the clearing.[38]

These lines make clear that the panther is being hunted and knows that its time has come with "a storm." The allusion to the storm and being hunted, following the white media's lies, makes clear that Melhem is critiquing the situation the party and its members are in and expressing her support. She represents the panther as alone and visible "in the clearing"—the white space left between these words and "I am here" are a powerful reminder of how white society has isolated and left the panther to defend itself. Melhem's respect for the panther and its struggles are clear, and she uses her sharp, simple, and short language to express this, including the poem in the section on "Heroines and Heroes."[39] This stanza, and the poem overall, uses a series of strategies of breaking language—using white space on the page, using short words as punctuation, and brief sentences to reinforce her message.

"Certain Personae" of Art and Politics/Politics and Art

The last volume of poetry D. H. Melhem published before her death in 2012, *Art and Politics/Politics and Art*, collects work she published in a number of locations, most of which are easily read as overtly political, openly merging politics and art. Like *Notes on 94th Street*, many of the poems inscribe strong antiwar messages that, given the different global context of war in the twenty-first century, means that they are specifically and deeply connected to wars in the Arab world. The collection is divided into three sections, the first of which is titled "Certain Personae."[40] I will focus on this section and in particular four poems written for Black American literary and political figures: Amiri Baraka, Jayne Cortez, Angela Davis, and Richard Wright, the first two of whom are included in her earlier study on the "new Black poetry" of the Black Arts Movement.[41] I read these poems together with the two earlier ones from *Notes on 94th Street* to construct a larger picture of how her poetics and politics of honoring Black literary and cultural figures are expressed.

Of the four short poems dedicated to Black American figures, three are short kwansabas, and the fourth to Angela Davis is titled "Song for Angela Davis in the Women's House of Detention."[42] The kwansaba is a poetic form of forty-nine words: seven lines, of seven words each, which mirror the seven principles of the African American holiday, Kwanzaa. Eugene B. Redmond coined the term and according to Melhem invented the concept in the Writer's Club 1995 workshop season in East St. Louis.[43] His revue, *Drumvoices*, is where many kwansabas have been published and are the first publication venue for the two poems here for Richard Wright and Amiri Baraka. As Melhem states in an author's note to her "Kwansaba for Richard Wright," printed in the text, "the closing passage of his *Black Boy* is so beautiful that I used it as the epigraph to the second part of my book-length poem, *Country: An Organic Poem* (1998), about the United States. The kwansaba is based on this quotation. I hope I did it—and this great writer—justice."[44] True to the genre, these kwansabas are praise poems: they honor and pay tribute to their subjects using a brief, limited form. The poem for Angela Davis is as well, though it does not meet the generic requirements to be a kwansaba. These generic constraints suit

Melhem's signature poetic style, and her use of language within them is precise and evocative of the mood she creates in each.

Kwansabas

The "Kwansaba for Richard Wright," as we know from Melhem's author's note included in the text, was intended to riff off of the closing lines to his memoir of growing up in the US South, *Black Boy* (1945).[45] *Black Boy* is as famous for its lyrical depiction of the suffering of African Americans in the US South as it is for its hopeful ending.[46] The classic book closes as follows: "With ever watchful eyes and bearing scars, visible and invisible, I headed North, full of the hazy notion that life could be lived with dignity, that the personalities of others should not be violated, that men should be able to confront other men without fear or shame, and that if men were lucky with their living on earth they might win some redeeming meaning having struggled and suffered here beneath the stars."[47] Melhem's poem reads as a pared-down rendition of these same lines, with only a few notable changes, and shifting the narrative voice from "I" to "You." Some of the subtle changes in words and focus lead the message of hope expressed by Wright to be a more powerfully militant expression by Melhem. For example, she slightly shifts that what should done without fear or shame to "confronting other men." Rather, she expresses this concept with "a life that could be / lived devoid of fear or shame." One reading of this is that she is moving the concept from confrontation to simply living life. This could be incorporating the idea that confrontation is a part of living life, but it also moves the focus from confrontation to life. Moreover, it subtly removes the gendered language used by Wright that takes "man" or "men" as the default, and replaces it with just living. This is consistent with Melhem's body of work that never uses male pronouns to be an assumed universal, though this was standard practice when she was active as a poet.

This feminist note is not incidental. Melhem's vision for women's rights and equality is very much consistent with that of her contemporary women of color and Black feminist theorists who insisted on women's rights at the same time as centering antipoverty, antiracism, and antiwar messages.[48] Several other small additions mark the changes to Wright's passage in Melhem's kwansaba. She adds the words "natural respect" to living life, perhaps referring to the concept of not violating others' personalities. Finally, she changes the way that Wright expresses the notion that people might "win some redeeming meaning" from the struggling and suffering, which Melhem expresses as "wresting some meaning from the pain you have endured." Melhem's words are more direct and point to an actively engaged process; it is not just about receiving but about a victory one must take—reminiscent of her imprecation to Jennette Washington about holding on to her "hard rage." Moreover, the stars in Melhem's poem bear "stoic witness" to Wright's pain and suffering.

Like all of the kwansabas, the praise poem for Richard Wright uses the break—here particularly evident in line breaks—as a form suited to this style of poetic composition. Each line can be read as a separate line, but each also spills into the next, creating a forty-nine word sentence or idea. The very first line, for example, is: "You kept watch as bearing scars, seen." The scars are emphasized in this first line—they are seen. We know from Wright's original that they are also "unseen," but this is not clear until the second line. The first and second lines run into each other and are made meaningful by Wright's original. But the second line is also interesting, as a standalone statement, "and unseen, you headed North, your hazy." The meaning here could be that he was unseen as he headed North. The notion of the Black American being always seen and unseen, invisible and hypervisible, is one of the important contributions of the book *Black Boy* and emphasized by the kinds of double meanings inscribed through the line breaks in Melhem's "Kwansaba for Richard Wright."

Kwansabas are praise poems that exist in the break: they break poetic conventions—their imposed brevity and word limits per line intentionally create unique word and sound effects that invoke a kind of syncopation and music. The soundscapes created therefore are powerful and evocative as much as they are on the written page. This is true of the poem for Wright, and even more so of the "Kwansaba for Amiri Baraka" and "Kwansaba for Jayne Cortez," the latter of which invokes syncopated rhythms most clearly to produce sounds that mirror drumming.[49] This sound effect reinforces the notion that poems are meant to be read and performed, and not to live merely on the page. The breaks used by Melhem in these poems recall the techniques used by Hammad, discussed in the previous chapter. Similarly to Hammad, Melhem's use of line breaks is clearly influenced by African American literary, linguistic, and musical traditions and meant to invoke and reflect them. At the same time, using these techniques also is proposed as a way of honoring the legacies and traditions of specific poets and literary figures, but also the larger African American creative traditions. The subtle and overt reference to Black poetic language is thus evidenced in these breaks. This is inscribed in all of the kwansabas in complementary but different ways that are original in each.

In its sparseness, repetition, and use of short, sharp, well-chosen words—as well as hard-hitting political messages—Melhem's work resembles that of Jayne Cortez. Cortez was a poet and performance artist whose production is associated with jazz, the Black Arts Movement, and the use of art as a way to advance political change—as hers was in the Black Freedom Struggle. She created lyrical and viscerally evocative sounds in her poetry, many of which were performed over African drumming.[50] The first line of Melhem's kwansaba invokes this: "Drums earth sweat hot jazz cool blues." "Drums" is one of only two capitalized words in this forty-nine-word poem—the other is "Yoruba." Both words are highlighted and honored through this capitalization, and opening the poem with the word "drums" further reinforces its pride of place among Cortez's own artistic production that Melhem explicitly shows she respected and admired.

The use of the break metaphorically is crucial in this first line of the poem. We can see this first in how the word "sweat" can be a verb and/or a noun. It is a word evocative of a bodily function that is produced with labor and work, but also any kind of exertion—including pleasurable exertions like making music. Using the word in a way that can be a noun or a verb or both, Melhem's poem once again prefigures a technique favored by Suheir Hammad in *breaking poems*. Like the examples given in the previous chapter, Melhem is breaking grammar and the rules of grammar. If "sweat" is a noun, she has simply listed a series of nouns and adjectives that call up images related to or describing something to do with music— drums, blues, and jazz—and associated them with words like earth, sweat, hot, and cool. Here, though used as a verb, we can then read the drums and earth as sweating—emitting or giving off, or even colloquially being bothered by—hot jazz cool blues. The lyrical surplus, as Moten would call it, located in this grammatical ambiguity is overflowing. Moten's musical metaphor is particularly apt here because of the poem's commitment to lyricism and musicality in its soundscape as well as its thematic content. The Black musical forms jazz and blues are here separated by two words that are both opposites and synonyms depending on context, hot and cool.[51] Here Melhem uses intraline enjambment as a sound technique to emphasize the multiple meanings and layered importance of all of these words. Both temperatures and metaphors for how popular, well-received, and/or culturally relevant something is, "hot" and "cool" are loaded with meaning in this line. Moreover, the word "hot" appears as a repeated word with multiple meanings in one of Cortez's performance pieces, "she got he got," another possible reference Melhem could be alluding to here.[52]

There are also multiple locations in which to read the breaks in the poem for Cortez—the lines come fast and the sounds are as important as the words on the page. Each line can stand alone—as in the "Kwansaba for Richard Wright"—but breaking the poem in different locations alters the meanings slightly. The two following lines for example, lines three and four of the poem, read:

> birth your poems from heart and bone
> burst from the navel of furious dreams[53]

"Birth" and "burst"—almost homophones when said aloud—could both be read as verbs continuing on from the Yoruba gods from the second line, following on across breaks for one long sentence. The heart and bone, however, may be bursting from the navel of furious dreams, tying together the symbols of the physical body. Like Hammad's project of breaking, Melhem here is true to Cortez's style of wordplay that could be described as "furious," much as the dreams Melhem attributes to Cortez. This is somewhat of a contrast to the dreams in the poem for Angela Davis discussed in the section below, described there as "unused."

Melhem's breaking language, which challenges Standard English, has much in common with Hammad's. She uses similar techniques like line breaks, enjambment, double meanings, challenges to grammar, sound assonance, and the juxtaposition of words to create sounds. She does not use all of the same techniques, however. She makes much less use of inter-anmination of languages—Arabic and English—and fewer grammatical breaks that could be read as spoken Black Language and/or Arabic. She makes more use than Hammad does of blank space on the page as a break. Though her soundscapes are different, the breaks in her poems are closely tied to sound, similarly to Hammad's. Another technique Melhem uses in this poem, somewhat uncharacteristically, is rhyme, "while finger snaps and left foot taps." This creates an effective mirror of the soundscape she is conjuring through the depiction of how these sounds are created. As a jazz poet, the finger snap and foot tap are characteristic of her performances, and even listening to recordings of her performances today that have no accompanying visuals, you can discern the sounds of tapping and snap-ping. This focus on sound adds power to Melhem's language and what she is trying to achieve in the break. The words "rise black within you" pay tribute to Cortez as a prominent contributor to the new poetry, the Black Arts movement, and employ very much the kind of language Cortez herself does.

The "Kwansaba for Amiri Baraka" works similarly to the previous two, in that it reflects back in its sparseness the work of Baraka himself and what he stood for. He was perhaps the best-known poet and writer of the Black Arts Movement, and something of an icon. As she does with the work of Cortez, Melhem features Baraka's poetry in her collection *Heroism in the New Black Poetry,* as well as in other locations. In the acknowledgments to this book, Melhem refers admiringly to his political commitments and how he inspired her when she sat in on his class on "Art and Marxism" at the New School for Social Research, describing his message to them and his method of teaching as follows: "Art, he demonstrated socratically, even when disguised as apolitical, is propaganda."[54] This brief homage is a tribute to their longer engagement.

As in her poem for Cortez, Melhem capitalizes only two words in the praise poem for Baraka, in this case the opening two words of the poem: "Proud Black." The importance and meaning of beginning a poem with these two words needs no explanation: Baraka's status as an icon of Black pride who was first known as a prominent Black nationalist and later as a Third World liberationist. His movement from a nationalist to internationalist stance is perhaps what is referred to in the poem's opening line, "Proud Black bridge to non-skin politic, you." Once again the use of line breaks allows multiple readings for both the meanings and sounds of the poem. Reading the first line as a discrete unit, the "you" at the end reverses the syntax and proclaims "you"—Baraka—as the bridge, proud and Black and leading to a politics, not determined or limited by color, though he remains who he is. These lines then follow with a series of verbs, which can also be attached to the "you" following the break: you pour (molten steel of poems), you pound (their music into stars), and you free (a series of things beginning with their drum).

"You free" could be read as a sentence with a zero copula—you are free—or it could be a transitive verb and Baraka is freeing something. If it is the latter, what Baraka is said to be freeing here is important, and Melhem's use of repetition—as in other poems—is crucial to the sound created to break English in this poem and create something new, as well as the message. Here the word repeated is "talk:" "talking blues talk / jazz talk race rising talk people power / talk across borders."[55] Talk and talking here separate the words blues, jazz, race rising, people power, across borders. Strung together these words have powerful associations with Black power on their own as music, race pride, people's movements, and working internationally. The use of "talk" as a repetitive sound device, but one with important meaning, reinforces the links and the power of the lines, remarking that Baraka is both producing this talk and way of talking but also that these elements themselves "talk"—convey culture, art, and meaning.

Like the poem for Jayne Cortez, this kwansaba creates a soundscape that uses breaking language as an effective technique to advance its conceptual engagement. The poem invokes another set of repeated sounds in the last two lines with "raising," "radiant," and "ray": "raising hearts raising fists / radiant with unity rays of constant change."[56] The way in which Melhem manipulates the break means that it could be the talk and talking and/or it could be Baraka the bridge that raises hearts and fists and is radiant with unity. The hearts and fists that are raised recall the classic symbol of Black power in the 1960s. This line also recalls the notion that the elevation of the race through education, art, and culture is inseparable from a Black politics of liberation—notions promoted by the Black Arts Movement. The concept of unity is also crucial to the movement: *umoja*, one of the seven foundational notions of Kwanzaa, represents this and therefore is important to the creation of a kwansaba. The idea that rays of unity would advocate "constant change" and that this is the closing imagery of the poem written for Baraka underlines his commitment to always making a change in the Black community and his struggle for the race.

"Song for Angela Davis in the Women's House of Detention"

The final poem by D. H. Melhem I discuss here is devoted to Black liberation icon, former Black Panther, political prisoner, and tireless advocate for justice—Angela Davis. The poem for Davis stands out here among the three others both because it is a "song" rather than a kwansaba dedicated to her, and also because she is not a poet or a creative writer, but a political figure. In this way, she can be read as more similar to Jennette Washington than she is to Amiri Baraka, Richard Wright, or Jayne Cortez in the context of Melhem's poetic oeuvre. The inclusion of Davis within the "Certain Personae" of *Art and Politics/Politics and Art* recalls the section of *Notes on 94th Street*, subtitled "Heroines and Heroes." This song for Angela Davis also names a specific location, the Women's House of Detention—the notorious Greenwich Village prison in which Angela Davis was held for nine weeks in 1970 under charges of murder, kidnapping, and criminal conspiracy before being extradited to California, where she was subsequently acquitted of all charges. It was shut down in 1971 only months after she was released. This prison had been over time used to incarcerate political prisoners, those women considered radicals and/or leaders of movements, and its inmates included other Black Panthers such as Afeni Shakur and Joan Bird, Andrea Dworkin, Valerie Solanas, and much earlier Ethel Rosenberg and Elizabeth Gurley Flynn. Davis, like others, spoke out about her treatment there in a number of speeches and publications including a 1970 article in the *Village Voice*, excerpted from her autobiography in which she documented at length the substandard living conditions, her unfair confinement to a solitary cell, and the abuse of herself and others at the hands of the guards. She also, however, recounts moving scenes of women's self-organizing in the prison, the warm welcome she received with fists raised of fellow "sister prisoners," and the solidarity demonstrations organized inside and outside the prison while she was held there.[57] It is no doubt not only Davis's work and actions and political commitments as a Black Panther but also her confinement in this prison that inspired Melhem to write this praise poem to honor her.

The poem opens with her first and last name, repeated twice as the opening line, "angela davis angela davis." Recalling the opening of the poem "for jennette washington," this poem opens by calling her name. It also evokes that it is a song, and even perhaps in the repetition a type of call-and-response. The repetition of the same name twice in the first line alerts us that repetition is key to this poem—the last two lines also repeat each other: "and the world drowns in unused dreams / and the world drowns in unused dreams."[58] The entire poem consists of two stanzas, the first five lines long and the second nine lines long. Therefore, like the kwansabas, the song for Angela Davis is compact and concise in its expression, focused on only a couple of ideas evoked through imagery and carefully chosen words.

The first stanza opens with a contrast between body and mind: her body is body incarcerated or, in the words of the poem, "caged," but her mind "goes out on to the street." Not only is the contrast powerful, but the choice of words is also meaningful. Referring to the body as "caged" of course recalls what is done to an animal, evoking the brutality of imprisonment and the dehumanization of people, particularly Black people in the United States, what Davis struggled against as a member of the Black Panther Party. That her mind is depicted as going "out on to the street" both testifies to the power of her intellect and ability to transcend the prison walls, but also that she was a woman of the people, working in protest movements and taking to the streets. The fourth and fifth lines read, "like a panther passing through stone / staining ground with immovable shadows."[59] These lines bring together the contrast between body and mind and join them in the unmistakable image of the panther—of course representing Angela Davis's political affiliations. It is Angela the panther who can escape the confines of the stone walls of the Women's House of Detention, and this testifies to the power of the party and its messages and meanings to not be confined or constrained by the system. The immovable shadows that she stains the ground with recall the dank conditions of the prison itself, documented by Davis. The use of the words across lines here to affect a break is important. The panther passes through stone and this stains (the) ground if the lines are read separately. If the words are read together as "stone staining ground," "stone" and "staining" might both be adjectives for the ground—something else the panther would then pass through.

The panther's fluidity of movement in any case is a clear message that is paralleled in the imagery around water—flowing and drowning in the second, longer stanza of the poem. Melhem's collection of poems opens with images of water, referencing the French painter Henri Matisse and the ways in which water gives life but also causes drowning. This is reactivated at the end of the collection to advance Melhem's poetic message in homage to Davis. In this stanza she writes, "every gutter runs grief to the sewer / until grief is flowing free." The notion of free-flowing grief is a stronger condemnation and political message of negating pain and suffering than in "Kwansaba to Richard Wright." Here, grief runs into sewers—urban images conjuring poverty and decay—until it is flowing free. She makes it clear that this grief is caused by "unused dreams" and cautions that this is what will drown the world. "Unused dreams" is a powerful image itself, the dream being an important reference point for Black culture—the dream of Martin Luther King Jr. and the deferred dream of Langston Hughes being two major literary reference points.[60] The space between the stanzas in this poem is one location in which to read "the break" as a creative intervention. The focal point of the poem in this reading is right in its visual center. Thus the sounds that work together in building the language in the poem recall the visual gaps. If we locate surplus meaning within the break, as much as in grammatical insufficiency as Moten suggests, then the words amplifying this meaning—filling the break between stanzas, where white space takes up the page—are: "truth is." The break this poem offers is Melhem's definition of truth. She demonstrates that truth does not die with a human body and is located within "unused dreams." Her "Song for Angela Davis in the Women's House of Detention," therefore, like the kwansabas that accompany it in "Certain Personae," carries a message of praise, of respect, and of solidarity in the struggle for truth and for justice.

D. H. Melhem's poetry is a powerful reminder of literary solidarity that is deep and sustained throughout her career as a critic, activist, and poet. Her homage to Black artists, poets, writers, activists, and political figures is connected to her larger worldview, her feminism, and the broader struggles in which she was engaged and to which she devoted her life. Her work prefigures that of Suheir Hammad in the issues she was committed to and her deep and long engagement in Black literary contexts and cultures of her times, also in New York City. In this sense it is also important to connect her poetry to June Jordan's Black-Arab solidarity work. Melhem engages the theory and practice of many African American intellectuals, poets, and cultural figures in her work, employing breaking language in multiple ways to both express this and honor their work. The epigraph to the "Certain Personae" section of Melhem's last book, attributed to the Persian poet Jelaluddin Rumi, can be instructive in thinking in these terms: "this is a subtle truth / whatever you love you are."[61] If we think about becoming what we love or who we love, that we *are* what we love, this leads us back to some of the kinds of solidarity statements expressed by Jordan in her poem "Moving towards Home," Lorde's commitment to fighting any sister's oppression,[62] or many of Hammad's expressions of coalition building, which evince love for people across backgrounds, languages, communities, and so on. Love and loving, including friendship, as solidarity leads us back as well to the kind of work being done by Atshan and Moore in their expression of finding a place for Black-Arab solidarity through work on shared community issues, including Black American uprisings and movements against police brutality and liberation for Palestine. Melhem's poetic production remained committed to Black American art, creativity, and struggle, and also evolved over forty-odd years. Her praise of this work and homage to it as a poet sets the stage for a different poet of a younger generation— Detroit born, raised, and based Saladin Ahmed.

Saladin Ahmed: Honoring Our Ancestors

Today better known as one of the first and most recognized Arab American science fiction writers, Saladin Ahmed is also a poet. He has deeps roots in the Arab American community of Detroit, Michigan; his paternal family is long established in the Detroit area. His father, Ismael Ahmed, was one of the founders of ACCESS, the well-known Arab American community center and one of the oldest in the United States, as well as Concert of Colors.[63] His great-grandmother was Arab American activist Aliyah Hassan, herself born in North Dakota, who is remembered fondly as a powerful community leader in Detroit, executive director of ACCESS from 1972 to 1981, and associate of Malcolm X, helping to organize his pilgrimage to Mecca where he first embraced orthodox Islam.[64] Ahmed penned a poem dedicated to his great-grandmother, "Important Things to an Eight Year Old," in which he ponders her important social contributions and his personal relationship with her.[65] It is discussed briefly below. Ahmed himself has a number of different connections and ties to the African American community in Detroit, and his creative work demonstrates a number of ways in which he engages Black America.[66] Examples of this include his essays, published when he was living in New York, as the "New York Newsline" column for the short-lived Arab American magazine, *Arabica*,[67] and his poetry published in African American literary venues like the journal *Callaloo: A Journal of African American and African Arts and Letters*.[68] I catalog some of Ahmed's connections in order to contextualize how they contribute to an analysis of his poetry as part of a larger coalition and solidarity-building project. It is not simply the fact of these engagements by Ahmed, but how they might be mobilized in this context that I am underlining here. In the introduction to this chapter I also mention that Ahmed is the only poet or author in this collection who is a man. I would like to clarify here that he is not included for this reason as a token, but because of the thematic and linguistic interest in his poetry. Though I am not focused on him as a male poet per se, it is interesting to reflect on his work in relation to feminist criticism and gender dynamics, for example Lorde's reflections on engaging the work and solidarity of men, also mentioned above.

The poem that Ahmed wrote for his great-grandmother, "Important Things to an Eight Year Old," admires her activism and in particular her connections to Malcolm X and the Black Freedom Movement. It exemplifies his own overall commitments and engagements and uses the voice of the poet as an eight-year-old boy to reflect on his great-grandmother. Ahmed regrets that he knew and appreciated the activist Aliyah Hassan only as his doting and kind great-grandmother, rather than for her immense work as a community organizer. He repeats that "no connections were drawn," because what was important to him as a child were her family stories, hidden candies, nonhalal steaks, and that she let him drink coffee at eight years old. He cites the things he wishes he had connected to in several lines that he describes as what obscured her to him, "the mountains of social justice / the oceans of personal achievement / the plateaus of religious scholarship."[69] Earlier in the poem, he also uses a three-line grouping in order to define her:

> She was . . . acquainted with Malcolm
> She was . . . one of his guides to Mecca
> She was . . . a jet-haired smoke screen, blinding FB's eye.[70]

In the later section of the poem, just before closing, he redefines her using the same poetic structure, but reformulating what she was to him:

> She was . . . at peace when cooking for him
> She was . . . happy when telling stories
> She was . . . very good at spoiling him.[71]

As a young man at her funeral, Ahmed regrets that he loved her more for the latter contributions than the former ones; the poem ends with an acknowledgement that these were both important to her as a person. In the poem, Ahmed highlights in two groups of three the things he finds most important in Aliyah Hassan's life, using the sounds of repetition and definition (she was . . .). Through this, Ahmed valorizes and gives attention to Hassan's work with Malcolm X and the Black community. In a sense Ahmed foreshadows or gives a sense of his own later commitments through his descriptions of this woman, who was a force in her community, a woman who advocated strongly for women, for Muslims, for Arabs in America and who built strong ties to African Americans herself.

"For Countee Cullen": Homage to Other Ancestors

It is in the context of this homage to his great-grandmother that I propose to read Saladin Ahmed's earlier "Poem for Countee Cullen," which in its title is dedicated to this towering figure of the Harlem Renaissance. As in the case of Melhem's "Kwansaba for Richard Wright," discussed above, where it is clear she is rearranging and working through some specific lines of his own text, Ahmed directly refers to Cullen's famous rhymed and metered poem "Heritage," with its well-known opening line, "What is Africa to Me?"[72] Cullen's poem was first published in 1925 in the volume *Colors*. The poem itself received much acclaim; it has been read in a number of ways including in relation to its connections to canonical white poets, its theological stances, and its claiming of Africa as a homeland as the title indicates.[73] Michael Lomax has pointed out that critical reception of the poem reveals a divide between white critics seeking to read it as a poem expressing "universal" issues, whereas Black critics have almost always read it as deeply engaging questions tied to race and racism.[74] An example of this latter position is that the poem is also used as the title and epigraph to Geneva Smitherman's article, "What Is Africa to Me? Language, Ideology, and African American," a 1991 study of the community response to the shift in language from using the word "Black" to the adoption of "African American." She uses the opening stanza of Cullen's poem to underline that the Black community is in a moment of rethinking and rearticulating its relationship with "Mother Africa."[75] This is so important because in Cullen's poem Africa is a search for the self, in America.

Paralleling this use of Cullen's poem by Smitherman, Saladin Ahmed's rescripting of it in an Arab American voice can be read as thinking about the same kinds of search for the self. Ahmed's search allows us to see this by someone of African descent in America through an Arab American lens. Like Cullen's work as a "New Negro poet," Ahmed's poem is defined as "new Arab American writing." The poem, for example, is published in a collection titled *Post-Gibran: Anthology of New Arab American Writing*. This anthology is an explicit engagement with previous collections of writing by Arab Americans, and it attempts to push the definitions of the community and its literary output further, countering some of the nostalgia present in earlier collections like *Grape Leaves: A Century of Arab American Poetry*, which includes Gibran.[76] Evident in naming itself as "post" Gibran, and emphatically not including his work, it counters the nostalgic relationship of so many Arab Americans (especially those of Lebanese origin) toward this poet, claimed as the forefather and progenitor of the Arab American poets who follow. This move can be similar to that of Ahmed's Detroit contemporary Hayan Charara in reconfiguring Lawrence Joseph's use of racial epithets and the "n-word." Ahmed's invocation of Cullen and reworking some of his lines in his new poem similarly both pays homage to and challenges a man he claims as a literary predecessor.

Saladin Ahmed makes his initial gesture toward Cullen by dedicating this poem to him. He opens his shorter, unrhymed, and unmetered poem—most lines of which consist of only one or two words—with five lines that contain a total of eight words. Four of these eight words are "remember" or "remembering." The use of repetition and the specific sounds of the word "remember" create a brief, staccato soundscape for Ahmed's poem, very different from that of Cullen's, and one that speaks to the "tribal rhythms" they both invoke. Ahmed is remembering Cullen's remembrance of the jungle and states that he himself remembers remembering the desert. In this way he sets up their parallel but different sense of belonging to something and somewhere different and Other in the American context. These places are defined in the very next lines:

Neither of us
Has ever been there
For both of us
It is home.[77]

Ahmed thus defines this jungle and desert implicitly as "Africa"—whether the geographical location or the mythical Africa of Cullen's poetic questioning, or both. Ahmed uses a line break creatively here as well. Though pausing after the word "home" gives the words a certain meaning and relevance in context, the next lines continue with "Where he found / Echoes of tribal rhythms." Continuing the sentence in this way implies that the echoes of tribal rhythms were found in this home—Africa—recognized by both Ahmed and Cullen.

Ahmed affiliates himself with Cullen and his search for home and self in his heritage and origin, while making it clear that this is an imagined Africa. Neither of them has visited this mythical location—Ahmed leaves it open as to whether this is literal or if it is a location impossible to visit because it does not exist. His evocation of "celluloid chatter" and "Tarzan fauna"—a clear gesture to the somewhat whimsical portrayal of African animals—shows his cynical take on the reality of this place. Most critics also read Cullen's poem itself as ironic; and he was clearly well aware that he was representing an equally idealized and overly savage and unreal "Africa." Ahmed's ironic tone itself therefore can also be seen as homage to the message and vision of the poet. In the final lines of the poem, Ahmed again draws parallels and affiliations between his Arab heritage and Cullen's Africa, while also pointing to connections to contemporary Black America. His line "I find Bedouin / Cattle drums" can be read as continuing the lines, "In Brownstone / Rainstorms,"[78] and/or it can also be read as beginning a phrase that then continues with "In cavernous / Hip-Hop clubs."[79] Ahmed's own heritage in both readings is connected to symbols that are affiliated with African American communities, the Hip-Hop clubs representing contemporary Black American music, the brownstones a typical architectural feature of Harlem, the quintessential Black New York neighborhood named a few lines before. The lines, "I find Bedouin / Cattle drums / In cavernous / Hip-Hop clubs" then allows Ahmed to find his Arab heritage in an instrument that he locates within African American musical venues. This example once again reinforces the ways in which Ahmed seeks to build relationships and solidify relationships beyond mere connections between these communities. He finds something that deeply connects him to himself within a Black American location, emphasizing the value of African America for him as he searches for his roots in diaspora. The final lines of the poem deepen this message.

When the poet claims he will sift "Camel hairs" out of "Oil puddle / Rainbows,"[80] he uses the double meaning of the word camel—an animal used to symbolize Arabs and also a cigarette brand. Thus here he might be locating a meaningful part of his Arab/Bedouin heritage, or he might be picking up a cigarette butt out of an oil puddle in the street. In the final lines, "Oil puddle / Rainbows," Ahmed finds the beauty in what is ugly. The oil puddle implies drops of oil left by a parked car; it would be on the street and the oil mixing with the water from the "Brownstone / Rainstorms" cited above creates the rainbow.

Ahmed's imagery and use of language, much like Melhem's, is spare. There are no extra words and certainly no meter or rhyme as in Cullen's work. The break in it can be located within the poem's sharpness. Every line breaks from the one before it and one after it; much like the kwansabas, each word carries meaning. That Ahmed invokes music and musical spaces to connect his poem to Cullen and the African American community is no mistake. Similar to the poems written by D. H. Melhem, music is central to poetic experience and African American poetic expression in particular. Music carries symbolic power, and so the linguistic force it brings is crucial to embedding messages about politics and justice. The breaks in language therefore echo powerfully in Saladin Ahmed's poem. They allow him to create a soundscape that resonates and reverberates in a number of directions. Like Melhem's kwansabas, Ahmed's poem written for Countee Cullen uses staccato sounds in particular to reflect the sounds of the drums he invokes. His poem, like Hammad's *breaking poems*, searches for a home, an identity, and a self. Language and lyricism works within it to draw specific, positive connections to African America by locating this home and a place to find himself. The solidarity and community building evinced within it thus very much dovetail with works by Hammad and Melhem, and Nye, as the example that follows shows. Ahmed's articulation of finding himself also resonates strongly with the search for self, embarked upon by Amal, the protagonist of *Mornings in Jenin*, the novel discussed in chapter 3. Before moving on to discuss *Mornings in Jenin* and prose fiction, I will analyze one final poem's use of breaking language that looks to a different kind of figure—an African American child—to honor.

Naomi Shihab Nye: Always Talking as Resistance

Composed in 2015, Naomi Shihab Nye's "To Jamyla Bolden of Ferguson, Missouri" honors an ordinary person—nine-year-old Jamyla Bolden,
killed in Ferguson, Missouri, by a stray bullet during the unrest there.[81]
This poem brings the discussion in this chapter back to Ferguson and
the Palestine-Ferguson connection raised in the first chapter, but with a
slightly different focus. Of the poets discussed in this chapter, Nye is the
least embedded and connected within African American communities
or issues of race and antiracism.[82] This is not to say that she has not been
socially or politically active on a number of issues; Nye has long advocated
for justice in Palestine, the country of her father's origin. She does not,
however, come out of a tradition of radical political organizing or work
within race politics in the same way Suheir Hammad, D. H. Melhem, and
Susan Abulhawa, or in the ways that Randa Jarrar and Saladin Ahmed,
do. A more mainstream poet, Nye's work has been much circulated and
acclaimed in the United States especially. She writes young adult fiction
and children's books and is also an educator. In the context of African-
Arab American solidarity work, therefore, Nye cuts a somewhat different
figure than other poets and writers in this study. One critic's contrast of
her poetic voice to that of Hammad, for example, implies this in her assess-
ment of how the two poets are received differently: "The steady, reflective
voice of Naomi Shihab Nye . . . stands in contrast to the hip, edgy voice of
Suheir Hammad."[83]

Though her work has circulated in mainstream locations, Nye has
written poetry and commentary that has a sharper political edge. Her
poem for Jamyla Bolden can be linked to a much earlier, less well-known
poem she wrote about Black political activist, singer, and artist Paul Robeson. In this poem, "Cross That Line," published in the Arab American literary journal *Mizna* in 1999, Nye refers to the Communist Robeson who
was pursued by Joseph McCarthy and the House Un-American Activities
Committee as a "brave friend" who could inspire Arab Americans to cross
lines they are not meant to cross, in the name of justice.[84] This brief poem
suggests Nye's interest in breaking conventions and breaking injustice,
as exemplified in her analysis of anti-Arab racism in essays like "Long

Overdue."⁸⁵ She has also written several poems dedicated to Palestinians, including a recent one for political prisoner Dareen Tatour, the young Palestinian poet jailed for using the word "resist." "Always Talking: A Poem for Dareen Tatour," inscribes Tatour in a powerful history of Palestinian poets and commends her resistance to Israeli oppression. It was circulated on the internet especially in Palestine solidarity communities as part of the campaign for Tatour's release.⁸⁶

In 2014, Naomi Shihab Nye thrust herself into the center of discussions about racism in the United States after the police murder of unarmed Black teenager Michael Brown, partly because she is originally from Ferguson, Missouri. This biographical detail has interpellated her into a position of being an Arab American interlocutor in intercommunity conversations during the very difficult period in Ferguson from 2014 onward. She asserted her connection to the place in order to participate in and contribute to the discussions arising in the wake of Brown's murder and the subsequent uprisings. Her own different history leads to a different way to offer solidarity. This comes through in her poetry—not only are her politics different from that of the poets discussed above, her poetic language, aesthetic, and soundscapes are as well. She makes no use at all of vernacular languages, Arabic or Black Language, or other kinds of spoken English. She does not make other use of linguistic citations and references to African America or that break grammar in the ways all of the other poets discussed thus far do. This does not mean, however, that her poetry is free of breaking language. Like Hammad's "first writing since," Nye's poem for Bolden is written in a context where people feel broken. She is using poetic expression to honor this murdered child, and others who have lost their lives, as a way to offer healing. To resist the idea of people, communities, and society being broken, Nye creates a poem. Within this poem she is able to break language, using sound, as part of this larger project of resistance and solidarity.

To further contextualize her poem dedicated to Jamyla Bolden, it is instructive to read Nye's short article published in the *Washington Post* in August 2014 just as the reactions to the state repression of protestors in the United States and the vicious Israeli war on Gaza were coming to a close. "On Growing up in Ferguson and Palestine" is an intervention in a mainstream US newspaper, in which the poet uses her childhood growing up between Palestine and Ferguson—she repeats a friend's joke "your parents really picked the garden spots"—to draw out the similarities between these places. In a few short paragraphs, she gives examples of racial/community segregation, racism, state violence and dispossession, and also the inequality lived by Palestinians in Gaza and African Americans in Ferguson.[87] Her father explains to her as a girl, for example, that when he was a child Jews and Arabs mixed, but no longer: "Now there was power and domination at stake." Most of the article, however, uses these examples only to build up the important parallels—and connections—between Ferguson and Gaza in the summer of 2014 and her dismay at witnessing the two communities of her childhood subjected to extreme state violence. She directly connects the United States supplying arms to both Israel and the Ferguson police force to the despair of ordinary people at the other ends of those weapons. She lauds the people who sent reciprocal messages of solidarity, imagining, "What if they could all march together? 1.8 million Gazans would really clog old Florissant Avenue." Her final message is one that implores people in the United States to take both situations seriously. She asks that as people decide how to change their local situation in Ferguson that they consider the question she ends her essay with, "Will the United States ever speak out in solidarity with scores of exhausted people burying their dead, staring up with stunned eyes, mystified?"

The poem "To Jamyla Bolden of Ferguson, Missouri" is written in this same spirit of questioning and anger about how a child of only nine years old could be killed by a stray bullet through her bedroom wall while doing homework. At only twenty lines long, the poem is addressed to the child and sympathizes with her at how unfair her tragic death is. The poem invokes the more idyllic past of Ferguson as a small farming community and is built upon Nye's identification with this young girl by remembering how she did her homework in the same place "fifty years before." The poem is posted on a Weebly page, #BlackLivesMatterPoetryReader, which collects poetry about the uprisings in the United States that are connected to the Black Lives Matter movement, and is also available through the more mainstream American Association of Poets website.[88] The title makes clear that Nye is dedicating her poem to Jamyla Bolden, and in the manner of

Melhem's footnote identifying Jennette Washington, she includes a note at the end to make clear who Bolden is: "(little girl 9 years old killed by a stray bullet through her window in 2015 at home in Ferguson, near the front lines of protests against the killing of Michael Brown by police)."

The soundscape that Nye creates in this short poem uses particular poetic techniques to underline its honoring of Bolden, sympathy for her family, and hope for social change. She creates this effect by using sound in three specific ways in this poem, at the beginning and at the end in particular. The sounds of the letter F from the beginning, as in the word "Ferguson" repeated twice at the beginning of the poem, recur again near the end, and are reinforced by other words beginning with and containing the letter F. This is not only alliteration but also an invocation of sound, with the S sound that intensifies at the end adding sonic power to the F in its similarity. The F sound for Ferguson and in the very first word of the poem "fifty"—indicating the age gap between the poet and the girl, the generations between which it changed from being a rural town to an urban ghetto—repeats with "friends," "farm," and "fed." The city it fed is named as "St. Louis" and the S sounds come quickly at the end—meadows, sweet potatoes, shovels, and the very important word "satisfactory," which is defined as "super" and in contrast to "sorrow." The use of the S and F sounds are mobilized as positive sound-pictures by Nye throughout the poem.

In the poem's penultimate line Nye uses the expression "S for Satisfactory," invoking the homework assignment Bolden was working on at the time of her death. She uses this expression to remind the reader of the circumstances of Bolden's death and to associate the S and F sounds with these positive ideas—"super" rather than "sorrow." This is contrasted with the powerful use of sound earlier in the poem and the expression that prefigures the later "S for Satisfactory"—she writes in line three: "If we didn't do our homework we might get a U—Unsatisfactory." In the very next line she once again addresses Jamyla Bolden, "Your dad says you didn't even get to see the rest of the world yet," using the words both "your" and "you" to keep the sound pattern active. And when she ponders how to absorb the gravity of the situation, even as someone over fifty who has seen too much of the world, she writes: "A girl shot through a wall—U! U! U!" In the following two lines she then repeats "you" four more times in order to seal this desperate sound with the desperation of how she feels. The repeated capitalized U's with exclamation points make a strong statement on the page. They have even more impact on the reader when the poem is read aloud/performed—the U/you repeating sound like cries or shrieks and then are soothed at the end with the softer sounds of S and F.[89] The combination of the S and F sound is the most emotive in lines eleven and twelve, the only two lines that start with a repetition, the same three words, "safe with our." In the first line the children are safe with their friends, in the second with their shrieks and summer shorts and happy hair.

Naomi Shihab Nye's "Poem for Jamyla Bolden" makes one short linguistic gesture in language to Black Lives Matter—the slogan and larger movement of Black youth arising from Ferguson, in lines 17–18 over the line break. These lines read: "and each life / even the little tendril of a vine, mattered." In the preceding lines, Nye conjures up Ferguson's history as a farm with details about the things that grew in the land there. The notion that each life mattered, "even the little tendril of a vine," is a comment by Nye in support of the young people standing up to proclaim that their lives matter—the rallying cry of their movement #blacklivesmatter—and a cry for Jamyla Bolden's to be sure that her mere nine years of life matter too. It is here that Nye's poem creates a powerful soundscape in the break in order to honor the life of this young girl and assert through sound that Black Lives Matter.

Conclusions: Homage as a Politics and Pedagogy

Jamyla Bolden, Countee Cullen, Angela Davis, Amiri Baraka, Jayne Cortez, Richard Wright, Jennette Washington, and the Black Panthers are the African Americans honored in the poems analyzed in this chapter. Arab American poets D. H. Melhem, Saladin Ahmed, and Naomi Shihab Nye all have dedicated their poetry to people in the Black community—mostly other poets, but also activists, community members, and a young child. This type of poetry is a direct way to show affiliation, to offer respect and recognition, and itself is a gesture of community building. In these analyses I have argued that this poetry of homage, centering and paying tribute to these figures of Black America, not only builds Arab American identity and communities through connecting to African Americans but also builds solidarity between the many diverse communities of Arab and African Americans. They do this by drawing out connections, valorizing artistic achievements, and highlighting struggles for justice. Melhem, Ahmed, and Nye in their own ways have linked their poetry to their actions and engagements in communities, to feminist commitments, and also to their politics. I am underlining this here, because the poetry of homage is also a politics. Coalition building and solidarity can be challenging; poetry can be both a reflection of these processes and a way into them. Further, drawing together earlier and more contemporary poetry reminds us of the histories of solidarity and connections between communities that are often obscured.

Poetry can also be pedagogy, and this is particularly true of praise poetry. Even if it is not obvious or apparent, poetry teaches. Poems do not always spell the lessons out, but rather offer clues, ways in, spaces in the breaks to invite new understandings and connections. An example of this can be how Suheir Hammad teaches us who June Jordan is, after June Jordan and others taught her about Palestinian poetry. We learn through poetry—we are exposed to images and allusions and we go and look them up.

In the anthology *The BreakBeat Poets*, many poets share anecdotes and analysis about how they have learned from both written poetry and the poetry of hip-hop.[90] Here we see Arab American poets teaching about and learning from Countee Cullen, the Black Panthers, Angela Davis, Amiri Baraka, Jayne Cortez, Jennette Washington, and Jamyla Bolden among others. We learn not just about these figures, but about their work and political affiliations—the Welfare Rights Organization, The Women's Detention Center, and so on. In a sense, my pedagogical project in this chapter mirrors that of the poets, in telling not only the stories of these poets and their works but also reclaiming their connections to the stories and histories of these Black American figures who they honor. By putting them into this context and connecting them to larger contexts of Arab American writing, African American figures can take a more central place in how we read and analyze Arab American literary production. These kinds of generative links, and the literary solidarities they represent, can help us as critics and readers of literature push our understandings of the relationship between communities from the limited ways they have been understood in the past, the three main strands being in competition with each other, through hierarchies of whiteness, or in relation to the replacement paradigm.[91] It also underlines Black and other critical race feminisms' focus on interlocking structures of power and oppression as well as how these are connected to literary and linguistic projects. This chapter therefore reads the literary, linguistic, and artistic project of the poems as unified with their political and pedagogical project/s. Politics and pedagogy are fused together in the language of poetry.

The languages of all of these poems are different, as are the specific political projects and artistic aims of each. But they share with each other, as well as Suheir Hammad's *breaking poems*, a commitment to engage in coalition building that presents visions and writings of how African America can engage and be engaged with Arab America. The break—conceptualized as a framework of reading and interpretive tool—and how breaking language is used in the poems is a way to understand the soundscapes created within them that push forward imagining justice and liberation. Linguistic and poetic breaks, like breaks in conventional grammar, make us stop, they make us question and think, and they manifest other kinds of breaks. All of the poems here present things that they need to break socially, politically, and/or conceptually and they inscribe this through their breaking language. In the analysis of Saladin Ahmed above, I underline how he identifies certain African American spaces as locations in which he can find his Arab identity, inscribing this through his staccato breaking language. This is a project very closely connected to the overlapping but distinct project of finding home through language in a very different kind of text, explored in the next chapter. Chapter 3 moves from poetry to fiction, analyzing Susan Abulhawa's expansive novel *Mornings in Jenin*. I propose that in this epic tale of Palestine, Abulhawa deploys "broken" English in multiple ways to break language and convention and inscribe a powerful pedagogical, political, and ultimately poetic project devoted to the liberation of Palestine.

3 Palestine, or a Language as Home

Susan Abulhawa's Mornings in Jenin

"There is a kind of liberation that can only come from being a part of the liberation of others," Palestinian American novelist Susan Abulhawa declared upon returning to the United States after participating in the Palestine Literature Festival (PalFest) in 2013. In an article published on the Electronic Intifada website, she reflects upon what she learned from conversations and thinking more deeply about coalition building and the meaning of "reciprocal solidarity" and "natural allies." She ponders who has supported the Palestinian struggle historically and continues to do so today. The article's title, from which she specifically distances herself, is controversial, "The Palestinian Struggle is a Black Struggle."[1] The struggle for Palestine, and all liberation struggles waged by "the wretched of the earth," she identifies as shared struggles. In a move that recalls Suheir Hammad's author's note in *Born Palestinian, Born Black*, Abulhawa defines Blackness in her short article, "blackness is what has been and is the recipient of colonialism and supremacy, with all that this entails in clashing forces of internalization of inferiority, resistance, black power and black empowerment."[2] Here, Abulhawa links oppression to resistance, thereby allowing her definition to expand when she talks about Palestine specifically and the need to demand—not beg—for the dignity of having freedom and a home. She calls this the "essential blackness of our fight. In this way, our struggle for liberation is spiritually and politically black in nature." Careful to resist the appropriation of Blackness, Abulhawa works

116

within a spiritual and political definition, citing inspiration from and giving credit to Africans and African Americans who have supported the Palestinian struggle. One of the main goals of her article is to call on Palestinians and Palestinian/Arab Americans to recognize the contributions of Black Americans to their struggle, honor these, and act with this in mind. She is calling for a larger project of solidarity moving forward—for the liberation of Palestine and also other liberation struggles. This conjures Audre Lorde's imprecation not to appropriate and call something yours but to fight for all struggles as if they were.[3]

Abulhawa's article is one of a pair, the second of which, "Confronting Anti-Black Racism in the Arab World," furthers the project of solidarity and coalition building by responding to comments and critiques on the first.[4] In this companion piece, Abulhawa takes up the complexities of anti-Black racism in Arab contexts today, including the histories of the Arab slave trade in Africa, the importation of North American and European racism into Arab contexts, and contemporary racism against migrant laborers from Africa to Arab countries. Echoing earlier work, like that of Stan West and the Jadaliyya roundtable on anti-Black racism, both cited in the introduction above, she also encourages Arabs to recognize the myth that Arab and African are entirely separate and not linked identities and ideas, and to recognize shared genealogies. Both of these articles also focus on the positive relationships between communities, possibilities for connection, and solidarities that have existed throughout history. In both, Abulhawa names and honors Africans, and particularly African Americans, who have regularly and consistently stood up for Palestinian liberation. She also underlines the need for people to recognize and take accountability for painful histories, as well as to work for shared struggles with solidarity "in heart and in action."

The Poetry of Fiction: Genre and the Creative Use of Language

Susan Abulhawa's epic novel of Palestinian history and resistance can be productively read against the background of these two articles and her commitment to Black-Arab solidarity, though it is not an explicit focus of the work itself. Rather than explicitly engage any particular literary form identified with Black America—like the kwansabas for example—*Mornings in Jenin* is most easily identifiable as an American immigrant novel. Race therefore plays an important and central role in the book, which indirectly and subtly decenters American whiteness as its Palestinian protagonist finds a way to thrive, in her "living room" in the United States, as June Jordan has put it. This element of the novel enhances its main and overriding message and point—the history of Palestine and its need for liberation. The Abulheja family's travails through British and Israeli occupation and emigration outside Palestine are all directly connected to the major events that shook the region and the world in the twentieth and twenty-first centuries. Ostensibly an American "book club novel," appealing to broad audiences, this 322-page text demonstrates that fiction marketed as mainstream within the North American and British markets can be politically powerful and experiment with its languages of expression at the same time.

Mornings in Jenin is a deeply moving tale that uses the Abulheja family's stories to make direct parallels to the crucial events in the history of Palestine, from the tragedy of the 1948 Nakba until the Israeli army's sustained attacks on Jenin in 2002. While the story is decidedly personal, the novel's political stand firmly advocates for liberation and justice in Palestine. One important argument I advance in this chapter is that Abulhawa is able to write such a challenging and politically powerful book about Palestine, which tells the history of the Nakba and claims a liberated Palestine as a home, because she masters the form and style of the "book club" immigrant novel so well. Within a larger project to write "the" Palestinian novel, Abulhawa manipulates a mainstream genre through which she is able not only to record and teach Palestinian history, but also many of the languages that make up Palestine, including spoken Palestinian Arabic.

Mornings in Jenin is a long narrative that experiments with language very differently from the poetry discussed in the previous two chapters. Like Hammad's poems, Abulhawa uses spoken Palestinian Arabic in a variety of ways and to important effect. But poetry demands linguistic experimentation: unexpected use of language is part of what defines poetry and sets it apart from other kinds of writing. Using breaks in multiple creative ways, as chapter 2 demonstrates, is part of what makes a poem a poem. What is important about this novel, therefore, and one of its most important features, is its extensive experimentation with spoken language/s. This is most visibly located in the use of Arabic to create a "broken English" effect. Narrative prose by definition uses language differently than poetry, and my readings here take generic considerations into account when analyzing how this "broken" language can be read as breaking. The concept of the break, and how it can be used in language to create sound effects imbued with meaning, can help us to understand Abulhawa's larger projects. *Mornings in Jenin* is concerned with home—finding and establishing a home—and reclaiming Palestine as a home, lost through occupation. Therefore, her breaks in language, moments in which language cannot be understood, can be productively read together with Moten's claim that home is written in those places of occluded language. Using the spaces between sounds to create home and find an articulation of self is part of the project advocated by other theorists of Black Language as well, like Smitherman, Baldwin, and Jordan, as explored in the introduction. The analysis below will read meaning and home into these breaks. I further analyze the effects of the soundscape created by Abulhawa and put this into conversation with those of the poetry in the first two chapters above.

This chapter proposes that through *Mornings in Jenin*, Abulhawa creates a soundscape that is Palestine. She achieves this through her use of multiple kinds of breaks in language, including the use of "broken English," and a large number of spoken Arabic, and specifically Palestinian, words and expressions. Though marketed to the mainstream, the novel is not simplified or dumbed-down in either content or language. In fact, Abulhawa challenges her readers to learn and assimilate Arabic words using a number of different techniques, merging her pedagogical project with her poetic and political one. This is reflected in the words of the protagonist Amal, remembering her life in a Palestinian orphanage in Jerusalem: "Our bond was Palestine. It was a language we dismantled to construct a home."[5] Within *Mornings in Jenin*, Abulhawa—like Amal and her friends in the orphanage—dismantles, explores, and constructs language in multiple creative ways, which can be analyzed as breaks in language and breaking language. The linguistic resources she draws upon help her to convey political messages that establish the language and soundscape of her novel as home.

For Amal, Palestine is a language where home is located, and Abulhawa insists on this point in her construction of the novel's soundscape in multiple ways. The novel's extensive and varied experimentation with Arabic words and expressions, at times conveyed in "broken English," as well as other techniques, recall Hammad's in some ways. As a narrative, *Mornings in Jenin* draws upon language readily identified as "broken" on an even larger scale. But Abulhawa, like Hammad, offers resistance to Palestine and its language being broken or seeming broken. If her project is reconceptualized within the framework of breaking language, her use of words, syntax, grammar, and other linguistic elements all exist in the break. *Mornings in Jenin* inscribes Palestinian Arabic language, culture, and memory into a different landscape and soundscape—the United States—in the process recording history and creating a home.

Abulhawa's extensive use of Arabic to produce a Palestinian soundscape can be read as engaging with the notion developed by Smitherman and echoed by Baldwin of how spoken Black language is deeply tied to the self for African Americans. As she puts it, language helps answer the question, "Who do I be?"[6] Like Smitherman documents and advocates for Black Americans, Abulhawa reclaims Palestinian oral traditions in this novel, making her "medium the message."[7] Although many of the underlying ideas and principles are the same, some elements shift between Black Language and Palestinian Arabic in English. One major difference is the foreignness and unfamiliarity that mainstream Standard English has with Arabic at all, let alone with specific elements of spoken Palestinian language. Abulhawa's location of home and the self through her Palestinian Arabic soundscape powerfully uses breaking language to manifest a break with how Palestine has been understood within English-language fiction. This chapter will first look at the novel as an intertextual commentary on Palestinian fiction, especially the work of Ghassan Kanafani, situated in relation to the Black community in the United States, through an investigation into Abulhawa's use of names and naming. Finally, it moves on to a more sustained textual analysis of how breaking language in the novel creates home. I will show this through examining *Mornings in Jenin*'s use of repetition, translation, transliteration, and finally connecting histories.

Ghassan Kanafani, Women's Perspectives, and Intertextual Breaks

Just as breaking language manifests a break in how Palestine is typically written into English-language fiction, *Mornings in Jenin* also inscribes important breaks with elements of Palestinian fiction and literary figures. Within this novel's larger political project of advocating the liberation of Palestine, it also rewrites Palestinian history. The novel recounts many important and central events, while also telling one family's story. Crucial to the narrative is that the stories are all woman-centered and privilege Palestinian women's perspectives. Without marginalizing or demonizing men, women are centered and their lives and struggles are the focus of the book.[8] While the Abulheja family tree—included at the very opening of the book before the main narration—places men at the top in the conventional, patriarchal fashion,[9] women's stories fill the novel and women's perspectives dominate it. Amal is the book's central protagonist, and her mother, Dalia, and later her daughter, Sara, are her main reference points throughout *Mornings in Jenin*. While men are never sidelined or made unimportant, this centering of women's stories and experiences is an important political statement in narrating the history of Palestine. This is done in multiple ways and permeates the entire narration, including the book's structure, language, use, and how it configures its intertextual relationship with one of the most important figures of Palestinian literary history: novelist and political activist Ghassan Kanafani.

 Mornings in Jenin is an intertextual rescripting of Kanafani's acclaimed novella, *Returning to Haifa*. Abulhawa openly alerts the reader to this in her author's note: "The seed for this book came from Ghassan Kanafani's short story [sic] about a Palestinian boy who was raised by the Jewish family that found him in the home they took over in 1948."[10] For a reader familiar with Arabic, especially Palestinian fiction, this link to the classic work is obvious, though likely it would not be to an English-language readership, necessitating the note. Moreover, Abulhawa makes clear that this is not a hidden or secret intertextual relationship in which an author cleverly borrows from or alludes to a previous work as a sort of wink to her readership. The rescripting of Kanafani I suggest here is not unlike some of the kinds of homage that I discuss in chapter 2 as honoring African American literary and cultural figures. It is markedly different, however, and the concept of the break offers insights into how we might think about Abulhawa's recasting of Kanafani's story as part of her larger political, artistic, and linguistic project/s. Here the rescripting is a break with the past. Abulhawa uses breaking English language in her narrative homage to rewrite and rework elements of Palestinian history within a soundscape that offers a hope for justice in Palestine, differently than Kanafani does.

Like *Returning to Haifa, Mornings in Jenin* is easily read as a pedagogical project. The book-club format lends itself to this; as one reviewer suggests, "this novel is one that could and should be taught in high schools and universities as a tool to educate youth about Palestine."[11] Kanafani's voice as the spokesperson for the Popular Front for the Liberation of Palestine comes through in speeches delivered by his characters in *Returning to Haifa*. Sharing a similar goal, *Mornings in Jenin* educates its readers through how characters quote and refer to news stories and speeches. Rewriting this specific story, by this specific author, is also meaningful. Assassinated in a Mossad car bombing in 1972, Kanafani died at the premature age of thirty-six, at the height of his literary prowess. Critics believe that he might have developed into one of the Arab world's greatest novelists and that his best works were yet to come.[12] Abulhawa's intertextual rescripting can thus be read not only as an homage, but also an expansion of what his vision might have been had he not been murdered. It is also important to question what such a reference point means in a novel directed primarily to an audience for whom the story upon which it is built means little, but for those who know it, means everything. This underlines the book's many diverse readerships and how multiple levels of analysis coexist and operate within a single text.

Some of the details of these two stories can help illuminate how Abulhawa's feminist political vision in *Mornings in Jenin* uses the break to rescript Ghassan Kanafani's *Returning to Haifa*. In both stories, young babies are taken from Palestinian parents in their homeland during the chaos of the Nakba and raised as Jewish Israelis, learning of their origins as adults. In both stories, the Jewish-raised adult men meet their Palestinian families and grapple with their origins and their relationship to their communities. But the stories diverge in several ways. Kanafani's work is best characterized as a novella and Abulhawa's is much longer and expansive. She is able therefore to engage this story in more depth, as well as relate it to other periods of time—her book spans generations. Kanafani's text is limited to a short period of time just after the 1967 war. Another major difference is that *Returning to Haifa* is geographically limited to Palestine (and mostly to one room in a house in Haifa), whereas *Mornings in Jenin* moves from Palestine, to Lebanon, to the United States, and other locations.

This is crucial to the difference in how the Jewish-raised men confront their original families. Amal's brother David/Ismael meets her for the first time in the relatively neutral territory of Philadelphia, rather than the stolen house in Haifa that serves as the scene of confrontation between Khaldoun/Dov in Kanafani's text. Finally, Palestinian women are not major figures in Kanafani's story: the mother is often depicted weeping, and most of the words in the text are placed in the thoughts of the father. In Abulhawa's story, on the other hand, everything is filtered through the consciousness of Amal. We see a shift in generational thinking, however, when her daughter Sara—a Palestinian American raised in the States and student activist working with Students for Justice in Palestine no less—interrogates and probes the edges of the conversation.[13]

Moreover, in Kanafani's story, the baby Khaldoun is somehow left behind in the chaos and confusion when his mother is pushed in a human tide of people being forced from their homes and out of the city.[14] Abulhawa changes this scenario considerably. Moshe, the Israeli "adoptive father" of Ismael, who is later renamed David, actively steals a Palestinian baby for his barren wife Jolanta who has lost her family in the Nazi Holocaust. After kidnapping the child, he sedates him with alcohol and steals away with him hidden in a sack. Late in her life Jolanta feels guilty, remorseful, and indeed offers to help her son search for his Palestinian family.[15] All of these differences are crucial to reading Abulhawa's intertextual project through the break. Her novel breaks with his story, but also with simplistic ways of understanding the Nakba. While the Jewish father in *Mornings in Jenin* initially appears more plotting and evil than the parents in *Returning to Haifa*—the latter couple are simply given a home and baby by Israeli authorities—he and his wife also prove to be more complex characters who are humanized by showing their range of feelings. Their vulnerability makes them more real, though the intensity of their crimes does not encourage the reader to empathize with them. Abulhawa's story thus can be read through this intertextual break with Kanafani, building his vision into a feminist one, which deepens its humanity and expands its politics of solidarity.

Diaspora, Alienation, and a Backstage Pass to Black America

I dwell on *Mornings in Jenin*'s relationship to *Returning to Haifa* here to highlight its complex politics of solidarity and feminist vision, both of which can be read in the break. This also allows me to allude to the work's other major conceptual break—how it embeds itself within Palestinian literary contexts through its use of Kanafani's work, but also breaks with this both by rescripting the novella and acting as a diasporic "immigrant" novel, complete with a reading guide in the back. This conceptual break is mirrored within the plot by the major break Amal makes with Palestine, leaving for the United States. This move happens almost exactly halfway through the book and is marked symbolically by a new section titled "El Ghurba," defined parenthetically as the "state of being a stranger."[16] This halfway point in the book is also where Abulhawa shifts her linguistic strategies. Below I discuss how the break and breaking language are useful conceptual tools to understand how *Mornings in Jenin* constructs its Palestinian soundscape in varied ways.

When Amal moves to the United States in the second section of the book, she begins commenting on language extensively. The linguistic strategy of writing "broken English," which I discuss in more detail below, gives way to a more prominent thematization of and metacommentary on language use. One example is Amal's contemplation of how she became "Amy" after she leaves Palestine—first leaving her refugee camp in Jenin and later her orphanage in Jerusalem—and immigrates to Philadelphia. As she settles into her new life in the United States, however, Amal learns that even changing her name to Amy does not allow her to become fully a part of the United States. This realization happens almost immediately, and Amal's initial alienation is highlighted throughout the book. This is true both when surrounded by the generosity of her first hosts, the Arab American Haddad family, and also when she lives in a university student residence with racist colleagues who refer to her "not infrequently as 'the Arab,' pronounced 'ay-rab' or as 'the rag head.'"[17] She speaks of this alienation in stark terms. What she calls a "sewage incident" in the university panics her college classmates, but for her the smell evoked "sweet nostalgia and longing for old friends."[18] She states unambiguously, "The divide could not have been greater, nor could it be bridged."[19]

Amal's blunt narration of her alienation in "America" soon becomes more nuanced; she is able to define what is alienating and different to her as "white America" immediately following this. Abulhawa uses the neighborhood, West Philly, defined by Amal as a place where "white people ordinarily did not go,"[20] as the first place she develops a measure of comfort and feeling of being at home. In this section of the novel, Abulhawa discusses the racial tensions faced by Arabs and Arab Americans in the United States and their status in a society racially divided between Black and white. Her use of African American characters and settings as a device to explore Arab and Arab American struggles for belonging in the United States echoes that of other Arab American novelists, some of whom were discussed briefly in the introduction.[21] Similarly, Randa Jarrar, whose works are discussed in chapter 4 below, uses a number of relationships between her Arab protagonists and Black and Latino characters both to draw together and also distinguish the communities. She also includes characters whose identities cross these lines—Arab/African Americans, Black Arab Americans—which allows her to delve further into these dynamics.

Though the depiction of African America is not a central focus of *Mornings in Jenin*, it is important to its definitions of "America" and adds layers to its message about liberation and community solidarity. Therí Pickens's critique of the three standard ways of understanding relationships between African and Arab Americans, discussed in the introduction, offers us ways to understand what the novel is doing here. In addition to competition and replacement paradigms, she proposes that we too often locate Arab Americans within a hierarchy that reaffirms the superiority of whiteness as the standard against which everything is measured.[22] Building upon Pickens's suggestion to shift our analyses, I read Abulhawa's intervention as resisting the depiction of the communities as competing—Arabs being "the new Black," or seeing Arabs and Blacks within the hierarchy of whiteness. The analyses below focus on the way in which Abulhawa uses breaks and breaking as a strategy to disrupt dominant ways of understanding intercommunity relationships together with linguistic registers in order to insert a soundscape of a Palestinian home in the US context. Her discussions of African America decenter whiteness as being all that America is and claim Black America as a space in which Amal's Palestinian self can speak, feel at home, and "breathe."

Like other Arab American fictional characters before her, Amal Abulheja finds comfort in the United States among Black Americans that she cannot feel with whites. Abulhawa underlines her focus on how a feeling of belonging and home is connected to language, speech, and sounds in the lines that close the first chapter after Amal leaves Palestine, "America 1973": "What I knew for sure was that people in West Philly thought I was beautiful, not different, and my accent was not a call for mistrust. The very things that made me suspect to the white world were backstage passes in the black neighborhoods."[23] Amal stresses that her looks and accent made her stand out in one world but were what allowed her to fit into the other. The metaphor of a backstage pass is loaded with additional meaning, given the racial allusions of the word "pass" in the United States.[24] Amal articulates that her difference and "Arabness" and/or "Palestinianness" are the things that give her this positive "pass." It is important to note here that Abulhawa does not depict Amal as "passing" as Black in these settings. Amal is appreciated for her looks and not chided for her accent, but she does not simply become Black. Rather she is accepted for who she is within a community in which she feels at home. This is an important distinction in reading the text and thinking through the lens of Black and women-of-color feminisms that stress solidarity through difference as creative and generative.[25]

Amal's provisional belonging in West Philly, we learn, is not merely granted to her but rather is earned through persistence and trying. This is why it is relevant that she does not "pass" as Black. Her belonging is not derived from her phenotype, looks, or mere existence, but rather based on active participation in the community. This recalls Abulhawa's arguments about reciprocal solidarity and natural allies in the articles I referred to in this chapter's opening. It is also consistent with her feminist commitments. Though African Americans may seem "natural" allies because of shared histories of struggle with colonialism, imperialism, and white supremacy, one should not simply take these for granted, but rather recognize the struggles of others on their own terms. This also recalls Abdulhadi's engagement with and analysis of Palestine solidarity activism in the 1980s in the United States, in particular how coalitions were built.[26] Thus because Amal does not live in the neighborhood, she does not try to fit into it as an insider, but rather she goes there every weekend, works there, and connects to people. She describes the neighborhood lovingly in its ugliness and beauty:

> In West Philly, nature and architecture hunkered down with the ghost of slavery, letting litter and urine move in the place of flower bushes. Young men loitered in bell-bottomed jeans and Afros. In the beginning they whistled, called me "mama," and made references to my backside. But as my face became a constant part of the weekend landscape, they called out my name in a rhythm that whistled, acknowledged my backside, and welcomed me, all in one word. Old women, imposing matriarchs, gossiped on their porches and kept watch over the neighborhood as best they could. They too eventually turned their mistrusting expressions into generous smiles when they saw me coming.[27]

Amal testifies here to how she gains her acceptance in the neighborhood through her constancy. It is relevant—and becomes more so as Amal becomes Amy—that this acceptance is eventually expressed by the young men wearing bell-bottoms and Afros literally calling out her name. As mistrust melts into generous smiles, Amal begins to find a space that offers her some feeling of being at home.

In West Philly, Amal also learns to appreciate Black culture, especially music. Music is a recurring trope in the depiction of African Americans in Arab American fiction, not to mention other fictional traditions. Jazz in particular is invoked by many poets and authors—from the works of Etel Adnan, to Diana Abu Jaber's *Arabian Jazz*, to specific poems of Suheir Hammad and her extensive engagement with John Coltrane, Sam Cooke, and others.[28] It should also be noted that invoking Black American musical traditions as a metonym for Black culture can be a tired and worn trope. I argue here that locating African America as Amal's American adopted home is a break paralleled by breaking English in multiple ways with Arabic, in order to create the rhythms of a Palestinian soundscape which will engage Black American rhythms. Thus the musical and rhythmic metaphor functions beyond a mere metonym for Amal: "It seemed to me that black folk brought a beat to every task. . . . Their enslaved culture had given birth to rock and roll, I learned—a kidnapped race that came to define the entire culture with its music."[29] The rather well-worn cliché about African Americans "having rhythm" here is mobilized to underline how Amal learned about the history of slavery, its connections to music, and the crucial contributions Black Americans made to musical culture in America, as an outsider who shares a history of struggle. Abulhawa's soundscape is used to break Standard English, and Amal's struggle here is paralleled to that of Black Americans who have created their own breaking soundscapes as the descendants of enslaved people. To put it another way, the two communities sharing a landscape create different soundscapes through breaking language.

Another example of the community bonds reinforced through language is in Amal's reaction to a robbery at work. Amal is not afraid of "crime," as an oppressed person who fled extensive state violence and war and grew up in a refugee camp, which was similarly or more impoverished than West Philly. This is reflected in a scene in which she does not call the police when a young man, Jimmy, holds up the shop where she works. Instead, she calls her boss, Bernard—also called Bo Bo—who approves of her decision. Bo Bo's name is almost a homonym of "po-po," a word meaning "police" in Black Language. With Arabic pronunciation,

it *is* a homonym because Arabic does not use the *p* sound. This character's name is thus a wordplay that reinforces his role as a replacement for
this official state institution which is so oppressive to Black people in the
United States. Bo Bo offers an explanation for his alternative solution of
putting Jimmy to work to keep him within the community, "It's an old web
that squeezes black folk until they got no more juice."[30] As a Palestinian
woman, Amal relates to Bo Bo's decision not to have Jimmy arrested and
understands how cooperating with oppressive state institutions can be a
trap for the Black community. She fully comprehends the bind in which
Jimmy, and the community at large, is trapped by an oppressive state.

Almost as soon as Amal lands in the United States from Palestine,
she begins to make important connections with Black America/ns as a
dispossessed and displaced Palestinian woman searching for home. Abulhawa thematizes the notion of intergroup connections and solidarity
directly, identifying Black America specifically as the America in which
Amal can feel at home. Like other Arab American fiction, *Mornings in
Jenin* depicts African Americans in sympathetic, if tangential, roles and
shows that there is more to the United States than white America. Amal's
"backstage pass" underlines the performative elements of identity and
also racialization. Her appreciation of Black music and culture both
underlines her belonging as connected to sounds and words, but also
to the soundscape that Abulhawa creates as a Palestinian home, which
itself can fit in within Black America. Amal's look, name, and accent,
herself as a Palestinian, can find a place in this break—the break with
white America and the sounds that are created in *Mornings in Jenin* to
make a home.

Amal to Amy: The Importance of Names

When the young men on the corner call out Amal's name, it contains a
whistle, an acknowledgement of her backside, and a welcome. But this
happens in West Philly. In the larger white world that Amal inhabits in the
United States—including the university—she cannot function as herself
and indeed turns her back on her family, community, refugee camp, and

even herself. To do this, she changes her name to "Amy." She describes her first years in the United States:

> I had, for the previous five years, tuned the world out. The Yom Kippur War came and went in 1973, as did further turbulence in Palestine, and Jimmy Carter's Camp David Accords were soon to be signed—all without response from me. I deliberately avoided political discussions, did not write to the people who loved me, and let myself be known as "Amy"—Amal without the hope. I was a word drained of its meaning. A woman emptied of her past. The truth is that I wanted to be someone else. And that summer at Myrtle Beach, I was Amy in a bathing suit, lounging on the sand as far away from myself as I had ever been.[31]

Here Amal connects her apathy, lack of political consciousness, and inaction with herself becoming a "word drained of its meaning." It is important symbolically that she identifies herself as a word. She changes her name because she wants to become someone else. In the novel, we see this as a negative breaking with the past—one different from the generative breaks discussed above—and is a result of feeling broken. I propose that this broken feeling exists in a break that exhibits creative linguistic tension. The tension between Standard English and Arabic, Arabized English, "broken" English, and various other kinds of spoken English exists throughout the novel. Amy is a word and name that fits easily into a Standard English soundscape of white America and in fact does not work well in the Palestinian soundscape of *Mornings in Jenin*. This layering of meaning in words and names refers back to earlier passages, where Abulhawa makes use of this device.

This is not the only time that Amal's name is the subject of a meaningful reflection within *Mornings in Jenin*. The first discussion of her name comes much earlier in the novel and punctuates one of its most dramatic and devastating scenes. The chapter, "June in the Kitchen Hole," depicts the June 1967 Israeli invasion and occupation of Jenin in great detail. Young girls at this time, Amal and her cousin Huda save themselves by hiding in a hole in the kitchen floor during what later became known as the Six-Day War. Traumatized for fear of losing her young life,

Amal thinks about her father, who she desperately wishes was with her and remembers him saying, "'We named you Amal with a long vowel because the short vowel means just one hope, one wish. . . . You're so much more than that. We put all of our hopes into you. Amal, with the long vowel, means hopes, dreams, lots of them.' Only six years old then, I grew with the belief that I alone held my father's dreams, all of them."[32]

These two reflections on the name "Amal" are self-conscious explanations of the Arabic word to the English reader, underlining and highlighting both her name's literal meaning and also how this meaning engages with the ideas presented in the text. This is one of the main techniques Abulhawa employs in *Mornings in Jenin* to use and promote the Arabic language. These examples clearly have a didactic purpose, teaching the meaning of Arabic words; a literary purpose, imbuing the work with sounds and effects with a larger theoretical impact; and an ideological purpose, intersecting with the larger political ideas about social justice and Palestinian liberation. Amal's relationship to the Arabic language, her family, background, and country are all thus explored within these discussions of her name's meaning.

Amal's reflection on her father underlines the importance of sounds, not just words. It teaches the reader that the sounds in her name are connected to the concept of hope, but that the long vowel of her name, pronounced "Amaal," is what makes it plural and thus enlarges and expands this idea. Abulhawa constructs the traumatic scene of the terrified girls during the invasion carefully and uses this reflection on sound both to heighten its tension and to stress how important the meaning of her name is. The power of this discussion of naming is rooted in how Amal's father, Hassan, stresses the plural nature of this hope. When he says, "we put all of our hopes in you," the reader notes he said neither "we put all of our hope in you" nor "I put all of my hope in you." The hopes are plural, as is the community that loves and supports her. Collectivity is stressed here over the individual. Just as Amal is pluralized through her name, those who believe in her and are counting on her are also a plural group.

The idea that Amal means multiple hopes and is herself a plural representative of a collectivity rather than a mere individual is paralleled in the word's actual sound. The word's sound here is as important as its meaning. Unlike the poems of Hammad, Melhem, Ahmed, or Nye, Abul-hawa's novel does not create a soundscape of short, condensed sounds or juxtapose words and line breaks. Abulhawa's novel's soundscape does, however, similarly layer meaning into words, just in other ways. This is why it is so important that a reader who knows English but not Arabic is offered an explanation of the sounds of two words—the singular Amal and plural Amal, with the short and long vowel sound—that look the same on the page. Though expressed in a narrative context and not a poem, it recalls Hammad's technique in *breaking poems*, where words with just one vowel sound or letter change have vastly different meanings: sickle cell amnesia/anemia or iced teeth/tea. Such a change in this particular word's meaning and sound is not simply linguistic play. The explanation of meaning underlines the larger sense of hope that Amal's father had for her and the community when she was born, which is crucial to *Mornings in Jenin*'s message of liberation. Hope is encoded in the very sounds of her name's vowels; she is the embodiment of a community's hopes.

The next time Amal reflects on her name, she has changed it to Amy because she lost hope. As the first passage cited above puts it, "I was a word drained of its meaning." Or as she echoes later in the book, "I was a woman of few words and no friends. I was Amy. A name drained of meaning. Amal, long or short vowel, emptied of hope."[33] The name change allows Amal to cope with living outside Palestine at first by becoming Amy. This is solidified in another long reflection on her name: "*Amy*. Amal of the steadfast refugees and tragic beginning was now Amy in the land of privilege and plentitude. The country that flowed on the surface of life, supine beneath unwavering skies. But no matter what façade I bought, I forever belonged to that Palestinian nation of the banished to no place, no man, no honor. My Arabness and Palestine's primal cries were my anchors to the world. And I found myself searching books of history for accounts that matched the stories Haj Salem had told."[34]

Her Arabic and English names are juxtaposed, as are "the steadfast refugees" of Palestine with the "land of privilege." By reading these three passages together, it is clear how Abulhawa emphasizes Amal/Amy's character formation through the Arabic language. Even when Amal rejects her belonging to the Arab world—as in the example cited above where she does not pay attention to the news—her character is necessarily infused with the Arabic language. But we see that Amal's name change to Amy is never a simple story of assimilation, even as she tries to disconnect herself from her difficult past. She is unable to do so because being an Arab and a Palestinian, connected to the Arabic language through her name, is her "anchor to the world."

When Amal/Amy moves to the United States to study, she searches for her history and tries to locate the stories told to her by a community elder, Haj Salem, within official histories of Palestine. She cannot escape that her identity is inextricably linked to the history of her people and of Palestine. Later, when she falls in love with her future husband, she acknowledges that she must return to her original Arabic name: "How it hurt, ever sweetly, satisfyingly, to be Amal again—not anonymous Amy."[35] Years after she is married and returns to Palestine with her daughter, she reflects, "Despite the turmoil, it felt right to be there. I could feel meaning coming back into that word that had been drained of hope and left as dumbfounded letters. I was Amal there, not Amy. 'I like hearing people call you Amal, Mom,' Sara said to me when we were in Jenin the following day."[36] The ideas explored by Abulhawa in relation to language and naming come together in a dialectical relationship—sameness and difference, sweetness and pain, short and long vowels—that are given more meaning through sound. The very last lines of the book are a letter to Amal from her brother: "Dearest Amal, with a long vowel of hope."[37] An insistence on describing sound closes the novel.

Arabic Experiments, the Languages and Sounds of Home

The analyses above show the self-conscious, metatextual quality of *Mornings in Jenin*'s extended reflections and meditations on language. To explore more fully how Abulhawa develops an experimental soundscape in the novel, in the break and through breaking language, this section discusses her extensive use of Arabic inscribed directly into the English language of the novel. The importance of Arabic, particularly Palestinian Arabic, is underlined by the sheer number of Arabic words, expressions, and sounds she uses in the novel. She incorporates Arabic using many different techniques, including writing both translated and untranslated Arabic words with transliterated Latin letters, using unidiomatic translated words and expressions, and including certain categories of words in language that is marked clearly as Arabic rather than English. All of these experimentations with language work together to produce one unified creative language that belongs to *Mornings in Jenin* alone, and they function to create a soundscape that deepens the meditations and reflections on language presented in the examples above.

Breaking language conceptually helps to read the ways in which *Mornings in Jenin* emphasizes the sounds of Arabic, particularly the Palestinian vernacular, in its own ostensibly English language narration. The many and multiple ways in which Abulhawa uses Arabic in the text can be placed in productive conversation with the poetic projects of Hammad, Melhem, Ahmed, and Nye, though they operate differently. Like these poetic works, *Mornings in Jenin*'s linguistic project goes beyond using Arabic to add local spice and color to the novel, making it "more Palestinian." The use of vernacular Arabic and evoking the sounds of the Arabic spoken in Palestine are an integral part of the aesthetics of the novel and are dialectically related to its political and pedagogical project. Susan Abulhawa thus challenges her readers to read and hear Arabic, through this asserting Palestine as a home, with language identified as this home. Abulhawa is "making the medium the message," as Smitherman would say. The language of Abulhawa's text conveys its message through multiple breaks in Standard English. *Mornings in Jenin* creates a Palestinian soundscape through breaking language that mirrors how it breaks down what the English-language immigrant novel is and can be.

Home, Names, and Family

A specific and important element in creating a soundscape is through the extensive use of Arabic words referring to family relationships and roles. This is the most pervasive and important use of Arabic in the text. While on the surface it may seem a simple technique of peppering English with Arabic words, as an exotic local spice, I propose here that the use of these words is a deep and meaningful contribution to *Mornings in Jenin*'s

Palestinian Arabic-infused soundscape. The novel's construction of Palestine as a language and a home is built through these everyday words. It is not only the words and their sounds that are important here, but also the way people are referred to by their roles and titles as part of the Arab Palestinian family structure. This then helps to preserve elements of the culture and history of Palestine even as the text bears witness to the ways in which colonization and occupation try to destroy it. This Arabic language creates breaks in the English text, inscribing the resistance and resilience of the Palestinian people. Once again the break in language represents a breaking concept—Palestine is whole, its family structures must be maintained, and it is a home. The Abulheja family, with the other village families of Jenin, not only represent Palestine, they *are* Palestine.

Through these techniques of breaking language, *Mornings in Jenin* addresses Smitherman's question: Who do I be? Even as individual family members are killed and the occupation forces try to destroy the family unit, the family perseveres. It is as family members in Arabic that they "be who they be." In relation to shared histories and building connections, such tales strongly invoke African American resistance to the dismantling of family structures under slavery; the importance of family roles and names is also important to African American literary and vernacular traditions. Smitherman, for example, discusses the origins of the naming patterns whereby Black men refer to each other as brothers (brothas); Black women as sisters (sistas); and older women, mothers, and older men, especially in the church, as elders.[38] Though these are not spelled out as such by Abulhawa, this backdrop for thinking about the literary histories and parallels become clearer in how *Mornings in Jenin* uses Arabic to break English. Some specific techniques used to break English with these terms include using them in Arabic with definitions in the glossary, using them in Arabic without defining them in the glossary, repeating words with and without definitions, representing them within everyday speech in idioms, and using expressions that employ call-and-response.

Referring to people by their family relationships in Arabic is pervasive throughout the text. Most of these appear in the glossary at the back of the novel including the following names and titles (with the definitions given): Abu (father of), Ammo (paternal uncle), Amto (paternal aunt), Baba (dad),

Binti (my daughter), Haj and Haje (male and female for person who has been on Haj), Ibn/Ibni (son, my son), Jiddo (grandfather), Khalo (maternal uncle), Khalto (maternal aunt), Sitti (my grandmother), Teta (grandma), Um (mother of), Wleidi (my son), Yaba (dad), Yumma (mom).[39] These eighteen words are used frequently and liberally throughout the entire book, lending the feel of spoken Arabic to its pages; they all are commonly used in everyday speech, often affectionately. In a book of 322 pages, I have noted more than 150 uses of these words, which averages more than one every other page. Some of these words, such as "Abu" and "Um," are used across all Arabic dialects and formal Arabic; others are more specifically marked as Palestinian—"Yaba" and "Yumma" for example.

The first way in which using these Palestinian Arabic words to refer to people and reinforce their family roles strengthens the novel's commitment to cementing the family—the large extended Abulheja family in particular—is as a metaphor for Palestine and thus an unshakeable unit. It also reinforces the idea that the pluralizing long vowel in Amal's name represents not just her father's hopes and dreams, but those of her people. Using so many of these words and sounds gives this novel an "Arabic accent," while making that accent easy to understand. Using easy-to-learn and remember family words imitates spoken language. Many words are similar to English words, making them understandable to an English readership. Context, repetition, and the glossary make this even easier. At the same time, these words mobilize the power and sounds of spoken Palestinian Arabic. The repeated sounds of Arabic reinforce the text's location and, particularity, the Palestinian people's connections to each other, their land, and their home. As the Abulheja family suffers from displacement, death, and disintegration throughout the text, we see the parallels with stories of other colonized and enslaved peoples across the world. The ways in which the Arabic language breaks English here captures the characters' struggles and resistance and echoes both Smitherman and Baldwin in their claims for how languages of resistance are forged out of necessity. The use of Arabic words for family members can be read as this kind of resistance and holding onto family ties even as an oppressive force tries to break them.

These Arabic breaks in the English language can also be read as a way to inscribe a parallel break in the production of knowledge about Palestinians and Arabic in mainstream English-language locations. The multiple functions of these breaks can be thought of as an interventionist tool, therefore, that produce their own knowledge through language. Through repetition, the English-speaking reader is being taught common, basic words in everyday spoken Arabic. These words also echo and invoke powerful meanings for Arabic-speaking readers of the English text. Through this Abulhawa is subtly able to demonstrate how words seemingly meaning the same thing actually can invoke and mean something different. This can be understood intuitively, in relation to the way in which we refer to the people closest to us—family words often carry deep emotional connotations and meanings. Thus, the word "yumma" means "mom," but the two words do not necessarily express or carry the same range of connotations and emotions. Particularly for a community under threat of extinction, holding on to the very particular words for mother, father, or grandfather carries distinctive connotations. This is summed up succinctly in June Jordan's analysis of language as power in "White English/Black English," where she argues for the preservation of Black Language to instill pride in Black children and maintain positive Black selfhood and presence. About white and Black English she states clearly, "The two languages are not interchangeable. They cannot, nor do they attempt to communicate equal or identical thoughts, or feelings."[40] Taking up Jordan's analysis in this particular context, there are several shifts that reaffirm her theorization of language and work specifically here. The Palestinian Arabic words are not entirely distant from English words, especially when written in Latin letters, but neither are they familiar. The family role of yumma, who she is, and what she represents in a Palestinian family, is not captured by the English word "mom." They both may generally mean a female person who has given birth to children in a family, but what these two words each implies is different. The feelings the words evoke are not identical. In an unequal society, they also are never equal.

It is important to note that this does not mean that a given word, "yumma," or another always means the same things to every speaker of

Arabic or Palestinian Arabic either. But following Jordan's argument, the power that communities of people invest in the words used in their spoken languages can empower them to find a self and create home. This is particularly true of oppressed people. Using language marked and understood as Arabic is even starker within English-language settings: the word "yumma" is invested with stronger power when set against other words in English than when it is embedded within Arabic. In standing out from other words, these Arabic family titles and words punctuate the novel—they force us to pay attention to them and their particularities. This is part of the power Abulhawa harnesses by using so many Arabic words, especially spoken Palestinian Arabic words, in *Mornings in Jenin* and how she inscribes messages about home and liberation through this breaking language.

"Ibni, Ibni"

One particularly powerful example of a repeated family-related word shows how its meaning, special relevance to the novel's plot and message, and sound work together to deliver an important aesthetic and political message. "Ibni" is repeated many times, in many different settings; the English equivalent word is "my son." This word is repeated in both mundane and dramatic circumstances. The story of Amal's brother Ismael, Yousef's twin, being stolen by a Jewish settler right out of her mother Dalia's arms is where it is repeated the most times, underlining the importance of the word. In the harrowing kidnapping scene, the word recurs six times in a row. The first time, it is translated for impact, "'Ibni! Ibni!' My son, my son, Dalia screamed, her eyes bulging in search of her son. Dust at her face, cactus at her feet. 'Ibni! Ibni!' She scanned the ground, looked up, and Hasan's tall figure was not there. 'Ibni! Ibni!' Some people tried to help her but gunshots tolled and Dalia was shoved along. *Is this a dream?*"[41] This use of the word "ibni" reinforces the tragedy that frames the entire novel and recalls the intertextual reference to Ghassan Kanafani's *Returning to Haifa*. This also recalls Abulhawa's feminist rescripting and demands we think about the specific relationship between mothers and sons, one focused on by many Black and women-of-color feminist theorists.[42] Abulhawa uses the repetition to create sounds capturing the despair and loss of Dalia, making the Arabic word echo through the English-language text.

This is not the only time the word is used in relation to this part of the story. As noted above, Moshe—the man who kidnaps Ismael to be raised as the Jewish Israeli David—recounts this same scene in the chapter immediately following the scene mentioned here. This chapter is labeled "Chapter Five, 'Ibni! Ibni!,'" reinforcing once again that to shout "my son, my son," does not sound the same nor carry the exact same meaning as "Ibni, ibni." He recalls, "He heard the woman yell, 'Ibni! Ibni!' and that made him believe that she had seen him take her baby"[43] and "The Arab woman's face, and her scream of 'Ibni, ibni,' would haunt Moshe's years and the awful things he had done would give him no peace until the end."[44] Much later in the book, on his deathbed, these very same two words are what haunt him still: "How he had learned to love her Arab child and had turned to drink to hush her cries of 'Ibni, ibni,' that remained as clear to him as on the day he had seized her son from her arms."[45] The Arabic word is repeated in all of these passages. The number of times it is repeated, by both Moshe and Dalia, in different sections of the book—as well as the word being used in other contexts—underlines the importance of this word's meaning and sound and the fact that it is Arabic. In scope, it recalls the sound of "U/you" in Naomi Shihab Nye's poem for Jamyla Bolden, which represents tragedy and trauma. In the novel, this repetition serves all of the functions listed above: it teaches the meaning of an Arabic word to an English-speaking readership, it highlights the importance of family and family relationships, it punctuates the text in important moments, and it reminds us that words do not always communicate "equal or identical thoughts or feelings," even if we think we know their meanings.

This example of "Ibni, ibni" reinforces Abulhawa's meticulous recounting of the history of the fictional Abulheja family, as she records a history that is not at all fictional. Crucial to the narration here is the preservation and building of family relations that are constantly being broken by the colonization and occupation of Palestine. She does this partly through her use of words, of which "Ibni, ibni" is one of many examples.

This has a powerful parallel in the ways in which African American songs, narratives, and poetry use linguistic aesthetics to challenge ways in which the institution of slavery broke apart African American families.[46] The Abulheja family are dispersed and separated by being kidnapped—as in the case of Ismael/David—murdered, driven mad, sent to an orphanage, exiled to the United States, and so on. But the use of Arabic family names among and between them continues all the way throughout the novel, even on its final pages when Yousef is thinking about his father, Baba.[47]

Broken English, Breaking English with Idioms

More challenging to readers and more compelling as a literary device than repeated words to do with family relations is Susan Abulhawa's use of different techniques to render commonly used, everyday Arabic-language idioms in *Mornings in Jenin*. The novel employs many different words and expressions that "do not translate" into English. Abulhawa treats these in a variety of different ways, all of which work together to function as breaks in English. Some of these examples read very much like "broken English" or "Arabic-accented English"; some are explained in detail, others are not. Included in these examples are a large number of words that appear on the surface to be connected to religion. Arabic contains many idiomatic, everyday expressions that contain the word for "God"—Allah—with varying degrees of religious connotation, depending on context and usage. At times, they have no real religious connotation at all. These are often difficult to render in English, because direct translations make expressions sound religious even if it not intended to sound this way.

Much like the use of Arabic family words to render certain concepts— Does "yumma" mean the exact same thing as "mom"?—many expressions here are shown not to communicate "equal or identical" thoughts or feelings. Abulhawa often shows how larger concepts operate by elaborating their contexts and meanings in great detail. Another technique she uses at some length is to provide literal, nonidiomatic translations of Arabic expressions that sound purposely odd in English.[48] In some ways this strategy of breaking English is more visible because it reads on the surface as different and odd to the ear. The effect in creating a soundscape that inscribes Palestinian Arabic in English is different from, but complementary to, the use of untranslated Arabic lexical items.

African American Echoes: Calls-and-Responses

Translating Arabic expressions directly and literally into unidiomatic English makes these phrases visible, while also giving the English language a "broken" or "accented" feel. This strategy of breaking English fuses the linguistic, aesthetic, theoretical, and political project of *Mornings in Jenin*. One prominent example of this is a passage that again underlines connections to Black American aesthetic forms and how they are relevant to Arab and Palestinian experience. In this example, Amal has arrived in Beirut to visit her brother Yousef whom she has not seen since she left Jenin refugee camp to take up a scholarship in the United States. As she walks out into the arrivals hall, she is immediately struck by the sounds of Arabic, which she identifies as "calls and responses": "But the guttural silk tones of Arabic rippled through me as I heard the melodic calls and responses of my language. It's a dance, really. A man at a desk was offered tea as I walked through the metal detectors. He said, 'Bless your hands' to the one making the offer, who responded, 'And your hands, may Allah keep you always in Grace.' Calls and responses that dance in the air."[49] As she emerges and is met by her brother's friend and comrade, he greets her in Arabic, "'Al hamdulillah ala salama,' he said, extending a hand. 'My name is Majid. Your brother sent me to pick you up.' 'And God keep you in safety, too,' I replied. *Calls and responses.*"[50]

   This passage invokes call-and-response as a definition for the Arabic language. Call-and-response here clearly evokes the musical and literary form associated with African Americans—people who were enslaved adopted this form from its deep roots in African cultures, transplanting them in North America and elsewhere.[51] Many contemporary Black authors refer to and activate call-and-response in different ways within literary works to harness its power and thus inscribe their works within a longer Black diasporic tradition, with a continental African heritage. As a quintessential African American art form, call-and-response is a technique that scholar Maggie Sale, for example, has argued demands art and literature to be meaningful and functional to the community, rooted in language patterns and ways that people speak.[52] Abulhawa here draws on this idea, linking the way in which spoken Arabic always uses calls that demand responses to this particular tradition, naming it as such. This directly connects *Mornings in Jenin* and its use and theorization of language to Black American language, literary, and political praxis, in how it writes the story of Palestine. Calls-and-responses here serve several specific purposes within the narrative in addition to building bonds of solidarity and connections with African American traditions. This example also shows the way in which being polite is defined as musical and itself is connected to a sense of being and self in the world. This scene also reinforces the ways in which familial and social connections knit individuals into the fabric of society—something Amal has missed since she has become Amy in the United States.

Explicitly defining the way in which people speak to each other in Arabic—particularly the use of a specific response to a phrase that is said as a greeting, thank you, and so on—as "call-and-response" emphasizes links to African American culture and music. These expressions and contemplations are pervasive throughout *Mornings in Jenin*. The book makes use of many different techniques to use, explain, and theorize language and its connections to aesthetics and politics. The novel ponders human relationships in great detail, particularly how to express gratitude. The example of landing in Beirut and listening to Arabic expressions of thanks is paralleled by an earlier example about two dozen pages earlier, when Amal first lands in the United States and is unsure how to use English. She wants to express her thanks for an American woman's generosity, but is unsure exactly how:

> "Thank you," I answered unsure of the proper American response to her gracious enthusiasm. In the Arab world, gratitude is a language unto itself. "May Allah bless the hands that give me this gift"; "Beauty is in your eyes that find me pretty"; "May God extend your life"; "May Allah never deny your prayer"; "May the next meal you cook for us be in celebration of your son's wedding . . . of your daughter's graduation . . . your mother's recovery"; and so on, an infinite string of prayerful

appreciation. Coming from such a culture, I have always found a mere "thank you" an insufficient expression that makes my voice sound miserly and ungrateful.[53]

Amal cannot make sense of how one simple phrase in English, "thank you," can express what she wishes to say when she feels extremely grateful. Once again Abulhawa's purposes for including these examples of "broken English" are multiple. She gives a number of literal, unidiomatic translations of Arabic expressions to make a point.[54] She uses expressions that have the word Allah/God in them and those that do not; in some cases she translates the word and others does not.

The first thing that her use of these many expressions to express "thank you" does is to show warmth of personal connection that they inscribe. The person thanking refers to something more specific in their words connected to a personal relationship or wishing well upon the person. This underlines the notion of community and building relationships. The linguistic techniques that Abulhawa uses here are also varied. Though all of the expressions would be considered "literally" translated and not idiomatic English, they are not all the same. For example, at times she leaves the word "Allah" untranslated and at others she translates it as "God." This choice demonstrates how she varies her breaking techniques to give the sounds of her "broken Arabic" a depth of expression, to make us question how and why she is using them. Once again the seemingly "broken Arabic" in fact is Abulhawa's strategy to create a new soundscape for a Palestinian Arabic story, revising the English language ones from which Arab voices are emptied. The breaking language Abulhawa uses in *Mornings in Jenin* is positive and generative and reconfigures and redefines what it means to be broken but then also to break. She represents sounds and words that do not sound naturally like English, but uses them to break with what is problematic English and convey ideas and thoughts through the sounds and invocations of an Arabic that is translated unidiomatically. This once again recalls the strategies of James Baldwin in identifying white English as the problem in the language and arguing to valorize Black languages of expression.

Later in the text, a further example shows how Amal has eventually come to terms with the fact that "thank you" does not express the same thing as the expressions she is used to using. Though both may be ways to express something, they don't convey an identical feeling. Abulhawa exploits this literarily to make other points. In portraying the depth of the relationship that Amal forges with her new "adoptive family" when she returns to Pennsylvania from Lebanon, pregnant and without her husband, Abulhawa once again uses such an untranslatable Arabic expression. Amal thanks the man who has welcomed her into his home: "Touched and without adequate words—'thank you' conveying a dearth of gratitude—in Arabic I said, 'Allah keep you in Grace and a bounty of goodness upon you. This kindness of yours, doctor . . . Ammo Mohammad . . . is humbling.'"[55] Underlining the emptiness of "thank you" allows the text to do more work than simply show a flowery or religious expression. Rather, the bond forged between Amal and Ammo Mohammad—Ammo is the Arabic word for uncle—is strong and unshakable.

The use of expressions of thanks, as well as others that have the word Allah within them, is common in Arabic, and Abulhawa generously spreads them throughout *Mornings in Jenin*. Some expressions are more directly connected to religion—almost always Islam, though they are also used by Arab Christians, and Amal points this out specifically when she is living in the orphanage run by nuns. Many of these expressions are not, however, particularly religious. Though they invoke the word for God, such phrases are simply culturally or linguistically appropriate to use in certain circumstances and do not mean that the speaker is thinking about or referring to God. They also do not indicate that the speaker is particularly religious. Such expressions are notoriously difficult to translate and one of the vexed questions Arabic-English translators face.[56] Not only do many such expressions not have idiomatic equivalents in English, but the question of how to deal with the word Allah/God is always present for translators. For example, should you use the equivalent expression "God" and neutralize, or "domesticate," the expression for an English-speaking audience? As this is the closest equivalent word and appears to "mean the same thing," it has the effect of making an expression that sounds very exotic or foreign easier to digest for this readership and bringing the characters in the book closer to the reader.

This can be an important political statement in a reception environment hostile to Arabs, Muslims, Palestinians, and so on. However, the
counter argument goes, does this not take away some of the specificity
of the meaning of the word Allah? In some settings, people might argue,
Allah is the more appropriate word—it connects the expressions to Islam
specifically often and also invokes the unique sound of this word, with its
doubled long *l* sounds and round vowels. At the same time that it might
sound more different, unique, or "foreign"—this is known as a foreigniz-
ing technique—it also might serve the opposite purpose. By integrating the
word Allah so seamlessly into the narration, an author or translator might
then mitigate stigma attached to the word in English, gathered from sen-
sationalistic journalism and racist diatribes against Arabs and Muslims.
As this brief example shows, the way in which translation choices work
for particular words and phrases between Arabic and English complicates
the notion that there is one right or wrong way to deal with them. In
more theoretical terms, it also challenges the dichotomy so prevalent in
translation studies that proposes these two techniques—domestication
and foreignization—as mutually exclusive. Many scholars are beginning
to explore the limits of this way of thinking about translation for Arabic
in particular, in how the alternately hostile and exoticizing approaches to
the Arabic language in English mean that foreignization and domestication are not necessarily the best concepts for exploring the translational
dynamics between these two languages.[57]

In *Mornings in Jenin*, Abulhawa uses and manipulates many of the
same structures and techniques that translators of Arabic fiction into English do to break language. She employs Arabic words and expressions in
ways that both mirror and challenge common practice, and her uses of
unidiomatic expressions, transliterations of Arabic words, and other linguistically "difficult" expressions far exceed that of what most translators
would dare to experiment with. Translators rarely use phrases that might
be read as "broken English" or try to give their texts an Arabic accent
for a number of reasons. One reason is that it is generally assumed that
translations will be written in a language deemed to be proper or Standard
English. This comparison helps to reveal where Abulhawa's language is

aesthetically and linguistically experimental and challenging. Though it is translating Palestinian history for English-language readerships, and it does bear many of the signs of translated fiction, the novel's use of language is much more formally and artistically connected to the language projects we find in African American novels. Her language is more akin to works identified by Gates as speakerly texts, like those by Zora Neale Hurston or Toni Morrison's *Beloved*, Alice Walker's *The Color Purple*, and June Jordan's *His Own Where*. This is one reason why the theorizations of Black Language, which these texts engage so thoroughly, offer insights into how breaking English can work through "broken" English in *Mornings in Jenin*. Abulhawa shows the beauty of a different language—here Palestinian Arabic—and does this both by describing it and showing it in multiple ways as the examples above demonstrate.

Some of the further work *Mornings in Jenin* does can be interpreted by connecting the insights developed above in relation to how Abulhawa deploys strategic essentialism, a common ploy of self-orientalization and exoticization. Strategic essentialism is a concept articulated by postcolonial feminists like Gayatri Chakravorty Spivak to think about how feminists and other people of color can exhibit a temporary unity around a shared ethnic, racial, national, or other "essentialized" identity.[58] Many women of color have used this technique as a way to undermine stereotypes and reclaim positive and beautiful elements of their cultures. In "Nobody Mean More to Me Than You and the Future Life of Willie Jordan," June Jordan discusses how not only she, but also writers like Alice Walker and Zora Neale Hurston, were harshly criticized for literary works depicting Black Language. Suheir Hammad was criticized for using "vulgar" language like June Jordan before her, and Hurston was strongly condemned for showing the negative elements of Black culture, as Abu Jaber was criticized for "airing the dirty laundry" of the Arab American community with the release of *Arabian Jazz*.

Abulhawa's depiction of Palestinian people speaking Arabic in a flowery and loving way may similarly seem like an exaggeration that activates stereotypes about Arab culture and language. Read through this concept, however, it can also be seen as part of her larger project of humanizing Palestinians and building the will for political solidarity. Her multiple techniques—showing and telling how expressions work, repeating family terms, focusing on expressions that have a specific response, leaving many words untranslated—are all ways in which she does this specifically. Though she does use a number of single words, more of her breaking language consists of expressions. And most of these are placed strategically at meaningful points in the text to highlight or punctuate a moment. An example of this is when Amal receives condolences upon her mother's death. Ammo Jack O'Malley is an Irish UNRWA worker central to the text and close to the people living in the camp. He uses an Arabic expression, repeated after the English one in the same sentence, "I'm so sorry, Amal. El baeyeh fi hayatik" and then follows with, "Yer Englizi is getting ahsan, eh?" He often mixed the two languages like that. "Yes my English is getting better."[59] In both of these sentences Ammo Jack mixes English and Arabic and in both the English equivalents are given for the Arabic. Once again, we are made to realize that the Arabic expression might not mean the exact same thing as the English one; this is confirmed by the glossary where Abulhawa notes that "El baeyeh fi hayatik" means "may your life be extended."[60]

The example of Ammo Jack's Arabic, like the others above, demonstrates how Susan Abulhawa's use of Arabic is more complex than simply giving the text "spice and flavor," though it may do this as well. Arabic expressions punctuate certain moments in *Mornings in Jenin*—Dalia's death, Amal's arrival in the States, Amal's arrival in Lebanon, and so on. The explicit reference to Arabic as a language that uses "calls-and-responses" not only links this work to African American literary and musical traditions, but also shows how theories and insights developed out of African American intellectual traditions inform it. Understanding *Mornings in Jenin* as using breaks in English and breaking language is a way to draw out and valorize this project. In the novel, Arabic finds and shows the beauty of things, people, places, and ideas that are deemed to be ugly, frightening, and hateful in her readership's environment. Moreover, Abulhawa demonstrates the inner beauty and "genius" of Arabic, to reconfigure Baldwin's characterization of Toni Morrison's words about a reviled language. *Mornings in Jenin* uses many different techniques to demonstrate how words do not convey identical or equal meanings or feelings, and that concepts can vary between languages. Most importantly perhaps, the novel insists strongly on Arab Palestinian culture and its connection to language. This insistence on language—words and sounds—is deeply bound to community building, togetherness, and family in the large extended sense. Even if all of these are torn apart, language is one way in which to knit things back together. Preserving and honoring language itself breaks the hegemony of English in a novel like *Mornings in Jenin*, where the soundscape invokes family and community to offer a sense of home.

Language, Translation, and the Glossary

As noted above, *Mornings in Jenin* contains an extensive glossary at the end of the novel, following the author's note, just before a list of references.[61] Compared to similar glossaries, Abulhawa's is fairly extensive, running just under four pages long and containing 115 words. This is one reason that it merits commentary. As a novel that uses so many Arabic words, expressions, and phrases with all of the different styles, techniques, and purposes discussed in this chapter, *Mornings in Jenin's* glossary is integral to her larger project. The glossary is not a common feature of Arab American novels; it is a more prevalent feature of works of Arabic literature translated into English and is arguably falling out of favor.[62] Including a glossary once again reveals the novel's function as a didactic project suitable for teaching settings and book clubs, but this also aligns it with works translated from Arabic and implies that a knowledge of Arabic is crucial to understanding it. This particular glossary makes available mostly short, direct translations; for example, "baba" is given as "dad" and "areej" as "fragrance."[63] In a few cases there is a contextualization; for example, the expression "La hawla wala quwatta ella billah" is translated and commented upon, "There is neither might nor power but with Allah. It is a saying to express one's powerlessness to reverse tragedy."[64] The literal translation in this example is accompanied by an explanation.

One specific example bears a longer investigation as it is not only a translation and contextualization but more of an intervention that speaks to the larger politics of the work, the way in which the Arabic language is used within it and also the way in which Arabic is used in English today. The longest single definition given in the glossary is attached to the common Arabic expression, "Allaho Akbar."[65] The translation given by Abulhawa differs from what we are used to seeing in English, and she explains this as well as providing a longer explanation: "*Allaho Akbar*: God is bigger. Western press explains this phrase as meaning 'God is great,' which is an erroneous translation that strips it of spirit and context. 'Allaho akbar' is used in nearly every conceivable context among Arabs, and always as a humbling reminder that God is bigger than any event or circumstance and therefore faith in Him is the answer."[66] Abulhawa picks out this particular expression to make a direct political point and challenge the stereotyped and problematic ways that Arabs and Muslims are mistranslated and misrepresented in English. Surely this is one of the most frequently misunderstood and misused expressions, particularly in the media—as Abulhawa points out—to show Muslim and/or Arab "fanaticism" or "fundamentalism." The definition here thus reclaims the words as an expression containing so much within it—the humbling reminder— while pointing out its daily use in a variety of circumstances.

Within the novel, Abulhawa indeed uses this expression many times and therefore demonstrates what she claims in the glossary, that this expression is used in "nearly every conceivable context."[67] It occurs frequently and not only in context but also in relation to its sound. One example comes when Yousef is found alive after having been believed dead: "'Allaho akbar,' over and over. Tens of them, hundreds. A cacophony of 'Allaho akbars' merging into one powerful chant as people converged."[68] Less than ten pages later, when the war of 1967 begins and the students clear their classroom in a frenzy, the narration describes them as "rushing beneath a sound banner of 'Allaho akbar.'"[69] Sound is once again crucial to the expression when Abulhawa uses extra letters to show how it sounds with elongated letters when writing down the way in which the girls in the orphanage heard the adan, "'Alllaaaaaaaho akbar . . . alllaaaaaaaho akbar. . . .' Poured in a musical lilt from the sky."[70]

This particular expression shows how Abulhawa's complex linguistic, literary, and political projects come together. "Allaho akbar" is a place where we can see the importance of sound, as the narrative uses explanations of it in relation to a "cacophony" and "sound banner," but also elongates some of its letters in order to demonstrate different ways it might actually sound to the characters. This comes together then with the relatively long discussion of the expression that takes a firmly critical and interventionist political position demonstrating what is wrong with the way it is usually understood and redefining it. This not only makes sense in relation to the larger aesthetic, political project of language in the novel being linked to Black American projects of breaking English and redefining language on its own terms, but also the role of *Mornings in Jenin* in Palestinian solidarity politics.

The Arabic Language, Literary Solidarity, and Teaching History

The glossary is not the only supplementary material that Susan Abulhawa uses in the novel to make it cohere as a readable, compelling work of literature. As I have noted throughout this chapter, the novel is well crafted and thoughtfully constructed. It contains a family tree outlining the Abuheja family and their relationships to each other, which also reinforces the importance of family. It offers a list of resources, a minibibliography of further reading, at the end. It includes an author's note that gives thanks to people who helped in the writing of the book and also explains its origins. It has a guide with questions to help readers think about various elements of the book. Along with all of these, as in many books—but not many novels—there is a table of contents. This is notable in the context of language use because seven of the eight chapter titles are Arabic words and expressions, and all of them are immediately followed by English translations in parentheses. This supplementary material supports each other and also the main narrative of the book. The way the table of contents uses Arabic words can be read as breaking language, teaching Arabic, and underlining concepts. The pedagogical tools of language indeed have their own breaking effects. In particular, they add power to the book's use as a teaching text for solidarity work with Palestine and a break with mainstream English-language knowledge produced about Arabs, Muslims, and especially the politics, history, and culture of Palestine.

The table of contents is composed as follows, with the intervening subdivisions omitted:

I. El Nakba (*the catastrophe*)

II. El Naksa (*the disaster*)

III. The Scar of David

IV. El Ghurba (*state of being a stranger*)

V. Albi fi Beirut (*my heart is in Beirut*)

VI. Elly Bayna (*what there is between us*)

VII. Baladi (*my country*)

VIII. Nihaya o Bidaya (*an end and a beginning*)[71]

Though I have not included them here, it is relevant to note that these eight well-constructed chapters are subdivided into many more, some of which also have Arabic titles, but most of which do not. A study of these chapter titles reinforces the importance of the Arabic language, the importance of understanding history, and the way the two are inextricably intertwined. Once again, the meanings of words—posited as equivalents by giving a translation—are shown in fact not to be equal or identical in expressing thoughts and feelings, recalling earlier examples.

Even more important, however, is the way in which Abulhawa chooses to define the specific and particular Arabic words that she uses as chapter titles. Some of these are standard definitions of words, or at least not unusual ones. "El Nakba," for example, is almost always translated as "the catastrophe," referring to the loss of Palestine in 1948. "El Naksa," however, is usually translated with a word like "the setback," and here Abulhawa chooses the more powerful and more idiomatic phrase, "the disaster." This choice of translation prefigures and draws attention to the terrifying scenes in *Mornings in Jenin*, which depict this war. The final four examples—chapters V through VIII—all have standard translations that might be considered both literal and idiomatic. It is worth noting that the spelling of these five words/expressions indicates that they are transcribed from colloquial, rather than standard, Arabic. This reinforces the sounds of the words and sets up the Palestinian soundscape of the novel before the narrative begins.

Perhaps the most interesting definition of a term here is in the fourth chapter. Abulhawa gives the definition "state of being a stranger" for the term "El Ghurba." More commonly defined as "exile" or "being abroad," this is a term that has embedded in its Arabic root the concepts of being alien or strange, different, estranged, and in the West. Defining El Ghurba as a state of being is relevant to the themes and content of the novel, as Amal as well as other characters like Majid experience that state when they are outside of Palestine, in the United States and England especially. Like all of the other words defined in parentheses in the table of contents, "El Ghurba" cannot be found in the book's glossary, though it is used in at least one passage in the text.[72] It is similarly not the only word from the table of contents to be used in the text of the novel—"El Nakba" also appears within the main narration, though it is spelled "nakbe," reflecting more closely the Palestinian pronunciation, and is not defined in the glossary either.[73]

These three examples in particular—but the four others as well—are evidence of how Susan Abulhawa uses *Mornings in Jenin* to create a Palestinian soundscape that uses breaking language to disrupt English-language knowledge production about Palestine. The pedagogical practice breaks with this mainstream teaching through using breaks in language. By naming the two first chapters after key moments in Palestinian history, the first marking 1948 and the second 1967, Abulhawa offers a history lesson through the chapter outline itself. Reviewers have commented upon and appreciated this function of the book. Marcy Knopf-Newman points out, for example, that it is one of the first novels in English that delves into the history of Palestine in depth.[74] She suggests it might be useful for teaching American high school students. Robin Yassin-Kassab similarly comments positively on Abulhawa's commitment to recording the history of Palestine in novelistic form.[75] Elsewhere I have argued that part of this book's importance is its role in popular education contexts informed by activism, such as its being chosen as the inaugural book in the "One Book, Many Communities" project launched by the Librarians and Archivists with Palestine group. The main pedagogical technique used here is to define a word the first time it is used within the text and then to repeat it without translation, so that the reader assimilates it through use, context, and the practice of familiarization.

The extensive chapter outline, with the Arabic language titles and their translations, is one more example of *Mornings in Jenin*'s tight and effective construction as a novel and how well it masters its form. The narrative parallels Palestinian history closely, and the family's history is a mirror of the country's larger history. Its characters live through major world historical events that shape their country, their region, and also their own personal lives. But they do not only live through and bear them as victims; at different moments they are agents and actors in this history as well. All of this is contained within the chapter titles. By expertly crafting the shape of *Mornings in Jenin*, Susan Abulhawa is able to make a strong intervention on behalf of Palestinian liberation in a paperback English-language novel, marketed to mainstream audiences. This novel's political commitment to Palestine and unrelenting critique of Zionist colonization is unusual to see in a work so widely and broadly marketed to this audience in North America, the United Kingdom, and beyond. This mastery of form and its use of Arabic is part of what makes it appealing at the same time that it teaches.

This is one more way in which *Mornings in Jenin* can be read in relation to African American fictional experimentations and creative interventions with language constructed in the break and as breaking. Many texts by Black American authors that are politically committed to Black liberation and challenging to mainstream white American audiences also use language in experimental ways and have found a mainstream readership. Works mentioned above—for example, Nobel Prize laureate Toni Morrison's *Beloved*, Zora Neale Hurston's long-neglected, but now canonical *Their Eyes Were Watching God*, or Alice Walker's National Book Award/Pulitzer Prize–winning *The Color Purple*, adapted for film by Oprah Winfrey—all are known for this practice. More recent works too, like Jesmyn Ward's 2017 *Sing, Unburied, Sing*, also extensively use Black language and are lauded in mainstream American literary circles. None of these literary projects is the same; the languages developed in them work differently and to different effects. But thinking through *Mornings in Jenin* in a framework informed by Black American linguistic and literary theory helps to tease out some of the ways its artistic and political contributions are rooted in its language/s, especially in the break. The way Abulhawa manipulates these to create a breaking English invokes a Palestinian soundscape to make this language a home.

Conclusions: Sounds of Solidarity,
Breathing in Palestine and Black America

"The future can't breathe in a refugee camp, Amal. The air here is too dense for hope," Ammo Darwish tells Amal. "You are being offered a chance to liberate the life that lies dormant in all of us. Take it."[76] A Jenin village elder uses these words to convince Amal to leave the camp for educational opportunities in Jerusalem, after the death of her parents. In a novel full of poetry, these lines stand out as particularly poignant. They also resonate specifically with other moments in which breath and the inability to breathe are used to express oppression. The basic human need for air to breathe links and ties people together, as Therí Pickens powerfully explores in a phenomenological reading of Suheir Hammad's poetry, focused initially on breath and breathing.[77] Pickens focuses first on her use of breathing in "first writing since," discussed in chapter 1 above, as well as other poems, including some of the *breaking poems*. Pickens's chapter was written before 2014, when thousands of people in the streets of New York City chanted "I can't breathe" in demonstrations against the New York City Police Department for its choke-to-death murder of an unarmed Black man, Eric Garner. Garner died saying these words. Ammo Darwish's words stick with the reader more powerfully in the wake of Garner's strangulation, which recalls this symbolic cry that echoed and prefigured it even as much as Suheir Hammad's poems. Being able to breathe or not being able to breathe is used as a metaphor in poetry and fiction, but is also shown literally to be the line between life and death. This metaphor and this reality serve as a location of connection between these communities. The literary connections that reflect the community connections in literature, language, organizing, and politics—including the renewed activism since 2014—also help to produce it. If we understand literary works as expressions, plots, characters, themes, and words of struggle and resistance, then these connections become even more important.

Mornings in Jenin is open to such a reading because of its political stance for Palestinian liberation, because it has been used specifically in such solidarity work, such as reading groups,[78] and because it evinces connections to Black communities. My analyses that emphasize and draw out the content and themes connected to Black America therefore also do political work, linked to Abulhawa's pair of articles cited in the opening to this chapter. Abulhawa's own larger project of naming where solidarity is located and working to embed this in her community has echoes in the novel. It is therefore important to underline how she depicts Black America as a place to feel at home, and where Amal can be herself—be who she be, recalling Smitherman's expression—and also speak in her own language, with her own accent. *Mornings in Jenin* creates a soundscape that is home through language. The theoretical lenses offered by Black American writers thus open up new and deeper ways of reading Abulhawa's style, form, and language.

Susan Abulhawa's *Mornings in Jenin* breathes new life into the English-language novel, giving it energy infused with a politics and aesthetics that underline freedom and liberation for the Palestinian people and other oppressed peoples. Her skillful use of form, language, and especially breaking English as a way to advance its political content allows *Mornings in Jenin* to become an "international bestseller" in ways that other Arab American literary works have not.[79] Chapter 4 also focuses on several texts that use major experimentations with English, including breaking and "broken" English, layering Arabic in multiple ways. Randa Jarrar's novel *A Map of Home* and two short stories from her collection, *Him, Me, Muhammad Ali*, use many similar techniques to *Mornings in Jenin*. They also experiment even more extensively with different registers of Arabic and English vernaculars. Like Abulhawa's characters, Jarrar's protagonists move between the Arab world and North America, producing different expressions of racial and racialized selves, with different connections to Black Americans. Jarrar uses allusions to Arab and African American music, literary texts, figures, and symbols by inscribing a mix of spoken and formal languages in complex ways, problematizing stark lines dividing what is Arab and what African American, and in turn leading her to challenge ways of expressing a politics of solidarity and coalition building through language.

4 Stories to Pass On

Randa Jarrar's Languages of Race, Sexuality, and Gender

"It was not a story to pass on," is repeated throughout Toni Morrison's devastating novel *Beloved*. But the novel's protagonist does pass her story on, and Sethe's story of killing her child rather than subjecting her to the horrors of slavery has not only become one of American literature's most haunting portrayals of the terror of African American enslavement, but also created a language in order to express what cannot—or should not—be expressed. The very idea that a story should not be passed on, while at the same time writing it down for others to read, also motivates Randa Jarrar's short story, "Lost in Freakin' Yonkers." Jarrar's story honors and refers to Morrison's classic novel implicitly in this way. On a more explicit level, the story names *Beloved*, when its protagonist Aida checks it out of her university's library, frustrated she could not find even one book by an Arab woman writer. She types the words "Arab," "American," "Woman," and "Fiction" into the library catalog search engine. When she finds nothing, she sighs, "Defeated, I read *Beloved*, and when I'm done it's nearing midnight."[1] The defeated Aida is also nine months pregnant, and these subtle and overt intertextual references to Morrison's text as the substitute for fiction by an Arab woman author makes an even more powerful statement.

The intertextual connection to Toni Morrison's *Beloved* is neither accidental nor superficial. Jarrar's style, theme, plot, and language demand that we notice a heavily pregnant protagonist who turns to this particular novel to give her comfort through her struggles being disowned from her family and in a violent relationship with her boyfriend. References to books and works of literature punctuate all the important moments in this short seventeen-page story. When she is tired and frustrated, she reads *Beloved* as solace in a bathroom stall on campus. Jarrar gives pride of place to a book by an African American woman that has connected feminists across communities over time. As Henry Louis Gates Jr. has pointed out, Morrison's novel is the "ur-text" of the African American experience,[2] one of the most iconic works for women-of-color feminists, and has served as a link between women of different feminist communities, particularly in the 1980s when it was first published.[3] Gates himself praises *Beloved* as a uniquely powerful work: "It is one of the few treatments of slavery that escapes the pitfalls of kitsch. Toni Morrison's genius is that she has found a language by which to thematize this very unspeakability of slavery."[4] Gates's emphasis on language is not accidental here. Morrison's genius is located not just in how she depicts slavery, but that she is able to create a language through which to do this. Her mix of vernacular Black Language and other registers of English is masterful, and this kind of experimentation is reflected by Jarrar's use of language in "Lost in Freakin' Yonkers."

This story will be analyzed further below, followed by readings of Jarrar's novel, *A Map of Home,* and two other short stories from her collection *Him, Me, Muhammad Ali.* The analyses of Jarrar's work focus on where her language uses breaking English to connect to, illuminate, and emphasize other kinds of breaks. Like Abulhawa, Jarrar layers languages into her English by using the break in multiple ways. This chapter reads Jarrar's intervention as breaking language that parallels her intertextual invocations of African American literature and music. She creates a soundscape of language informed by Arabic, using representations of "broken" English of various kinds, including spoken Egyptian and Palestinian Arabic in her English, as well as differently marked spoken englishes, that gesture to Black Language, Spanglish, and others. Jarrar uses language to train her ironic eye on society with humor as part of her strategy to address and challenge racism, misogyny, and compulsorily conventional (hetero) sexuality. This allows Jarrar to propose language as solidarity between people of color in facing white racism. How this solidarity and social justice message is inscribed through the language will be analyzed below first in relation to intertextual links to literary works and then by exploring how humor functions and the way in which family members, and also minor characters, are portrayed. This section concludes with a discussion of women-of-color solidarity and breaking language.

As in the works analyzed in the chapters above, Jarrar's short story is concerned with creating a language of expression which, when read through the framework of breaking, challenges and confronts a number of personal and political issues of social justice. Similarly, Jarrar draws upon and honors African American literary resources—it is a Black feminist text that helps Aida come to terms with her own identity. This is a literary expression of the kind of solidarity activism documented by Abdulhadi and Naber, discussed above in the introduction. It also echoes the work of a poet like D. H. Melhem, discussed in chapter 2, who was deeply inspired by, engaged by, and involved in the work of Gwendolyn Brooks, among others. Suheir Hammad, discussed in chapter 1, in fact talks about how she arrived at a knowledge and appreciation of Palestinian poetry and creative production through the work of Black Americans, in particular June Jordan. Jarrar's fiction can be read as part of a lineage of both Arab American writers and poets before her, and also women of color—in particular African American women—with whom she engages in a literary conversation.[5] These literary connections give the text its identity, help Aida express who she is, and also build the solidarity bonds across languages, literatures, and communities toward shared politics and commitments.

Literary and Intertextual Solidarity

The importance of literature is not expressed in only one passage in "Lost in Freakin' Yonkers." All of the short story's important moments are punctuated by literary references, often tragicomically. For example, pregnant Aida gets mugged one night when walking home alone in the dark. Depressed, she sardonically comments that the only thing the thief got away with was "my backpack, which contains three interlibrary loan books by Sahar Khalifeh, all in Arabic. He must have felt like one lucky motherfucker."[6] This scene works in several ways within the story. The interlibrary loan system allows people to check out books not available in one library from another, and this advanced book-loaning system is contrasted here with the idea of mugging someone for cash and valuables, late one night on a street. It is comic that the thieves would have stolen something presumably of no value to them, but it is tragic in that this is something valuable to Aida.

Jarrar adds to the comic impact of the scene by using a swear word (motherfucker) to refer to the person who stole them. This scene lets us know that though her library has no books by Arab women, she has managed to get ahold of several. The irony of them being stolen in a street crime displays her resourcefulness. Aida is carrying around three novels by Sahar Khalifeh. A Palestinian woman novelist writing in Arabic, she would likely not be as immediately recognizable to Jarrar's English-language reading audience as Toni Morrison, though a number of Khalifeh's novels are translated.[7] Khalifeh's portrayals of Palestinian women's lives and struggles, as well as their strength and activism under occupation, are well known in Arabic literary contexts. Jarrar credits literature as saving Aida from the miseries of her life, but also shows this as part of what is driving her mad—interlibrary loan books being stolen presumably have to be replaced or she will be charged a fine she is unable to pay.

Sahar Khalifeh and Toni Morrison are balanced by reference to another literary great with important symbolic resonance to Arabs and especially Palestinians—Mahmoud Darwish. We learn through details scattered throughout the story how Aida's family reacted when she told them she was pregnant by her verbally and physically abusive boyfriend. We learn that she has had a tenuous relationship with her family, especially her father, before this and that he disowns her completely when she reveals her pregnancy. This comes in the form of a note delivered to her by her mother:

> Having quoted poetry on every single special occasion, he was not going to stop doing it now. The note he sent back said,
>
> > Each river has its source, its course, its life.
> > My friend, our land is not barren.
> > Each land has its time for being born,
> > Each dawn a date with a rebel . . .

If you have the child, we will no longer be your family.
We will be dead to you forever.

"Holy shit," I said out loud after reading it. I couldn't believe it.
Darwish? Infuriated, I took the train north, to our house.[8]

When she reaches home, Aida confronts her father: "'You sent me a poem?'
I said. 'I'm pregnant and you quote me Darwish?' I was trembling."[9] This
passage concisely reveals further details about Aida, her family, and their
relationship to literature. We find out, for example, that the protagonist
was raised by a father who cites poetry, "on every single special occasion."[10]
This is one hint that perhaps Aida is more like her father than their open
conflict suggests. Jarrar punctuates the story with literary figures and references, mirroring Aida's father's citations of poetry. The protagonist's anger
focuses here on the fact that he "quoted [her] Darwish." Not spelling out
who this is, indicating that the reader is meant to know that this refers to
Mahmoud Darwish—the iconic Palestinian poet of resistance—is a nod
to her Arab/Arab American, and especially Palestinian, readers. This also
alerts us that her father is likely meant to be Palestinian himself.

One way to interpret this through the framework of breaking is in how
Jarrar creates a textual break. She gives a great deal of information in this
short story "in the break," or between the lines, adding layers of meaning
to the text. The short story is a narrative genre like the novel, creating language in similar ways, but its brevity means it must also make use of other
linguistic techniques, as does the poetry discussed in chapters 1 and 2. In
order to layer deeper meanings in the story through language, Jarrar offers
supplementary information within such breaks, to those who can read
into them. Like poetic techniques, presenting words, sounds, and ideas
directly, but also in the breaks between them, is effective in a genre like
the short story. This also resonates with other uses of breaks, which manifest conceptual breaks with ideas and ideologies, such as how Abulhawa
challenges us to "break with" the production of knowledge about Arabs
and Palestinians with her breaking language.

Jarrar works with the idea of breaks manifesting other breaks extensively. For example, Aida's complaint has an irreverent ring to it. Mahmoud

Darwish is considered one of the greatest Palestinian national poets and literary figures and an important symbol of Palestine. She resents the fact that her father attempts to manipulate her through this poetry, to lay a nationalist Palestinian guilt trip on her—he implies that she has betrayed her nation by getting pregnant. She does not appreciate that he is trying to divest her of her origins because she followed an unconventional path by falling pregnant without being married. Her own citation of and reference to women writers implies that she sees Darwish, like her father, within a lineage of patriarchal male literary figures. Her search for Arab women in the library is presumably an action she takes to counter this. Her situation is gendered and coded female: she resists being disowned through the symbolic evocation of an iconic male figure of the Palestinian resistance. As much as she rails against the racist US society that doesn't respect Arabs, Aida also firmly critiques patriarchal conventions that respect and cite Darwish even as she struggles to access the work of Arab women writers.

This passage is central to the story. As a narrative device it also allows Jarrar to insert the story of a minor character, Mona, who is Aida's friend and coworker. These Arab American women have their nonconforming sexuality in common—Mona's family shuns her because she is trans. We learn that it was Mona's idea for Aida to write a note to her father informing him of her pregnancy, because this is how Mona came out to her family as trans when she started taking estrogen before transitioning. When the protagonist asks if her father ever got over it, she replies, "'Oh no, honey,' said Mona, whose birth-name was Munir. 'He left my mom and married another woman, said maybe she'll give him straight sons.'"[11] Thus the proudly trans character is used to parallel the story of the young woman pregnant outside marriage; both are portrayed positively and in need of better community and family support. Understanding and embracing people who are queer and nonconforming—including other trans Arab American characters—are a feature of the collection *Him, Me, Muhammad Ali*, taking Arab American fictional expressions of diverse realities in new directions.

Other minor characters also play important symbolic roles in "Lost in Freakin' Yonkers." Two of these characters are African American and

one is Jewish, underlining Jarrar's symbolic and literary links. As in Jarrar's novel *A Map of Home* (discussed in the section below), Kahf's *Girl
in the Tangerine Scarf*, and Erian's *Towelhead*, the protagonist Aida briefly
has an African American love interest in the story. This is cast as an open
rebellion against her father and one which her mother colludes with, "She
covered for me when I went to prom not with the Arab American ninth-
grader and friend of the family Baba had chosen, but with a young black
man I'd picked up at a club on an earlier night when Mama had covered
for me."[12] Unlike this unnamed man, who is directly contrasted with the
family's Arab American identity, most of the characters in the story are
not identified by race, but are racialized through names, context, and language. This is a technique that allows Jarrar to inscribe messages about
people of color coming together to fight against white racism; in the end
of the story this manifests in one long speech by Aida expressing feminist
solidarity with women in her community.

The plot, characters, intertextual references, and themes are all closely
tied to Jarrar's use of language. The work's narration, and even more so its
dialogue, are infused by spoken languages—represented as "broken English," slang, and swear words. Jarrar uses all of these as techniques of breaking to create a soundscape bringing the story to life with the language/s
of every day speech. Like *Mornings in Jenin*, Jarrar's soundscape in "Lost
in Freakin' Yonkers" also preserves the sounds of Arabic. The story, however, also diversifies this as an extensive project, reflecting difficulties in
moving between languages and sliding between different spoken versions
and registers of English. One effect of this soundscape is humor, through
the use of swearing and slang. But this is not the only effect. Similarly to
Toni Morrison's *Beloved*, which the story itself invokes, and other African
American writers, "Lost in Freakin' Yonkers" also makes the "medium the
message," as Smitherman put it. The languages created by Jarrar are the
story, and the sounds evoked make it what it is.

Ibn il-sharmoota: Vulgarity in Context

The importance of language in the story thus begs the question of how to
understand the extensive use of "vulgar" language, the English and Arabic

curse words that pepper the text. Contextualized within a self-consciously literary project like the collection *Him, Me, Muhammad Ali*, this language use in "Lost in Freakin' Yonkers" draws attention to itself and must be read as a vital part of its message. I suggest that this be read with Smitherman's arguments about Black Language. She demonstrates how, contrary to the ways in which people have characterized and demonized this language and its use of what is termed vulgarity, it is not simply about using "bad" words. When Smitherman reminds us that Ebonics is not "broken English," sloppy speech, or slang, she insists on it as a "set of communication patterns and practices resulting from Africans' appropriation and transformation of a foreign tongue during the African Holocaust."[13] As a technique of breaking, what can be read as vulgarity or "improper language" can also have different potential, particularly within a racist setting of struggle, and instead represent resistance and fighting back.

Jarrar's text has much in common with the project of representing resistance in "vulgar" language. Aida uses such language when quarreling with her boyfriend and explaining how she counters both racial and gender abuse. She describes this but also enacts it through her language; words not normally seen in literary works penetrate her text and form its soundscape. For example, Aida regularly undermines her boyfriend by speaking to him in demeaning Arabic—when they are having sex and at other times—and translating it to him as words of affection. For example, "'Habibi ibn il-sharmoota. Yarab tmoot.' (My love, you son of a whore, I hope you die.) 'What's that mean, baby?' He wants to know, and I lie, 'It means I'll love you forever and ever.'"[14] Rather than just let the words in Arabic penetrate the English and stand alone, Jarrar allows the non-Arabic-speaking reader to enter into the private joke. On one level, she layers Arabic within the text to represent how people speak, but does more than this on another. Aida speaks to James in a language he does not understand. This is her own secret language, but she shares it with the reader in a kind of literary complicity. This complicity is shared unevenly with readers, though, reminding us of the way in which words do not always represent identical or equal thoughts or feelings. Though a non-Arabic speaker can work out what it going on and participate as a sort of insider, the reader who knows Arabic can appreciate this intervention more fully.

In a technique recalling *Mornings in Jenin*'s repetition of Arabic words and expressions, Aida also uses certain Arabic phrases over and over. This infuses the English language text with Arabic, breaking the flow of a single language and teaching these words to non-Arabic speakers. It also offers the author's/protagonist's own explanations of these words to readers who do and do not know Arabic. Three pages after the exchange cited above, for example, she repeats her cursing with no translation, "'James,' I say, 'what the fuck is this shit, yilan abuk ibn il-sharmuta yarab tmoot?'"[15] Though Jarrar and Abulhawa both use the technique of repetition that teaches, the effect is somewhat different. Abulhawa makes Palestinian words and expressions about family and values stick with an English-language readership to advance knowledge of Palestinian language and culture. Jarrar, on the other hand, emphasizes "vulgar" words to undermine the authority of her racist white boyfriend. The soundscape created by Jarrar thus invokes spoken Arabic, but hers is a harsher soundscape than Abulhawa's, which underlines her messages about racism and sexism.

Aida's cursing at her boyfriend in Arabic and willfully mistranslating it into English operates on multiple levels. First, Aida gains verbal and linguistic control over a situation that she has little other control over. This recalls the struggles of Sethe in *Beloved*, and Morrison's challenge in finding a language for a story that was "not to pass on." I read this as a feminist breaking strategy, challenging male domination. On another level, even as Aida tricks James, she also schools him. In one scene she curses him while they are making love, saying, "'Habibi, ibn il-sharmoota. Yarab tmoot' and he moans, 'yeah you hot Arabic princess baby I love you too.'"[16] James has "learned" what the Arabic words mean, according to her mistranslations, and we as readers can feel superior to him along with Aida, because even non-Arabic-speaking readers have learned these words. Aida then goes further and consciously resists his misnaming her as "Arabic." While showering after they have sex, she informs him that she is "not Arabic." He questions whether or not she has lied to him about this, and she replies, "No, you moron," and continues, "'I am not a language; if you must, you can call me Arab. But never Arabian or Arabic.' While shaving he replies, 'All right, so you ain't a horse or a language. Got it'."[17]

This brief exchange is important to the story's language politics. There is a clearly articulated feminist message in Aida teaching James through language, and the text teaches this to the reader. The breaks in English—the Arabic expression, its mistranslation, and then this intervention into how people wrongly talk about Arabs as Arabic—allow for a break in problematic productions of knowledge about women, Arabs, and Arab women. What on the surface therefore might seem to be teaching swearing or "vulgar" Arabic words to the English-language reader can be read as a break that advances an important message about the naming of the community. Jarrar uses her breaking language to intervene in an ongoing Arab American community conversation about the misnaming of Arabs in America as Arabic and Arabian. She underlines the more politicized identity—Arab—and shows that James is able to learn quickly—it is in his mouth that the implications of the misnaming are articulated: she is not a horse or a language.

Feminist Solidarity, Women-of-Color Solidarity

The dialogues between James and Aida continually show her reclaiming her sense of self in negotiating her relationship. This difficult relationship is posed against Aida's work with other women in a multiethnic, multiracial beauty salon, where she comes into her own as an empowered Arab American woman. Aida works there with Mona, reads fortunes, and serves Turkish coffee in cups she bought at a local Armenian shop. Jackie, who works at the adjacent Laundromat where she washes her boyfriend's clothes, is racialized as Black through her use of expressions coded as Black Language, for example, her familiarly calling Aida "chil'." She helps Aida with her laundry when she is too heavily pregnant to do it. Two of the women who she regularly mentions affectionately are meant to be Jewish, Mrs. Liebowitz and Mamie the widow. The latter is mentioned by name when she is having her nails done and holds up her middle finger, "I see the profile of a Black man. 'MLK Day,' she says, 'it's comin' up.'"[18]

There are other instances of women-of-color solidarity, for example, when heavily pregnant Aida mistakenly backs into a car driven by another woman, who is racialized as Black through her language, like Jackie. As

Aida apologizes profusely, "'It's a-rye,' the woman says snapping her gum, 'It's my boyfriend's car anyhow. Fuck'm. Don't worry about it, hon.' She gets in her car and drives away."[19] In contrast to the violence of being mugged at knifepoint for her library books, or her boyfriend hurling a dictionary at her so hard she had internal bleeding, or her father's disowning her for getting pregnant, the women she meets in the community offer her a space to grow into herself. At the very end of the book, she backs up into another truck, and this time the male driver and a nearby cop are not as understanding and threaten to give her a ticket, forcing her to pay for the damage with money she does not have. Aida lets loose with a rant that closes the story:

> 'Please, I'm broke, I'm having a kid,' I tell the cop, then turn to the man, who has a mustache and looks eerily similar to the Egyptian comedian Adel Imam, 'and you, sir, your truck's not so bad. I live with a drunk and my parents disowned me, I haven't seen my mother smile in over a year, I haven't seen my father, period, and I have these bags of potatoes I fry and eat on newspapers. Why on newspapers? Because. Because my boyfriend throws dishes at me when he's drunk—he's always drunk—and in my entire life every man who's claimed he loved me hit me. And I had to read those old Jewish ladies their fortunes every Shabbat for weeks and lie about their impending deaths . . . and there's not a single book by an Arab woman in my college library, so please cut me some slack, will ya?'[20]

The words spoken by Aida, ending with a vernacular English, "will ya?" reveal her concerns and preoccupations. As she lays her struggles out before him, she begins with her difficult living situation, moves through her precarious work as a fortuneteller for "old Jewish ladies," and then finishes with her crowning moment—there's not a single book by an Arab woman in her library. The fact that she equates not finding literature by an author who shares her background in the library with being abused by a drunken boyfriend or disowned by her father serves a comic purpose here but is also serious. It elevates the importance of literature once again, tying the story together. It stresses the need for ethnic belonging and solidarity with other women.

The story closes with all the women—including the "old Jewish ladies," Mamie and Mrs. Liebowitz—standing outside the strip mall and clapping. It is this powerful scene of women's solidarity that buoys Aida in the end and pressures the owner of the truck to rethink how he spoke to her, saying that the truck belongs to his boss who is a "bastard" anyway. The cop then walks away without giving her a ticket.[21] This fantasy ending allows Jarrar's story to feel humorous and light, because of its comic use of breaking language strategies. This contrasts with the message and feeling of a work like Morrison's *Beloved* or even Abulhawa's *Mornings in Jenin*. These novels mobilize their soundscapes to a more devastating effect. Jarrar's soundscape uses breaks in language to highlight and challenge racism, misogyny, and compulsorily conventional sexuality, as well as the production of knowledge about Arabs and Arab Americans. Her particular techniques, however, also inscribe humor and irony within these breaks—as well as an idealistic or idealized fantasy of improving society—a technique explored in more detail in the analysis of her novel, *A Map of Home*.

Language as the Sounds of Self in *A Map of Home*

Aida's feminist fantasy rant is prefigured in some ways in Randa Jarrar's larger exploration of Arab American identity, gender, race, and sexuality in *A Map of Home*. This novel's distinctive and realistic narrative tone, noted and appreciated by critics, draws on numerous linguistic techniques to punctuate humorous and tragicomic moments.[22] Though the text's use of language is striking and important, most critical work on *A Map of Home* has focused on themes of home and identity, or her use of humor, rather than investigating language in any depth.[23] One notable exception is an article by Albakry and Siler that outlines how Jarrar uses Arabic in the text; it stands out as one of very few studies that delve into language use in Arab American fiction. Albakry and Siler propose that Jarrar models bilingualism in the text and conclude that, "Jarrar's accomplishment should be considered as a window for Western readers to experience a particular instance of Arab-American experience so as to encourage communication and mutual understanding."[24]

While fostering communication and mutual understanding may be one of Jarrar's accomplishments, my analysis revises Albakry and Siler's study, proposing an interpretation of *A Map of Home*'s layered languages as breaking English and thus rooted in the disruption of power. As Smitherman teaches us, "There is a fundamental, dialectical relationship between language and power, between language and oppression, and between language and liberation. Surely it is only the unwise who consider language a 'mere' instrument of communication."[25] Building on this notion, I argue that Jarrar's use of language is a means of both exploring the oppressive nature of race and racialization, and also inscribing the potential for liberation from limiting categories of existence, especially those bounded by race, gender, and sexuality.

A Map of Home uses language creatively in many ways, including by representing "broken" English, much like "Lost in Freakin' Yonkers," through including translated and transliterated words and expressions, among other techniques. We can similarly read this breaking language as challenging and reconfiguring race and racialization, as well as conformist notions of gender and sexuality. The readings below will show how these work together. Because this is an almost three-hundred page novel, rather than a seventeen-page short story, the linguistic play within *A Map of Home* is more sustained and therefore the novel investigates and works through some of the issues in more depth. The novel is more comparable to *Mornings in Jenin* in length, though the story of the Ammar family and Nidali herself does differ from the epic scale Abulhawa uses to present the tale of the Abulhejas and Amal. Though regional events, most notably the Iraqi invasion of Kuwait and the expulsion of its Palestinian population, do structure the book, *A Map of Home* is more personal. Rather than Amal Abulheja's more politicized look at Palestine, Lebanon, and Pennsylvania from the Nakba through to the Lebanese Civil War in *Mornings in Jenin*, Jarrar's novel delves into the inner working of Nidali's mind and details her coming of age between Kuwait, Egypt, and the United States through cynical teenage eyes. The ways it uses language is intimate and personal, while simultaneously political and challenging. Below I draw out how *A Map of Home* uses the power of language in its breaks and breaking techniques to create a soundscape that invokes race and racialization to reconfigure a mainstream US soundscape, offering the potential for racial solidarity and bonds between people of color. The following discussion covers first the use of names, then moves onto terms for family members, the shaping of the self—especially as a racialized self with thematic ties to Black America—and ends with a discussion specifically of Nidali's relationship to Muhammad Ali.

Nidali Is My Struggle: Layered Arabic, Family, and Self

Like *Mornings in Jenin*, *A Map of Home* is a tightly structured novel; it is divided into three sections, and within each there are a number of named chapters. The first section is the longest at 143 pages and takes place in Kuwait, before the Iraqi invasion. The second section takes place "on the road" when the family drives out of Kuwait to Jordan and then travels to Egypt over 67 pages. The final 79 pages take place in the United States. Emphasizing the page count in relation to location is not an entirely accurate way to explore how geography and movement are represented in the novel, because the narration does move between more places than these— a visit to Nidali's father's family in Palestine, for example. The United States is discussed frequently in the earlier parts of the book in relation to the family's earlier residence there.[26] This structure and its connection to place are relevant to how language is represented and functions, particularly in expressions and discussions related to race and racialization. There is a significant difference in how Jarrar shifts her use of "broken" English in the three sections of the book. For example, the representation of Nidali's parents' accents—like making fun of the confusion between *B* and *P* sounds—only begins in earnest in the final third of the book, beginning on page 213. Below I argue that this use of language changes, as the novel represents an increasingly nuanced representation of how race and racialization are expressed differently in the Arab world (and Arab contexts) and the United States.

This change in the representation of "broken" language can also be easily compared to *Mornings in Jenin*. Jarrar also uses a similarly large number of Arabic words, expressions, and representations of Arabic— some translated, others not. There are over ninety Arabic words used in *A*

Map of Home, and a smattering of words from other languages, including Greek, Hebrew, and Spanish. Like *Mornings in Jenin*, words and expressions related to the family are invoked frequently in *A Map of Home*. There are ten words that name family members and relationships, some of which appear over one hundred times, like "Mama" and "Baba." Other words represent Nidali's mixed heritage, referring to her grandfather and grandmother in Egypt as "Geddo" and "Teta," and Palestinian grandparents as "Sido" and "Sitto." There are also recurring uses of words for uncle and aunt/auntie (Ami, Amo, Amaati, and Tante).[27]

My analysis of *Mornings in Jenin* proposes that insisting on naming family members in Arabic breaks English by focusing on their relationships and suggesting that such names are not simply interchangeable with their English equivalents. *A Map of Home* takes this further by differentiating local Arabic dialects. These words do not mean or imply the same things. Recall the way in which June Jordan articulates this about Black and white English, "The two languages are not interchangeable. They cannot, nor do they attempt to communicate equal or identical thoughts, or feelings."[28] *A Map of Home* uses language, for example, to represent Nidali's closely knit, intimately engaged, and at times explosive relationship with her mother and father. She uses their Arabic titles, "Mama" and "Baba," constantly and consistently throughout the text—they appear almost two hundred times each. Arabic sounds therefore permeate nearly every page of the English-language book, and these are not the only—simply the most frequently repeated—Arabic words/expressions. These words establish that Nidali's family relations are best and most closely expressed through the words that structure her thoughts and feelings. Words for family relations deeply infuse the English-language text with Arabic sounds, creating a soundscape that insists on recognition of these relationships, expressed in these terms. Moreover, the use of "Geddo" for an Egyptian grandfather and "Sido" for a Palestinian one emphasizes the diversity of the Arab world for the English-language readership of the novel and invokes specific locations and meanings for the reader who knows Arabic. These words therefore do different work for the text's different readerships. Similarly to how Jarrar references Mahmoud Darwish by last name only, as discussed above, this can be read as breaking technique in how it maintains Arabic sounds within an English-dominant text in order to say more than one thing at the same time.

Nidali's main struggle in *A Map of Home* is to understand her place in the world, in her family, and also her family's place in the world—as a person, a woman, a Palestinian, a Palestinian-Egyptian, and an Arab immigrant racialized in the United States. Jarrar plays with, manipulates, and makes fun of "broken" English extensively to conceptually advance this project. Reading Jarrar's intervention through the concept of the break and breaking English allows us to understand how the text uses its language to make its interventions thematically.

Using the genre of the young woman's coming-of-age story in an immigrant context, Nidali's struggles begin with her birth and naming, both of which embed her within her familial role. This is clear from the very first page when the baby's father names her: "he approached the box that contained the question, NAME OF CHILD, he wrote with a quivering hand and in his best English cursive, Nidal (strife, struggle)."[29] The story of Nidali's birth is one of intense conflict between her parents over this name, which both misgenders her as male and which her mother despises. Upon realizing his mistake in gender, a comic scene ensues, with Nidali's Baba running through the hallways. He accosted the nurse who was holding the birth certificate and, "grabbed a pen and added at the end of my name a heavy, reflexive, feminizing, possessive, cursive, cursing 'I'."[30] The shift in onomastic identity when Nidali becomes gendered female is mediated by a number of adjectives. Jarrar takes care to remind us that the feminizing letter here is an *I* and activates the double meaning that this implies in creating a self that is necessarily gendered female. The other adjectives foreshadow some of what Nidali faces in life, the cursive, cursing *I* using the alliterative sounds and opposite implied meanings of these two words to suggest some of the contradictions that she will combat continuously throughout the novel.

The onomastic play of this name breaks English in a number of other ways as well. The way her naming is embedded in a scene full of uses of Arabic words, racialized markers, and humor sets up the novel's focus on Nidali's search for self. The name Nidal, strife/struggle, or Nidali, my strife/struggle, invokes clearly the Palestinian identity and background of her Baba—father—and the heaviness he carries with him as a refugee. Ruz, Nidali's Mama, whose nickname is short for Fairuza, reinforces this explicitly. She berates him, saying she will change her daughter's name and threatening to withhold sex from him and die before he calls her this. She states that she prefers "my treasure, my life, my tune."[31] Responding to his jeering suggestion she might be called Mazurka, Sonatina, or Ballade, Ruz replies, "There's nothing wrong with Sonatina!"[32] This amusing interaction follows a more serious one, where Ruz's speech simultaneously disidentifies her daughter from her husband's Palestinian refugee background, and contextualizes the name for the English reader who does not know Arabic: "First you give her a stock boy's name, as though she'll be raised in a refugee camp, as though she's ready to be a struggler or a diaper-warrior, then you add a letter and think it's goddamn unique."[33] In these interactions, Jarrar exploits her text's multilingualism and uses her characteristically sardonic humor to depict the protagonist's parents' conflict to set up the story. The name Nidali represents the seriousness of her father's dispossession as a Palestinian and his ongoing status as a refugee, which in the novel will later be linked to the family's refugee status, when they must leave Kuwait—again because they are Palestinians—for Egypt and then the United States.

Language, Race, and Racialization

Several of the opening scenes of A *Map of Home* reinforce this creative use of breaking language as interventions on race and racialization. In one such scene the novel's protagonist and narrative voice, Nidali, fantasizes about what might have happened to her had her parents remained in Boston after her birth rather than moving to Egypt when she was a baby. Following her mother's complaint that she could have left Nidali's father and embraced "that women's liberation thing," Nidali imagines her life as a 1980s latchkey kid with a single mom, "It could have been like the Bill Withers song, '*just . . . the . . . two of us*': poor and Arab. People would have assumed that Mama, who has kinky black hair, brown skin, dark green eyes, and wears a lot of gold, was a Latina, and that I, a cracker-looking girl, was her daughter from a union with a gringo, and that would have been that."[34] Nidali expresses her fantasy by invoking a classic 1980s romantic song by the African American singer Bill Withers. In their article on language use in the novel, Albakry and Siler read this passage as establishing the narrative voice's proficiency as a native speaker of English and her high level of cultural literacy about the United States. They base this on her referencing what they call "American entertainment" in the form of a "famous jazz song."[35] Albakry and Siler do not, however, mention the larger context of this quotation, or the particular song invoked.

Nidali here invokes not simply American—but African American—music, and in relating to this song, imagines herself and her mother as together and happy, though poor and racialized within the United States. She first claims their identity—poor and Arab—but immediately follows with how they will be perceived—one as Latina and the other "cracker-looking." Her mother is racialized both by phenotype and hair, and also by the way she dresses, whereas Nidali is assumed to be white, presumably because she is lighter skinned. Nidali does not identify herself as white and distances herself even from the misidentification by saying she is cracker "looking"—invoking the derogatory term—and attributing the way she looks to a false assumption about her paternity. Jarrar here establishes both that Nidali is racialized in the United States and also how she is "white passing." This scene also establishes Nidali's familiarity not simply with "American culture" but also racial codes. Her fantasy is bounded by specific realities, and she is able to name them using the language of the United States and racialized cultural knowledge in order to articulate this.

Many scenes in the novel echo this one, reinforcing the differences in Nidali's later experiences as a teenager and those of her parents. A *Map of Home* uses language to outline some of the dynamics of race and racialization through the Ammar family's interactions with broader society; these fade into the background somewhat when they are living in the Arab world, only to rush back when the family moves to Texas.[36] Another example is how Nidali's mother Fairuza, or "Ruz," is racialized and contrasted with the white mothers who have given birth in the same hospital. This is depicted by emphasizing her color, "Her brown IV-ed hand rested on her enormous hip"[37] and also in her use of language, as in when she angrily yells at her husband, "'You think these people understand a word we're saying? You!' she shouted in Arabic, and pointed at a white woman nursing her child in the hallway, 'Your kid looks like a monkey's ass.' The woman smiled at her in English."[38]

In this example, Ruz breaks with racialized linguistic norms by not speaking broken English, but by having her Arabic translated into idiomatic English in a humorous way. In a setting where the character is racialized as an Other—by her language and her color—Jarrar therefore invests her with the energy of breaking language by putting this wittily subversive interjection into her mouth. The "broken" English can therefore act as a break—it interrupts the narration by being Arabic, but also by being funny and using a word considered vulgar—that itself acts as an intervention to challenge white spaces and society in the United States. Ruz's exclamation here can be read as prefiguring the way Aida challenges and also schools James in the scenes from "Lost in Freakin' Yonkers" discussed above.[39] Here, though Ruz and Waheed are shown to be in conflict over the name Nidali, the banter is playful, even in the subsequent examples, where Ruz swears at Waheed extensively.

These examples of language use are critiqued by Dina Jadallah, who finds them unrealistic, claiming that many of the instances of language play use expressions coded as or meant to represent Arabic sound contrived.[40] Reading these examples as breaking language, I interpret them somewhat differently. In line with Nancy El Gendy's argument that Nidali is a trickster figure, using her cleverness to make commentaries on all manner of social ills, I propose that the swearing and banter is not necessarily meant to be realistic but is somewhat exaggerated for effect. One of the examples that might be read as "contrived" is when Ruz compares the white baby to a "monkey's ass." While this is not a typical way to refer to someone being ugly, it does invoke the famous Arabic proverb whereby "even a monkey looks like a gazelle in its mother's eyes." This layering of meaning for the reader who does know Arabic enriches the textual experience, while still providing a linguistically challenging experience and "break" even for readers who do not. The reading of this scene as breaking English can be compared to how Jarrar depicts Aida as taking back control through translating and not translating Arabic expressions that she says to James. Making fun of the white patients and showing explicitly how they do not understand her also sets up a space for the family within the racialized systems of the United States and reasserting control. By speaking aloud in Arabic in the hospital, Ruz controls the soundscape and inserts Arabic into it. Jarrar maintains the sounds of English, but by using words and expressions marked as Arabic, allowing the reader to follow and understand while being challenged at the same time. As this example demonstrates, Jarrar's multiple layers of language use offer possibilities to challenge different readers differently, which as has been argued above in this chapter, is part of Randa Jarrar's larger project of breaking language and conventions.

Other than the anonymous white characters, like the mother in the hallway who smiled at Ruz and Waheed "in English" as she is being insulted, one further minor character fills out this scene—the nurse who attends to Ruz after giving birth and helps Waheed sort out Nidali's birth certificate. This nurse is identified as African American: "Baba regally relayed it to the black nurse, who he remembers was called Rhonda, and she stared at the name and sighed, 'Damn'."[41] Rhonda kindly cares for her mother and is there to help her father; further, she understands the burden of the name that Nidali has just been assigned. She is the only nonfamily member referred to by name in the opening of the book and the only Black character in this section. A Map of Home opens by showing how Arabs fit uneasily into the United States and must navigate their nonbelonging on a number of levels. Jarrar uses her characters to demonstrate how this society functions through racial categorizations and how the Ammar family negotiates their belonging relationally, drawing upon this familiar relational paradigm, whereby African Americans are the group against which all "others" are measured. Jarrar explores this in complex ways by using breaking language to reinforce such relationality thematically on a number of levels, offering suggestions for readings based on solidarity and shared politics.

Another way in which relational, racialized identities are established in the opening pages of A Map of Home is how Nidali's name congeals in the reader's mind as having a meaning—even for the reader who may not be familiar with Arabic. This name is clearly gendered within the racialized United States context, and Jarrar underlines that this is done not only through a letter but also sound. Nidali's name continually interrupts an English-language soundscape, as well as an Arabic one, because of its unusual feminine ending, which hints at the possessive. Nidali's thoughts about her name recur on a number of occasions and focus on the connection between her gendered struggles and her struggles being racialized in the United States. Toward the end of the novel, for example, Nidali reflects poignantly upon her name, showing that even as she continues to rebel against her father, she also has begun to appreciate where he is coming from: "I wonder if Baba never wanted me to be a woman because he never wanted me to struggle. It's funny that he called me 'My Struggle': for a long time, I thought he meant I was *his* struggle."[42]

In her reflection on her name, Nidali ponders why her father is set on her remaining a virgin until marriage and attending a local university rather than setting off on her own. She thinks in detail about how the two of them relate to the notion of struggle differently. Even as she admits to finally understanding that everything he has done for her is because he loves her so much, at the end of this chapter she decides definitively to pursue her dream of applying to a college in Boston—the city of her birth, far from Texas.[43] This decision thus links Nidali's long contemplation of her name with her own search for a metaphorical home, which has a geographic component, in locating a college in the town where the initial discussion of her unusual and contested name took place. The geographic and the aural are themselves connected: Nidali and her family search the world for a home, while Jarrar's textual world becomes a home through the creation of a soundscape that both uses and breaks Standard English.

Ana ana, ana ana, ana ana? Or Who Do I Be?

Name, self, and home are deeply connected in *A Map of Home* and mediated through geography and identity. Jarrar uses a number of breaking language strategies in addition to those already mentioned, including the repetition of Arabic words to craft a soundscape. One specific example is an early reflection by Nidali on the use and power of words. She thinks back to when she was ten years old, living in Kuwait, and ponders the difference between words having meanings and words being just sounds. She describes how she would look at a blank space and then "I'd repeat a question to myself, 'ana ana, ana ana, ana ana?—Am I am I am I am I am I am I?' over and over again. When I'd tricked my mind, it would float away, and I could see that I *am* just I. I'd see myself from outside my own mind: my life, my body, and I was not half something and half another, I was one whole, a circle."[44] The words Nidali repeats over and over again to herself—first in Arabic and then in English—she poses as a question, but the words themselves can also both be read as statements. Read in this way, however, the English words are reversed, unlike in Arabic. "Ana ana" can mean both the declarative "I am" and the interrogative "Am I?" The same word, "I," is repeated because of the zero copula in Arabic, a grammatical feature of Arabic that is not reproduced in Standard English—though it is a feature of Black Language—as discussed in the chapters above.[45]

By writing this line in Arabic and immediately translating it into English, Jarrar creates a soundscape that evokes how Nidali connects different, fragmented parts of herself, resisting splitting herself into halves, seeking to become whole. The text thus offers sounds that coexist on the page but are different. The languages exist side by side and permeate each other in print and sound. Crucially, the repeated and mesmerizing sounds of "ana ana, ana ana, ana ana" that calm Nidali are reproduced six times rather than three times in English, "Am I am I am I am I am I am I." The English also does not use punctuation. This can be read as the English words needing twice as much questioning and twice the number of sounds in order to achieve the same effect they do in Arabic. Moreover, I suggest, even though these words are offered as a translation, they are not equivalent or identical expressions, to use June Jordan's terminology.[46] By repeating these words and sounds as an incantation, Nidali can float away and be "just I." Nidali brings them together and uses them together in order to build up a coherent and authentic, whole self.

Reading Nidali's repetitions and translations through June Jordan's insights into Black and white English helps to elucidate how Jarrar is using breaking English creatively. Like so many people who speak Black English,

Nidali is bilingual and finds ways to bring her different language systems together to express herself. She reproduces words and sounds presented as equivalent because they are translations but that are not identical in order to question who she truly is. Readers who do not know Arabic still can grasp that the words in Arabic are not identical to the words in English—both in sound and on the page. This is all the more striking because the zero copula means that in Arabic just one word, ana (I), is repeated. As a bilingual person, Nidali must master the two languages competing within her to become whole. Geneva Smitherman articulates this question as the creation of culture and values to find the self through language: "the question of the moment is not which dialect, but which culture, not whose vocabulary but whose values, not *I am* vs. *I be*, but WHO DO I BE?"[47] Reading Nidali's reflections through these lenses shows how breaking English by infusing it with Arabic sounds allows her to reconstruct a language as whole through a different soundscape. This reflects the context of *A Map of Home* in which the racialization of the Arab and Arab American characters is experienced through language, in confluence with other elements, including skin color, as in the examples given above. Because of these parallel, though different, processes of racialization, African American and Arab American experiences can be read together. This adds more meaning to extrapolating the metaphor of breaking from language to other breaks in social convention and constructions of self. Nidali no longer wants to think of herself in halves; by breaking the concepts through language she can then make them whole.

Who Do I Be? Language and the Racialized Self

Nidali struggles to be "just I," seeking to answer Smitherman's question "Who do I be?" as a teenager of a mixed background, moving between geographical spaces. This changes over the course of the novel, as do the breaks in language. The first two sections of the book are set in the Arab world, the final section in the United States, and this has a significant impact on the text's language and soundscape. Arabic words related to family—Mama, Baba, Amo, and so on—recur in all these sections unchanged, but other words and expressions that break Standard English work differently. This use of language is deeply connected to the self and its changes across geography. As in the work's opening scenes in Boston when Nidali is born, this self is a racialized self when she comes back to America. The novel expresses and discusses not only race but also color and processes of racialization in different contexts, through language. Thus it is with the shifts in geography and the accompanying breaks in language that the racial self is expressed and explored through A *Map of Home*. To make this clearer, in Kuwait, Egypt, and Palestine, the focus of how people identify themselves and others is national and refers more to color than to race.[48] In Arab world contexts, Nidali is light-skinned and of a mixed background because her mother is Egyptian and father is Palestinian. These identity terms that resonate in the Arab world do not transfer to Texas. She becomes deeply aware of how not only her color but also her racial construction is seen as different from people identified as white. She also learns how she is perceived as different from her mother, who is darker skinned and assumed to be Latina in Texas. These changes in understanding herself as racialized in the book's third section hearken back to its opening and Nidali's imagination of life she never had as a child in Boston, an incarnation of the Bill Withers song.

The way in which Nidali develops a sense of belonging in the United States, as Carol Fadda-Conrey argues, "is shaped by and articulated through a translocal consciousness that incorporates her experience and memory of Kuwait, Egypt, and Palestine."[49] Like other Arab American texts, A *Map of Home* insists "on transforming the Arab-American as well as mainstream US landscapes by highlighting multiple nodes of experience and memory, particularly the pain and war trauma that are lived and relived within the US space."[50] Nidali struggles with fitting and not fitting into the landscapes of her school and community and is deeply aware of her life experiences that are so different from those of many of her friends and classmates. When Jarrar writes about these multiple nodes of experience, therefore, she transforms not only Arab American creative expressions but also American creative expressions more broadly. In what follows, I analyze several examples of how the confluence of language and race configures and reconfigures Nidali's expression of self to build a sense of racialized and gendered solidarity in A *Map of Home*.

Recalling so many other scenes from coming-of-age novels, especially to do with immigration or moving to the United States, Nidali has her own first encounter with racializing systems of social organization as a teenager in the high school lunchroom. Nidali likens the lunchroom to a map of the world, one in which she does not fit:

> People sat in a student center in between periods and for lunch, and this student center was like a map of the world: the white kids with money, the ones who showed up in their Beamers and their Pathfinders, sat in the top left; the white people with no money, the ones who drove Metros, sat in the top right; and the thespians, who were also white, sat in the middle (around where France would be). Then the black people sat in the bottom center; the Latino kids sat in the bottom left; and the nerds sat on the bottom right. I discovered that no one was interested in where I was from because people in this high school didn't ask, "Where are you from?" They asked, "Where do you sit?"[51]

In the next paragraph we learn that she literally makes this untrue. Not finding a space in the American racial map of the world exiles Nidali to a bathroom stall, where she eats her mother's homemade lunches.

Though the school geography and racial identity are identified here explicitly as Black, Latino, and white, we learn that when Nidali finally makes friends they are a mixed group of differently racialized young women. Camilla is originally from Croatia, a background the Black and Latina girls think might offer Nidali meaningful connections. As Nidali finds a place in school and its social structure, we see how her experiences are profoundly mediated by language and race. The lunchroom remains important in chapter 14, which manifests Nidali's new sense of belonging, contrasted with her former immigrant self, by shifting the narrative voice from "I" to "you." As when people speak about trauma in the second person in order to externalize something difficult to talk about, here the entire chapter is narrated in this way, reflecting the pain of becoming a new self in this context. In chapter 15 the narrative voice alternates between second- and first-person narration in a series of vignettes before the first-person narration returns for the rest of the book. In the passage below, for example, Nidali expresses the shift that comes when she returns to school after a bout with TB:

> Every day, Dimi wants to have lunch with you. Soon, so will Camilla and Aisha, who is black and Muslim and wants to hang out with you during Ramadan so y'all can give each other support. When these girls call the radio to request songs, they send you mad shoutouts. You don't know what a shoutout is, but you like that your name is on the radio, even if they mispronounce it. They are sixteen and drive beat-up cars and want you to hang out at the park with them when it's dark. You tell them your Baba doesn't allow it. "She said her papi don't play that," they'll translate to each other.[52]

A community of other young women of color embrace her, and she bonds with them over Ramadan fasting, music on the radio, and eating lunch together. The language used in this passage reflects that of the rest of the chapter in employing racially marked language, for example "mad shoutouts" and "her papi don't play that." In previous scenes, Nidali discusses how her use of English sounds bookish and formal to her friends, and it is partly by mastering the lingo of her Black and Latina friends that she is then able to find and embrace her own racialized self within the US context. The young woman who Nidali grows into in Texas is one who can move easily between languages and registers, and her linguistic expression makes her who she is as a racialized subject in this environment.

The passage where her friends translate her speech shows a progression from her earlier experiences with these same friends, as they share their languages. One example is when she begs Camilla not to smoke, "My mom will be enraged if she sees, or even smells, you smoking. Please extinguish it, please!" Irritated, Camilla ignores her, and Dimi intervenes. When Camilla claims not to have understood Nidali, "It sounded like Shakespeare or some shit," Dimi then translates, "She said her mami don't like her hanging around smokers."[53] Here Nidali is marked by her formal language, drawing a comparison to a canonical white, British man but then is translated into "one of them," her mother becoming the Spanish "mami." Another example is when she discusses how her friends constantly corrected her English when they first met: 'This one talks like she's on public radio,' they said, which at first I thought meant I talked a lot, because in Egypt when you wanted to make fun of someone who talked a lot you said, 'she's a radio!' but here they meant I spoke like a white girl on NPR, all boring and with nary a crazy emotion."[54] In her review of the novel, Dina Jadallah critiques Nidali's perceptions of Arabs, even calling it "slightly racist" and "Western-influenced" for identifying Arabs as "emotional." As this example suggests, however, Jarrar also uses emotion as a way to show bonds and links between people of color who come together against a coldly oppressive white society. It is a contrast to the Shakespearean English of their boring classrooms and the dispassionate white voices of the American public radio station, NPR. The use of strategic essentialism—similar to Susan Abulhawa's representation of Palestinian Arabic in *Mornings in Jenin*, discussed above—helps to explain what Jadallah sees as the excesses of Jarrar's depiction of "Arab" emotion. This can also be read as person of color's insider commentary, connecting to other Arabs and Arab Americans through identifiably shared cultural markers.

African American Thematic Ties:
Prom Dates, Rap Music, and Identity

As teenage Nidali finds her place in the United States in her mixed group of racialized, mainly Black and Latino, friends, she also begins wanting to date. The passage cited above, in which she reflects on how her name inscribes her father's love for her, also discusses how her father forbids her to have a boyfriend. He cites Arab and Palestinian cultural norms as the reason. Jarrar is doing more than simply depicting a stereotyped, domineering Arab father or Arab/Muslim culture as oppressive to women. I draw here on Cariello's argument that the novel invokes stereotypes and exaggerations as challenges to patriarchal norms but also to the stereotypes themselves.[55] This argument is congruent with Jarrar deploying strategic essentialism to investigate her setting and characters. She is operating here within a familiar position of Black and women-of-color feminism/s that centers women but attempts not to isolate or alienate racialized men and their particular concerns. Critical race feminism offers ways into thinking about Jarrar's text. Thus, at the same time Jarrar depicts Waheed as bossy and trying to control his daughter's nascent sexuality, she also sharply critiques the notion that somehow all Arab fathers or Arab/Palestinian culture itself is somehow responsible for restrictive conventions for sexual behavior of women and girls. Nidali herself also rejects such race thinking—that is, giving racial or cultural explanations for why certain people do certain things.[56] When others assign cultural or culturalist meaning to certain actions by Arabs and Palestinians, especially in relation to gender and sexuality, Nidali is quick to challenge them. Jarrar picks apart some of the complexities of these racial dynamics in relation to two specific characters in A Map of Home—Nidali's African American prom date and her boyfriend. As mentioned in the introduction to this book and elsewhere, the figure of the African American love interest is a fairly common trope in Arabic American fiction. A Map of Home is no exception.

In a powerful scene, Nidali reflects on the possibility that her father might react violently toward her if she comes home late with a boyfriend. She is also aware that such violence would prompt a racist reaction by other people toward her and her family because her father is an Arab. She recounts here a story she had heard of a "sixteen-year-old girl in Minnesota or was it Michigan or Montana or Minneapolis, someplace that began with M, whose baba had killed her. He was Palestinian and she was dating a black kid and working at a drive-thru, and so her insane baba had killed her."[57] The story here connects the father's murder of his daughter to her presumed sexual transgressions in dating, with a clearly racist rationale. The fact of the father being Palestinian and the boyfriend Black adds layers of complexity to how this story is used, and moreover because Nidali experiences this in a classroom setting, when her social studies teacher shows a magazine article about this girl to the class. The teacher singles out Nidali in front of the entire class and asks Nidali to "stand up and say a few words about my Palestinian dad."[58] Nidali is confused at first because she is not sure if the teacher wants her to confirm that "not all Palestinians are bad" or if she was reducing her to her Palestinianness. But as Nidali expresses very clearly, "Either way I hated her. I couldn't imagine her bringing in a statistic about a black or Latino criminal then asking a black or Latino kid to stand up and defend his entire race."[59] Nidali is able to analyze the racialized dynamics of this situation and draws an immediate parallel to other communities that experience similar racist treatment. Whereas it may not be so far-fetched that a teacher would ask a Black or Latino student to defend her or his entire race,[60] Nidali points to one of the most salient features of the racialization of Arabs and Muslims in the United States—the notion that violence that would normally be defined as criminal should be understood as inherently a part of Arab and/or Muslim culture.[61] Nidali makes her rejection of this culturalist argument more powerful by referencing and connecting to Black Americans.

This deeper analysis of race and culture is followed by a more mundane example—her prom date. In "Lost in Freakin' Yonkers," Aida's prom date is mentioned as a detail, deepening the race politics of the story. Like Nidali, she defies her domineering father throughout the story; one rebellion is refusing to attend her prom with the son of Arab American family friends, chosen by her father. Instead she goes to the dance with a "young black man she'd met at a bar." Nidali does not use her prom date to openly defy her father. In fact, she wins the right to go to the dance by negotiating with her father. Her date was compelled to accompany her because of her friends' persuasion: "I went to prom by myself, although technically I was with Juman, a fly black junior Dimi threatened to escort me. At the end of the night he kissed my cheek and told me to have fun; it was only 1 A.M. (The dictator was relaxing his grip)."[62] Unlike in the short story, therefore, the character Juman is neither an anonymous "black man" picked up in a bar, nor a symbol of rebellion against her father. Here he has a name and is a student like Nidali, Dimi, and their other friends. In *A Map of Home*, Juman functions in the role of a date to the prom as a way to show that Nidali is socially connected enough to the community of students of color to have someone to go to the prom with—even though previously she was forbidden from dating. This dating conversation involving Nidali's Baba is a stark contrast with the example from a few pages before about the murderous, racist rage of a different Palestinian father. Waheed is often shown to be violent and irrational, but when Nidali was on her date with "the fly black junior," Juman, he "relaxed his grip." We see therefore a diversity of expressions of male, patriarchal Palestinian authority toward daughters dating Black men here—even as Nidali contemplates this other young woman's "insane baba," she does not face the same sanction in relation to her own date. This is a further way in which Jarrar presents and complicates the lived reality of her characters, especially Nidali, in relation to how race interlocks with gender and sexuality in the United States.

Racial Selves: Language, Music, and Identity across Generations

Another way in which Jarrar uses the concept of the break connected to language, expression, and race is by engaging Black American musical traditions both symbolically and textually. In A *Map of Home* Jarrar does this consistently from opening the novel with the Bill Withers song to her extensive discussion of sampling in rap and hip-hop and through pairing African American and Arab musical traditions in multiple ways, likening both to poetry. Jarrar uses Black American culture relationally as a way for Nidali and her brother Gamal, who appears relatively infrequently in the text, to negotiate their racialized selves in the United States. Nidali and Gamal relate to Black culture and its symbols specifically, but at the same time are shown not to be Black, negotiating between cultural appreciation and appropriation.

One of the clearest examples of this occurs in chapter 16, "The Shit No One Bothers to Tell Us," which is subdivided into fifteen shorter sections, some only one paragraph long. Nidali's discontents with her family's adaptation to the United States are expressed here, as are many of the ways she, her brother Gamal, and her parents cope with their new lives. The numbered section five consists of one paragraph, in which music is discussed:

> Madonna is an uncool music choice. Gamal knows this so he steals Baba's credit card and goes to the record store to buy some hip-hop: Bizmarkie, Pete Rock and CL Smooth, NWA, Beastie Boys, KRS-One, A Tribe Called Quest, Erik B. and Rakim. He goes home and jams out. He remembers the stories about Arabia, how disputes over property, family allegiances, gold, and women were all solved by two warring

poets who stood on top of a big, sturdy boulder. The poets rhymed until
one was defeated, solving the case. Gamal knows he's not black, but he
comes from the home of the original rap battle.[63]

Gamal is often depicted in passing, either listening to hip-hop or rapping.
This passage lists the names of a number of classic and well known hip-
hop artists who were popular at the time the novel is set, giving a deeper
contextualization of the cultural scene. Jarrar does not simply name
one or two artists, but rather provides a small window into that musical
moment. These hip-hop artists are contrasted to a white artist, Madonna,
who is referred to simply as "uncool." We understand through this passage
that music for Gamal is not just about appearing cool, but is a deeper
exploration of self. He connects to Black music because it is related to Arabic poetry, his heritage, and vice versa. This passage shows him explicitly
remembering not only Arabic poetry, but also its origins and thematic similarities to rap music. The two engage each other and he deeply immerses
himself in both.

How this functions in terms of identity, appropriation, and solidarity is
complex. Jarrar is careful to not conflate Gamal's racialization with Blackness, and remarks explicitly that "he knows he's not black." This can be
read in contrast to Hammad's claim that she is Black and more congruous
to Amal's affiliation with Black culture in *Mornings in Jenin*—as someone else depicted as "not Black," but with positive, strong, and familial
bonds with African Americans. Because of the history of appropriation
and exploitation of Black music, materially and morally, by both white
artists and non-Black artists of color, including the exploitation of these
artists, this can be difficult ground to tread.[64] The relational formulation
of identities of people of color in the United States to Black Americans
is often expressed through affiliation to music. There is a strong parallel
between Gamal in *A Map of Home* and the character Matussem in Diana
Abu Jaber's *Arabian Jazz*. Matussem is a drummer in a local jazz group
and is racially derided by whites in his small town as "no better than a
Negro."[65] I have argued elsewhere that his affiliations to jazz music show a
putative solidarity between the Arab American characters in the book and
Black Americans.[66]

In *A Map of Home*, this engagement is far from superficial and drawn in considerably more detail than in *Arabian Jazz*. Jarrar shows the centrality of African American culture to the racialized identity formation of Nidali and Gamal in the United States as they navigate their teen years. Ruz's reaction to her children's interest and even obsession with rap music is different from theirs, however, and more in line with the kinds of discussions characters have in *Arabian Jazz*: "I can't tell which of those kids has a bigger identity crisis."[67] Neither Nidali nor Gamal, however, express any feeling of crisis—identity or otherwise—in the sense meant by Ruz. They instead formulate identity through the dialectic and creativity of solidarity in difference, as articulated by Audre Lorde, discussed above.[68] Their crises are different. Rap and hip-hop here are ways in which to relate to their Arab selves, and their appreciation and exploration of Black music is a connection to this.[69] The generational divide is crucial to understanding relational identification with African Americans as crisis or conflict.

The features that lead critics to label *A Map of Home* a coming-of-age novel point to the struggles between generations, especially in a context of immigration. The use of the music of a younger generation—Nidali is a teenager during the Gulf War—can be contrasted to the protagonists in *Mornings in Jenin*—Amal is already an adult during the Israeli invasion of Beirut in 1982. Jarrar uses shifts in the representation of broken English when the family comes to the United States as a break in order to make points about race, gender, sexuality, and how these are linked. The generational conflict is crucial in unraveling some of the ways in which the depiction and analysis of race is woven into the text. The musical examples depict generational conflict plainly. Nidali and Gamal find solace and belonging in hip-hop music, their mother sees this as an identity crisis, their father feels they need more schooling in what it is to be an Arab. Nidali and Gamal know they are "not Black," but nonetheless relate to and are drawn to this music and culture. They also adopt its language. Gamal learns and grows into a proud young Arab man from his hip-hop obsession, and this is paralleled by Jay-Z's music being enriched by the hook from Abdel Halim Hafez's song, discussed below. Music, poetry, and language that express the experiences of racialization they have internalized allow Nidali and Gamal to formulate their identities and a sense of home.

A *Map of Home*'s extensive engagement with parallels between Arabic poetry, Arabic music, and hip-hop is explored in a number of other passages. One of these moments is a humorous exchange between Nidali and her father. The chapter in which this scene is set is titled "Big Pimpin'," foreshadowing a discussion of Jay-Z, overcoding the chapter by citing his song in the title. The scene opens with Nidali spying on Baba, who is filling in her application for the local college she does not wish to attend. Jay-Z's song comes on the radio. Baba is struck by it, stops what he is doing, and asks Nidali what the song is. She rolls her eyes and says sarcastically, "Jay-Z. You know, hip-hop?"[70] He then implores her to turn up the volume. When she does so, he says in an outburst of "broken"—literally and unidiomatically translated Arabic—English, "sons of the whore!"[71] This interjection alerts us both to the fact that he is very agitated and also that what is happening is so dramatic that a break in language is needed. The use of this expression that is not idiomatically translated—"sons of bitches," "son of a bitch," or even "son of a whore" sound more like English—signals that Jarrar is using a break in language in order to break something down. Baba proceeds to explain to Nidali that the percussion section in this song was lifted from Abdel Halim Hafez's song, "Khosara." Nidali is impressed that Jay-Z sampled this Arab singer and wants to hear the original track. Nidali's fascination with the connections between the two songs, and the symbolic interweaving of Arab and Black American music, coupled with her father's dismay about the song being stolen, reflects not only a cultural and generational divide, but also debates about the ownership and appropriation of music within and across traditions.[72] This is an example of how breaks in language can signal lyrical surplus, as Moten calls it. These breaks in language lead to connections musically and also culturally and conceptually.

This scene, ostensibly about music and the sample, also allows Jarrar to delve into the politics of sexuality. When her father tells her it is natural to love the music of Umm Kulthum and Fairuz because she is a girl, but that it takes extra dedication to love an Arab man's voice, she retorts that, "Abdel Halim himself didn't like Arab girls."[73] When her father pushes her further and she says he was gay, her father responds with another example of English that sounds "broken": "Abdel Halim was not a gay."[74] As in all of the scenes when Nidali is frustrated with her father, she makes fun of his mistakes in English by saying, "He wasn't *a* gay, but he was gay."[75] This example uses nonstandard Arabic as a break naturally, and then reinforces it by having the protagonist call attention to it. In this example the soundscape Jarrar creates uses "broken English" to create breaks in the text that draw attention to themselves.

The conceptual breaks that mirror the linguistic breaks here once again connect Nidali's coming of age as an Arab American woman to language. As Nidali is connecting and bonding with her father, her heritage, and the traditions of Arabic music—feeling externally validated by knowing one of her favorite hip-hop artists liked Arabic music enough to sample it—she insists on breaking with things she does not agree with, such as the denial of gay sexuality. She forcefully argues that this side of Abdel Halim must be embraced. Her father continues to be in denial about Hafez's sexuality, claiming he can hear the longing for the girl in the song and calling his own daughter stupid because she does not hear it. Jarrar then uses another kind of a sound break in response, a line from Big Pimpin', "'It's just that jigga man pimp,' said Jay-Z."[76] As a literary strategy, this allows the words of the song, and its tune for the reader who knows the hook from Jay-Z's and/or Abdel Halim's version, to permeate the text, imbuing it with a musical texture. Music infiltrates the pages to alter the soundscape of the novel and by extension the soundscape of mainstream US society, in a way that blends the Arab and Black American musical experiences on the level of language and sound.

One final example of how Jarrar uses hip-hop, coded as Black music, and Arabic music—again by Abdel Halim Hafez—in a humorous intervention comes a few pages later in a section of chapter 18, "Dictations," subtitled "Combozishan #9." Nidali explains that her father ordered her to write essays about Arab topics every day in order to prepare her Statement of Purpose for university applications. Nidali takes up this challenge, tongue in cheek, and titles each essay with the word, "combozishan." This is a transcription of her father's pronunciation of the word "composition"—highlighting the use of *B* for the missing *P* in Arabic. These essays are full of examples of vernacular language and plays on and with words. She titles her ninth composition, "East is East and West is West, / or, / Abdel Halim vs. A Tribe Called Quest."[77] Her ironic tone and use of rhyme show Nidali's mastery of language and of the breaks with convention and tradition that allow her to show the "vast differences in culture yet freakish proximity in purpose of the two musical entities."[78] She juxtaposes words from "Electric Relaxation" with those from three famous songs by Hafez—"Asmar Ya Asmarani," "Kol Maoul Touba," and "Gana El Hawa"—in order to demonstrate this. The juxtaposition of the vernacular Black Language and slang used by A Tribe Called Quest in their 1993 song and the somewhat stilted, standard Arabic expressions of the 1960s translated into English seems ridiculous. For example, the two lines "Honey check it out you got me mesmerized, / Witcha black hair and yo fatass thighs" are placed on the left side of the page immediately next to two other lines, "Dark, dark goddess / who sent you after me?" on the right side.[79] The examples escalate in the use of explicit language on the left side, with the right side's lyrics remaining in the realm of the romantic. This is consistent with what Nidali states in her introduction by claiming "vast differences in culture."

The humorous juxtaposition here, however, is also meant to be more serious. It is not only the differences in culture, which are to some extent differences in language, which must be investigated, but also the "freakish proximity in purpose." Nidali claims that though the language of expression might look different—something visibly demonstrated with the two columns of words and explicitly manifesting the notion of the break—the purpose, the endpoint, of this music is the same. Nidali once again explores the bonds between Arabic and Black music and poetry as part of a larger exploration of self, identity, and home. This is paralleled in a break in the narrative structure of the novel—this chapter breaks with the others formally by being a chapter of compositions. This example, moreover, consciously evokes a soundscape that mixes the musical and poetic traditions. This passage can be read as an oblique inversion of Suheir Hammad's author's note, which defines what is Black: "Black like the genius of Stevie, Zora and Abdel-Haleem."[80] Rather than define herself as Black, and claim a Black-Palestinian identity like Hammad, Jarrar builds connections with

Black Americans differently in A *Map of Home*. Jarrar inextricably links Nidali's identity and coming of age as a racialized young woman to Black culture in many ways, especially through poetry, music, and language. But she does not claim Blackness as her identity or a part of her "self," like Hammad's poetry does. Jarrar's project builds a different kind of racial self through positive relationships with people of color, including Black Americans and Black American culture. This identification is a familial affiliation, but not a claiming of selfhood in Blackness.

The development of an Arab American racial self in relation to African Americans in A *Map of Home* draws upon Black characters and figures, as well as symbols, music, and culture. Black characters are used throughout the book in minor roles. Because white America is not theirs, Nidali and the other members of the Ammar family fit into their surroundings in relation to other people of color. In A *Map of Home*, multiple characters—Nidali's circle of friends, Juman her prom date, Rhonda the nurse present at her birth—reinforce a proximity to African America against which the Ammars find their place. This is similar to *Mornings in Jenin*, even if it is never stated as openly as when Amal avers that she felt at home in America only in West Philly.[81] It is not an identity of sameness, as in Hammad's poetry, but also is not relationally opposed to Black Americans as in early Arab American immigration and the racial prerequisite cases in which Arab Americans litigated to become white in the United States.[82] I propose here to read A *Map of Home* as invoking a relationship built on empathy and solidarity. Arguably, the novel may fetishize Black America or use the problematic model whereby African Americans appear as the ultimate Other against which the racialization of all other groups must be measured. Without negating the importance of thinking through this complexity, I am suggesting that we read the negotiation of Arab American racialization and identity in Jarrar's novel through the framework of breaking, suggesting generative and positive links between these communities. To conclude the discussion of A *Map of Home* in this chapter, the next section discusses one final example of a Black American figure invoked in the novel to draw out these points more clearly—the iconic Muhammad Ali.

Baba, Nidali, and Muhammad Ali

In a scene that occurs almost exactly halfway through the book, when the Ammar family is "In Transit," as the chapter title announces, a humorous scene demonstrates how Nidali mediates between Black American and Arab Egyptian locations. After being teased relentlessly for being Palestinian in the aftermath of the American-led war on Iraq, when her family is forced to flee Kuwait and take refuge in Egypt, Nidali's teacher in Alexandria calls on her to list the leaders of Egypt beginning with Muhammad Ali. Rather than give the expected answer about the reformer credited with being the founder of modern Egypt, she replies, "'Muhammad Ali was a boxer who converted to Islam in the sixties and when my parents were in Boston where I was born they saw him on the street and my mother took a picture of us together,' I said, as though being quiet all this time had taken its toll, 'and my father explained to Muhammad Ali Clay what my name meant and the great one said, so she's already a fighter.'"[83] The class continues to jeer at her, the teacher looks at her disparagingly, and Nidali subsequently stuns the room by screaming, "'Muhammad Ali! . . . Wali Ibrahim, Wali Abbas, Wali Sa'id . . .' and a bright green and yellow spotlight shone on me and no one else. 'Khedive Ismail, Khedive Tawfiq, Khedive Abbas Hilmi, Sultan Husayn Kamil . . .' the teacher's faint mustache suddenly grew into handlebars and curled up at the edges. 'Fuad, King Farouk, Gamal Abdel Nasser, Anwar Sadat, Hosni Mubarak, the end!'"[84] Nidali defies expectations here and shows her flexible knowledge of multiple locations and histories. Knowledge is shown to be important in this scene, echoing her father's constant reminders that as a Palestinian she must achieve a high level of academic and intellectual fluency. This scene also underlines what Albakry and Siler note in relation to her use of the Bill Withers song—Nidali has a vast cultural knowledge. This is not about Jarrar simply facilitating "intercultural communication" or showing her fluency in American and/or Arab cultures and idioms, but rather demonstrates the ways in which all of these are a part of who makes Nidali who she is. Her wide range of cultural knowledge is a part of her selfhood and identity and allows her to fashion herself into a young adult and independent person.

This passage also links Nidali's knowledge and mastery of these cultures to the Black American cultural icon who facilitates this breakthrough moment. She explains who she is through Muhammad Ali; he helps her silence her rude classmates. She uses her knowledge of history to assert her superiority over her classmates, and can do this in more than one space. Moreover, her American reference point is Black America. This not only deepens the significance of the novel's other Black American reference points—Bill Withers, hip-hop artists, and so on—but also suggests that these are her meaningful connections in America. The way in which Nidali expresses her connection to Muhammad Ali is powerful because she identifies with him as a "self" rather than an "other." Muhammad Ali is well known for being a boxer, but also for converting to Islam—she stresses this and refers to his preconversion last name, Clay, as well as his chosen Muslim name. Nidali refers to him as "the great one," a slightly Arabized English reference to his nickname, "the Greatest." The baby Nidali herself cannot speak at this point, but the boxer himself identifies her as a fighter because of the meaning of her own name. Jarrar inscribes a break here by showing Nidali about to break, but then recovering and breaking down information for her classmates. She powerfully links his fighting with her struggle and *the* struggle. This scene depicts the world's most famous boxer and one of Black America's most popular iconic figures identifying with the novel's protagonist as a baby. He sees her, learns what her name means in Arabic, and recognizes her. This mutual recognition is a crucial message and a way to symbolically link Black, Arab, and specifically Palestinian struggles in a way that has meaningful resonance across contexts.

This passage and the connections demonstrated within it can be seen as a direct foreshadowing of the eponymous short story in Randa Jarrar's collection, *Him, Me, Muhammad Ali*. The final section of this chapter, which serves as its conclusion, argues that "Him, Me, Muhammad Ali" builds off of this brief passage in *A Map of Home*—the story is centered around the narrator searching for a picture of herself, her father, and Muhammad Ali. In the story, Muhammad Ali is not only a symbol in a picture, but as an icon of African America and Black American resistance he performs a central function in the story which explores Black-Arab relationships and solidarity.

Conclusion: Dad, Kinshasa, and Muhammad Ali

"Him, Me, Muhammad Ali" revolves around the narrator's search for herself and her family's histories after her father's death. In the opening, she recalls how her father "sang about a photograph of him, me when I was a baby, and Muhammad Ali" that he had since lost.[85] As the narrator contemplates her father, her thoughts turn to her mother who predeceased him. Her mother died when she was just twelve years old, and she was subsequently sent from their home in Australia to live with her father in New York. Recalling this evening when her father told her about the picture, the narrator also remembers, "Whenever I was being stubborn, he'd bring up the photo as if, by touching Ali, some strength and stubbornness had passed along to me. I wanted to believe him, so I visualized the photograph, and convinced myself that I'd once seen it."[86] After she searches his house for the photograph to no avail, she decides to scatter her father's ashes in her mother's homeland, Egypt, according to his wishes, expressed long before his death, to make the great pyramid of Khufu his final resting place, "with the old African kings."[87]

The narrator's father's connection to Africa as a Black American is established from the opening lines of the story in which she introduces him to the reader, "If you're a regular reader of the *Sun*, you may have seen my father's 'Tut Is Back and He's Still Black' series of articles, which he wrote in revolt against Western museums' 'color neutral' depiction of King Tutankhamen."[88] This, combined with his desire to be buried with the old African kings, and his discussion of the photo of Muhammad Ali, are moments racially coded as Black in the opening of the story. As the story develops, his racial identity is discussed in more detail and relationally with the narrator's mother, who is Egyptian. This itself can be read as a moment of breaking—different but not unrelated to previous examples explored in this book. Jarrar chooses to take her Arab/Arab American characters' relationships with Black American characters to a new level, breaking literary and social conventions, producing a narrator/protagonist who is herself a Black Arab American—challenging and breaking down the notion of their relational identity by inscribing both identities in one character.

Their daughter who tells the story offers her own examples of ways in which she is racially and ethnically identified, misidentified, and coded throughout her life—as Egyptian, Ethiopian, Aboriginal in Australia, and so on. Race is a central feature of the twenty-three-page story and is explored in great detail. For example, identifying the narrator's African American father with the controversy over the King Tut exhibition in 2005 inserts the story within contemporary race politics in the United States. Recalling an earlier controversy about the display of artifacts related to Tutankhamen between 1977 and 1979, the more recent protests that deracialized King Tut, or racialized him as white, used "Tut is back and he's still Black" as a slogan.[89] Jarrar thereby links her fictional characters to contemporary events and firmly within US racial politics. The narrator navigates her American and Egyptian/Arab selves as an African American Egyptian/Arab American—something we have not seen in previous characters in Arab American fiction.[90] The protagonist serves as a break in racial codes as a Black Arab American, redefining expectations of how "mixed" Arab Americans are presented.

The way in which race politics play out in the personal and political level for this family is confronted directly in this story, right from the beginning of the narrator's parents' relationship, even before she is born. We learn that, though divorced, they were very much in love when they met and had a passionate affair that created the narrator. The location and setting in which the narrator is conceived, as well as the place where her parents meet, are crucial to the story and tie it to the importance of Muhammad Ali: "They met in Zaire. My mother was a journalist in Sydney—she'd just received her MA from the University in Queensland, but had hustled her way to cover the Ali-Foreman fight in Kinshasa. My father was writing for the *Post*—the only Black person on staff."[91] The ill-fated couple met at one of the most touted and famous sporting events of all time, the "Rumble in the Jungle," on October 29, 1974, and produce a daughter named Kinshasa—her name is alluded to only once in the story: "Their planes landed in Kinshasa, my namesake, within hours of each other." The story recounts their brief love affair alongside this iconic boxing match, which took place at four in the morning after a more than five-week delay.

The fight between Ali and Foreman is used symbolically as a geo-graphical halfway point between the locations of her parents' places of residence, "Zaire was precisely halfway between Sydney and New York. They would never meet halfway on anything again."[92] It is also used sym-bolically as a pan-African location that unites their diasporic family, as is the narrator's name, Kinshasa. The title of the story and the search for the photograph, which is unveiled near its end, binds this notion to the story, tying it together. Muhammad Ali is a well-known boxer, convert to Islam, and Black American icon, but he also symbolizes Black Power, Third World unity, and resistance to US imperialism. As a symbol there-fore he represents not merely racial, religious, or ethnic pride, but also an anti-imperial politics that underpinned Arab and Black American solidar-ity in the 1970s.[93]

At the same time that Jarrar's use of Muhammad Ali draws upon this potent symbolism, it reconfigures deeper layers of the work. There is a small plot twist at the end of the story, when the picture of Kinshasa, her father, and Muhammad Ali is finally located. Asking her father's best friend, Astor, if he had ever seen the photo, he replies that of course he had—he is the one who took it. Surprised, she asks to see it and they go together to his basement where he projects it onto the wall from a slide. She looks up and, "on the white wall, I was in both my parents' arms. There was no trace of Ali. I told Astor that and he laughed."[94] The narrator is rightly confused until he explains that Muhammad Ali was her father's nickname for her mother, "what he always called her with his friends."[95] Astor explains that her mother once accused her father of cheating on her, punched him, and broke his nose. The narrator is not sure if she should believe this or not, but she does not care: "I'd never seen a picture of all three of us together. In the photo, my father wore tawny bell-bottoms and an open, floral-patterned shirt. His fro was short, his eyes smiled in my mum's direction, and his left hand encircled my arm. My mum held me by the bottom, her short dress and knee-high boots magically matching my nude body."[96] This moment of coming to terms with herself, her fam-ily, and her parents together is one of the book's final reflections. The last paragraph sees her riding the same train her father died on to scatter his ashes beneath a tree in the house they shared in upstate New York.

The plot twist whereby Kinshasa's mother is identified by the name of the iconic Black American boxer who marries an African American journalist blurs the firmly defined racial lines between Black and Arab, African American, and African. This itself can be read through the break. The cultural politics in "Him, Me, Muhammad Ali" complicate and trouble the firmer and putatively "obvious" lines that have enabled writers to inscribe links, connections, and solidarity between Black and Arab American communities. This is a deeper layering of identity and affiliation than in other texts. In the case of Hammad's identification with Blackness in *Born Palestinian, Born Black*, her political affiliation comes from a rooting in Palestinian heritage, culture, and identity that itself is Black. The lines between what is Black and what is Arab are also unstable. In "Him, Me, Muhammad Ali," Kinshasa is born of a union of people who exemplify this solidarity. Even though their identities are politicized, we see that what brings them together is a flirtation, lust, and a torrid affair that results in pregnancy. The points of view represented in the story are not simply an Arab gaze on Black America or Black Americans, but also reflect African American ideas about Arabs and Egypt, and the experiences of a young woman racially and socially coded as Black in the United States. For example, she recounts how her father's family reacted to her parents' marriage: "When he returned to New York with my mother, Dad's family teased him; he'd travelled all the way to Africa to bring home the lightest-skinned woman he could find."[97] Numerous times in the story the mother and father are described as looking similar, with only slightly different skin tones. The narrator herself is taken as both Egyptian and non-Egyptian when visiting her family in Egypt. The racial confusion in the United States, in Australia where she is read at times as Egyptian and at times as Indigenous, and in Egypt itself where she is frequently identified as Ethiopian, layers meaning into Jarrar's explorations of race and racialization here.

The narrator Kinshasa in "Him, Me, Muhammad Ali" shifts the discourse around race in ways unprecedented in Arab American fiction, producing a different kind of formation of identity, self, and home. Suheir Hammad, for example, manifests a complex identity affiliation as Palestinian and Black, using literary, cultural, linguistic, as well as political links. Other writers express affiliation by phenotype in characters who "look Black" in their texts. Abulhawa explicitly claims a spiritual and political meaning for Blackness in her articles, and manifests this implicitly in her novel, also using language as a way to manifest these connections. Melhem, Ahmed, and Nye all work to build connections and solidarity through their praise poetry in honor of African Americans. Reading Jarrar's short story as a break with these—offering generative possibilities— helps to fill in another element of complex expressions of Arab-Black American affiliation and solidarity, through Kinshasa's mixed heritage as Egyptian and African American. Her pan-African birth, identity as both continental African and the descendent of enslaved people, conception in Central Africa, and moving back and forth between diasporic locations and the continent allow Jarrar to suggest further possibilities for links, connections, and solidarities that break with and from other models. This conversation between the African continent—Egypt specifically—and Arabs in the United States in the 1970s, when the fictional Kinshasa was conceived, is central to the work discussed in the next chapter, Radwa Ashour's memoir, *The Journey*.

5 "The Most Pressing Causes of Our Times"

Translating Radwa Ashour
Translating Black America

If "Him, Me, Muhammad Ali" is a fictional representation of the pan-African diasporic consciousness of the 1970s, Radwa Ashour's memoir *The Journey: An Egyptian Woman Student's Memoirs in America* is a nonfictional, though still literary, account of these same dynamics and relationships. With the encouragement of her mentor, Shirley Graham DuBois, the memoir's narrator, a young Egyptian professor of English named Radwa, sets off to study at the University of Massachusetts at Amherst. A few years later she becomes the first PhD graduate from the newly established W. E. B. DuBois department, named after the Black American leftist intellectual and DuBois's late husband.[1] Temporarily leaving behind her own husband, Palestinian poet Mourid Barghouti, she researches, writes, and successfully defends her doctoral dissertation titled *The Search for a Black Poetics: A Study of Afro-American Critical Writing* (1975). Radwa then returns to Egypt to rejoin Mourid and her life there. The very last chapter of the book pictures the narrator with her infant son, Tamim, in her arms as the Egyptian security services arrest and deport his father, foreshadowing the family's future by invoking the title of his recently written poetry collection, *Difficult Days*.[2]

Published in 1982, *The Journey* is a compelling, first-person account of Ashour's time studying in the United States between 1973 and 1976. She later became a renowned feminist activist, scholar, and novelist and passed away prematurely in 2014.[3] *The Journey* offers us, as twenty-first-century readers, a glimpse into the personal and political struggles of its author and the people who surrounded her in the United States in the turbulent and politically charged 1970s. The book is populated with people, references, stories, and anecdotes drawn from Ashour's involvement in Arab, Black, and Third World left progressive movement/s in Egypt, the United States, and beyond.

Ashour's memoir exemplifies a 1970s politics and aesthetic—*The Journey* openly embraces a firmly anti-imperial political analysis of everything from the ongoing US war in Vietnam, to the harassment of Arab students by the Jewish Defense League, to streaking on campus, to the Israeli invasion of the Sinai in 1973, to classroom discussions of German romantic poetry. She is invested in combating racism and sexism, but does not operate in the terms of what later becomes called "identity politics," or in the same terms that are used today. She discusses how homosexual groups on her campus have organized to defend their rights, for example, but does not use the language or conceptual categories we use today, like "queer spaces." Her ways of explaining and talking about people's rights and their interconnected struggles show how the vocabularies we use to discuss these issues have profoundly changed. Translating this text from Arabic to English in 2018 demands that we make both theoretical and practical links between the language and rhetoric of the 1970s and today, for example how race, racism, and colonialism relate to US imperial ambitions in Asia and Africa.

The Journey is an exploration of Black America. Ashour states in the opening pages that she wishes she did not have to travel to the United States, but she must do so in order to delve deeply into African American culture, politics, and literature. She is clear about how her project fits within a firmly defined politics of Third World solidarity. In her very first meeting with Ekwueme Michael Thelwell, who later becomes her teacher, mentor, and friend, Radwa as narrator explains to him—and her readers—that she has come to the United States only to immerse herself in the poetics and politics of Black Americans: "I told him that I wanted to study Afro-American literature because of my interest in the relationship between literature and the reality of people's struggles. I also said that

I taught in an English literature department, but didn't want to become someone so embroiled in their research that I spent my whole life studying things which are not at the heart of the urgent issues that matter to me—the most pressing causes of our times."[4] The urgent issues and "most pressing causes" of her times are not only what Radwa the narrator cares about, but also what Ashour the author believes must be conveyed to her readers. The memoir makes clear that she intends to use her studies in activist contexts and sees academic and intellectual pursuits—including poetry and other literary work—as part and parcel of political action making the world a more just place. Radwa announces this to Michael, and Ashour assures her readership that literature and poetry are not merely abstractions.

Ashour demonstrates how a commitment to people's struggles and effecting genuine social change involves understanding Black America. The memoir narrates a story that is personal and political, artistic and aesthetic. She explores a relatively unknown and underexplored part of the United States in Arabic, for an Arab audience, with Arab reference points. Black American literary works are charted within understandings of Third World solidarity.

The Languages to Translate: Race, Politics, and the Trace of the Self in the Other

Different from the works discussed in the chapters above, Ashour's memoir was originally written in Arabic. *Al-Rihla: Ayyam taliba misriyya fi Amrika* was published in Beirut and intended for an Arab—likely mainly Egyptian—readership. I have included it in *Breaking Broken English* for two important reasons. First, it exemplifies the Third World liberation and solidarity politics of its time by building connections between Arabs and African Americans, particularly literary and poetic links, and discussing this in depth. Second, it has recently become widely available to an international audience because of its translation into English.[5] The challenges of translating a book so imbued with the politics of its time offer insights into the complex relationships between language and power, especially in relation to race, Third World liberation, and intercommunal solidarity.

Similarly to juxtaposing the 1970 statement of Black solidarity with Palestine with the 2015 statement by Black4Palestine (discussed in the introduction above), the language of politics is different, even when the underlying principles and ideas—and the text itself—are the same. Ashour uses the Arabic language in her memoir to "translate" Black America to her Arab readership. The process of moving this work "back" into English I propose can be read usefully through the concept of breaking language, allowing us to probe connections between race, language, and politics across time and place. Thinking through the Arabic original and English translation in their contexts also offers insights into how breaking language/s work/s across time. Moreover, I am the translator of this work and from the day I took on this project, I was well-aware of my responsibilities and specific challenges that being entrusted with such a special task included.

As a feminist translator and researcher, I know that my contribution to bringing this work from Arabic to English in light of feminist translation theory would be crucial. I took seriously Gayatri Chakravorty Spivak's proposal in her now classic essay, "The Politics of Translation," that the translator must find the trace of the other in the self to produce ethical translations. The trace in this case is our connection as feminist solidarity activists, engaged in the struggle for a free Palestine, and students of African American poetics. But I also am aware that I was born in the 1970s, when this work is set, and that Ashour's language and "rhetoricity" is not ours today. This presents particular challenges to me as a translator—explored in detail below—and remains a tension in my translation, which appeared in print the very same week that I sent the revised, final draft of this book manuscript to the publisher.

This chapter analyzes my translation of *The Journey* from Arabic into English in order to reveal both the fault lines and the possibilities of its literary, linguistic, and political projects and how they inform each other. It examines how Ashour conveyed Black American poetry, literature, activism, and experience in Arabic to her Arab readership in the 1970s and 1980s into conversation with my own translation of these for a twenty-first-century English-language readership. This chapter analyzes the translation of *The Journey*, specifically the ways words, expressions, conversations, and ideas express skin color, race, and racism in Arabic and English. These moments of linguistic tension and difference are read as breaking language. Because translation is itself a break with an original language, here I suggest that additional creative breaks in English—including the same kinds of techniques of writing discussed above—are used in the translation to produce creative, generative meanings. I expose some of the desired effects of the English soundscapes created to convey that of the Arabic one.

The sections below examine in more detail how Ashour transposes and translates words related to race in the United States into Arabic and then how they are translated "back" into English. In order to do this, I propose to read *Al-Rihla* as a translational text. After setting up the parameters of this, the analysis is divided into two sections. The first examines how Ashour renders words and expressions to do with skin color, identity, and race in Arabic. My focus is on both positive and derogatory terms used to refer to and describe people of African descent, including Ashour herself. The second section looks at passages in which the notion of "race" is used and/or is challenged, with a focus on race politics. I also analyze how these are then translated "back" into English. In exploring these concrete and specific textual moments as breaks in language, this chapter therefore links together how race and racism, as they are embedded in Third World politics and international solidarity between Egypt, the Arab world, and the United States, are explored in these breaks, as both continuities and ruptures. I close by examining how Ashour works with breaking language/s through translating two Black American literary masterpieces into Arabic, iconic texts by Langston Hughes and Frederick Douglass.

Translational Texts and Texts in Translation

Because this text self-consciously mediates the experience of the United States for Arab readers in Arabic, *Al-Rihla* can be understood as a translational text even before it becomes *The Journey*. In Waïl Hassan's article on Ahdaf Soueif's *Map of Love*, "translational" texts are those that straddle two languages, "at once foregrounding, performing, and problematizing the act of translation: they participate in the construction of cultural identities from that in-between space and raise many of the questions that preoccupy contemporary translation theory."[6] Written in Arabic, Ashour's memoir performs a sort of "reverse" translation compared to works that translate certain cultural identities into colonial languages. Ashour's text, moreover, is not concerned with cultural identities but political solidarity between peoples. Using the notion of translational texts as a way to think about Ashour's memoir, I propose, can help us read breaks and breaking language within it in a number of ways. The premise of the text is Radwa making a break from Egypt to lead a new—though temporary—life in the United States. She intervenes in her own standard Arabic narration by naming ideas, concepts, and things that manifest progressive political stances in ways that challenge this type of formal, standard language. The English text must therefore attempt both to convey these breaks and also break English creatively and productively in its own way, to produce a new version of the text that is as compelling as the original.

If we understand *Al-Rihla* as a translational text, moving ideas, words, and concepts from an English-language African American context into Arabic, our challenge is to understand how it develops its translational language in Arabic and how the generative breaks in this language work. On the surface, Ashour's creative textual language is fairly easy to identify: she writes in standard, formal, but simple Arabic. *Al-Rihla* does not experiment with the vernacular or use everyday, spoken language in her Arabic text. Both of these features set her work apart from the others explored in *Breaking Broken English*. Ashour uses a colloquial Egyptian Arabic expression only once, in a joking conversation with a bureaucrat about her degree, right at the very end of the memoir.[7] Ashour even represents snippets of dialogue, for example when Radwa and Mourid are talking at home, in standard Arabic. Moreover, she does not engage the Black vernacular languages or their breaks with standard language/s in English within her Arabic text or refer to Black Language explicitly. The creative linguistic interventions and use of breaking language are different.

Radwa Ashour uses formal, standard Arabic in the memoir, but also does experiment with and use breaks in this language in meaningful ways. Her standard 1970s Arabic language of Third World liberation is a creative intervention into the discourse around race and Black Americans at the time. The Arabic she employs in the text explores and exposes the

intricacies of another world through shared affiliation, culture, and ultimately politics. Careful attention to how she draws upon and manipulates
terms, concepts, and ideas that come from English to discuss liberation
politics—especially but not exclusively in Black American settings—
offers some insights into the complexities of the translation of race in *The
Journey*. We can read examples of breaking language as ways to express
African American realities, with the purpose of teaching her readership
about them. Much as Abulhawa uses Palestinian words in the English-
language narrative in *Mornings in Jenin* as part of a larger pedagogical
project, Ashour here finds ways to write about issues and ideas important
to African Americans in her Arabic memoir. We can interpret how Ashour
uses these breaks in the Arabic language as parallel to breaking with conventional ideas and assumptions about race. The reproduction of these
breaks when the Arabic text is moved into English is a further challenge.
Examining how this does and does not work in translation offers insight
into issues of language and race across place and time.

Languages of Race and Liberation:
Does a Good Translation make Good Politics?

Studying *Al-Rihla* as a translational work while analyzing its translation
into English brings the complexities of how language informs race, politics, and solidarity to the fore. Despite this text's unwavering politics, the
way in which it expresses the way people look, act, and belong in terms
of their color, ethnicity, national origin, and/or race does not translate
smoothly between Arabic and English. It might seem counterintuitive
that a memoir with such clearly defined and "good" race politics in Arabic might not sound as though it had "good" race politics in English. As
the work's translator, this is one of the major questions I grappled with
throughout the translation process. Ashour's work consciously makes an
intervention into Arab racism by exemplifying how to write about Black
Americans in a relevant and new idiom and language. But because of
differences in languages and contexts, the way in which Ashour talks
about the many people, groups, and communities she engages with in the
United States is a fault line in the translation. One location of this tension

is the line between descriptive markers and identity markers. Simply opt-
ing for a word for word equivalency approach in translating *Al-Rihla* into
The Journey demonstrates how the time, place, and language of Ashour's
original text moves uneasily into twenty-first-century English. To further
investigate these word choices reveals issues of race and power, heavily
mediated through the translation's language.[8]

In *The Journey* this can be investigated first on the most micro level
of understanding translation—the different meanings and connotations
of using seemingly straightforward words, like using "dark-skinned" or
"brown" to translate the Arabic word "asmar." This works on the broader
level of the larger political identity category of "Black" being inscribed
when Ashour uses the word "sood" in Arabic. Using "sood" to refer to
Black people is a change from the common, but derogatory, "zinji," whose
origins are located in slavery. It makes a shift drawing upon the change in
community affiliation from the 1960s, the era of Black Power and pride.
As the more detailed discussion below demonstrates, how words and concepts become meaningful in their own contexts—the original and the
translation—must be located within the language politics of their times.
Published in 1982, Ashour's text is the product of the debates and issues of
the late 1970s, when it is set. This is the same era in which Smitherman,
Jordan, and Baldwin were engaged in heated debates in the United States
about language, as well as naming their community. The definition of
words and comments related to the Black community was hotly contested
at this time and discussed with great political urgency and sophistication
by people of African descent in the United States.

In the chapters above I refer several times to June Jordan's intervention
in these language debates in her powerful essay, "White English/Black
English: The Politics of Translation." This piece is a particularly strong
defense of her choice to write a novel entirely in Black English, *His Own
Where*. It isolates the conceptual category of translation as a way to think
about the differences between these languages. Not stressed above, this
is another part of her argument, which is compelling and relevant. In the
essay, Jordan explains how the two languages she is discussing—Black and
white English—may be mutually intelligible, but are not interchangeable,
"They cannot, nor do they attempt to communicate equal or identical

thoughts, or feelings."[9] She goes on to challenge the notion that somehow Black English is just a lesser or "slang" version of a correct or "standard" English, a notion also effectively dismissed by Smitherman. This question is still being debated and discussed today in scholarship.[10] Jordan warns us against making equivalents of things that are not the same and analyzes this on the basis of power relations. This is also the case in moving highly loaded, culturally significant concepts from one language, geography, and cultural reality—as well as time—to another. This becomes evident both in *Al-Rihla* writing its story of Black America in the 1970s in order to create the memoir, and also in its transformation into the English-language work that becomes *The Journey*.

In *The Journey*, Radwa Ashour breaks with words used to name and represent African Americans and challenges this in how she works with the Arabic language. It is crucial to underline this because she clearly intends her work to make a positive intervention into the discussion about and depiction of Black Americans in Arabic. Positively reclaimed words like "Black" and "Afro-American" are the two main examples. As Geneva Smitherman, among others, has pointed out, Black Americans advocated for changes in terminology to refer to their community consistently over time, and in the 1970s, these changes were part of community pride and rebuilding: "The black consciousness movement of the 1960s was thus not playing a Scrabble word game but asserting the right of Black America to define itself including the right to select its own name."[11] Written about fifteen years later, Smitherman's article "From Africa to African American" charts the use of these terms and their meanings historically, as well as providing a contextualization of their use within different Black communities in the States.[12] Ashour was certainly aware of and engaged in a project of promoting this usage and finding ways to translate and convey this to her Arab audience. She employs words that are direct translations of those being used and promoted in English in the 1970s to refer to individuals, communities, and literary works.

The Arabic words used by Ashour are translated literally from the positive, relatively newly adopted English terms and not from a locally developed Arab or Arabic perspective or context. She consistently uses the literal Arabic equivalents for these words throughout the entire memoir:

"aswad" (singular) or "sood" (plural) for Black and "Afru-Amriki" (as an adjective and a noun), meaning Afro-American, which she also uses in the standard plural form (Afru-Amrikiyoon/een). Ashour is careful to use these words consistently throughout the book; she is conscious of replacing words like "colored" or "Negro" with the positive terms embraced in the 1970s. This seemingly would make their translation "back into English" easier, though this is only partially true as I detail below. Moreover, Ashour eschews the racist, negative, or ambivalent words that were more commonly used to refer to people of African descent at the time—and still today. She does not use the terms "zinji" or "abeed" ("Negro" or "slave") in the text unless she is directly translating a derogatory word from English for a specific reason. For example, Ashour uses the word "zinji" to render the word "slave" in the title of Frederick Douglass's famous speech, which was reprinted in the *New York Times* in 1975 as, "What, to the American Slave, Is Your Fourth of July?"[13] She uses the same word, "zinji," to represent "Negro" when Douglass refers to "free Negros" in the speech.[14] Similarly, when translating a message by W. E. B. DuBois to the Congress of Black Writers in Paris, she represents his phrase "Negro American" as "zinji amriki."[15] She uses the word "abeed" on a number of occasions to render the word "slaves," for example when describing the people who sang spirituals longing for freedom while laboring in the South.[16]

In the passage discussing spirituals, Ashour's use of the word is subversive. Her explanation of the musical genre highlights the musical prowess of and contribution to culture of the enslaved people who produced them, though they are referred to by the word "abeed," giving it an ironic feeling. This word in fact is used as a racial epithet, not simply a descriptor of a state of enslavement, making it more similar to what in English is referred to as the n-word. It is important to note here in the discussion of reclaiming language and her strategies of creative language use that Ashour does not discuss or thematize her choice of vocabulary items. She models the use of certain words in Arabic by incorporating them into her narrative. Reading this strategy through the lens of breaking language offers us additional ways to think about Ashour's interventions into Arabic literary language at the time. She does not discuss her usage of terms and words as she does other issues—she engages language directly by just using it to inscribe messages. In this way, I propose, she models an Arabic language respectful to African Americans. The breaking effect here is that *Al-Rihla* creates a corrective soundscape in Arabic, challenging her readership and reflecting the politics of the African America/ns she is representing.

Because so much of the memoir is focused on the Black community and African America more generally, there are too many examples of the words used to catalog all their occurrences. I analyze several key examples in what follows. She translates, for example, the rallying call of the times, "Black is Beautiful," as "al-aswad al-jamil."[17] She invokes this motto in a long passage describing Harlem, talking about the Great Migration of Blacks from the South to the North, the intellectual production of Marcus Garvey, and putting all of this into the context of Black pride and liberation movements.[18] Ashour remains consistent in how she refers to other peoples and groups by their national origins, according to commonly accepted terms. For example, Puerto Ricans, Iranians, Indians, and Ethiopians are all referred to with direct Arabic transcription. She does not use the terms gaining popularity in this period like Boricua or Chicana, for example, to refer to Puerto Ricans and Indigenous Spanish-speaking people of North American origin, respectively. Other ethnic and/or religious groups she refers to as Latin Americans, Sikhs, and Jews, using the direct and literal Arabic words to translate them (Latin Amrikiyeen, Seekh, Yahood). The only group that this is different for are Indigenous Peoples, who she refers to in translation with the equivalent word for Indigenous, "Asli," though not by the names of individual nations, communities, and so on. She takes pains to note that she distinguishes between Zionists/Jewish people with Zionist politics and religious/ethnically affiliated Jews, as well as anti-Zionist Jews who support the Palestinian struggle.[19] It is relevant here that the term "Black" is not used as a skin-color descriptor, but as a political and community category. She uses it interchangeably with Afro-American throughout the text, similarly to how she refers to people as "Jewish" or "Puerto Rican."

But what complicates the question of race in the text, and becomes even more evident in translation, is that Ashour describes people frequently by their skin-color and appearance—particularly those with whom she feels a particular affiliation and/or affinity. This perhaps is not unexpected and makes sense in a memoir by an Egyptian author traveling to the United States and describing communities of people they have never before seen to an Arabic-reading audience. In English-language texts, however, such references to people's color and tone between recognized and recognizable racial/ethnic groups are less common, especially when they travel outside of in-group contexts. Though she refers to these kinds of ethnic/racial labels as well, her Arabic text focuses on color frequently. This is where difficulties in translation arise. The words and expressions are not difficult to translate, but the frequency of their use is. This is another example of breaking language—and the challenge of it in translation. To riff off of June Jordan, even when words may seem to be identical or equivalent, in fact they do not at all mean the same thing when used across language, time, and place.

Ashour's descriptions of people in the Arabic text generally read as neutral or positive discussions of color, which more often than not establish an affiliation between the author and the person being described. In these examples, Ashour does not use the term "Black" as a descriptor, because in Arabic the terms for color do not imply a racial or racialized identity in the same way they do in English. They do not necessarily invoke American race categories. The words she uses are positive or neutral terms: "asmar" (dark-skinned), "qamhi" (wheat-colored), "khamri" (wine/burgundy-colored). Thus at the same time that we see Ashour insist on using or normalizing the political, racial categorization of Black (aswad) in the text, she also resorts to other words to describe the people upon whom she and her narrative are focused—her friends, teachers, and others who are almost exclusively African American and Puerto Rican. Within the textual logic it is clear that these descriptions of color are meant to be a statement of affiliation and recognition—often these descriptions are couched in expressions of similarity, how people look like Radwa herself or "us," Arabs/Egyptians.

There are many examples of Radwa referring to herself by her skin tone, using the word "asmar," which could be translated as "brown," "dark-skinned," or even "brunette" depending on the context, or "qamhi," literally "wheat-colored," also implying a shade of brown. She consciously compares people—who are also identified elsewhere as Afro-American and/or Black in the text—with herself in terms of color in different passages.[20] For example, she talks about first meeting Ekwueme Michael Thelwell, her mentor in the Afro-American Studies Department, describing his hairstyle as an "Afro" (transliterated into Arabic as "afru") and saying, "his skin was light brown, like mine" (literally: "his skin was wheat-colored like me," "basharatuhu qamhiyatun mithli").[21] I have chosen to render the Arabic idiom "wheat-colored," an understandable metaphor but not easily recognized as having meaning in English, as "light brown skin." The more familiar or conventional expression used in English by African Americans to render what Ashour is conveying might be "light skinned." I did not choose to use this expression in the translation, as it makes sense within a Black community setting, in which we assume all or most people are of African descent. The norms of mainstream English-language North American publishing might deem "light skinned" an awkward rendition in this non–African American context, leading to the misunderstanding that Ashour was identifying herself and Thelwell as "white."

In the published translation, I gesture to the idiomatic expression "light skinned" by changing it into the somewhat unidiomatic and descriptive, "light brown skinned." I drew upon translation theory that at times advocates for the less fluent, in favor of a more foreignized/unidiomatic phrase to signal or make a point.[22] In the context of *Breaking Broken English*, my choice can be read as a break generated through translation. It attempts to give *The Journey* a soundscape that itself breaks English in a parallel to how the original breaks Arabic, in order to convey some of the text's indirect messages about race and racialization. Many such examples recur throughout the novel in different contexts. The reference to color descriptors continually reinforces how Radwa, and then also Mourid when he joins her, feel a part of and at home in the African American community. Describing this feeling of home and belonging, being welcome as opposed to unwelcome, Radwa's recollections recall Amal's feelings of being at home in West Philly in *Mornings in Jenin*. The narrator Radwa describes how she and Mourid spent most of their time with African American friends, "We would go around to their houses and mix in their circles as if we were a part of them."[23] Like Amal, Radwa describes this community as comfortable, familiar, and home-like in social interactions and shared experiences, but unlike Amal for her this begins with phenotype.

These examples demonstrate how in *The Journey* the translation of words for descriptions of color and/or race was not extremely difficult or problematic in terms of locating the equivalent expressions. We might debate which specific word or phrase is best used to convey Ashour's meaning in a given location, but it is usually made fairly clear when she is referring to color or appearance (asmar/brown, qamhi/wheat-colored, light brown skinned) and when a more abstract concept of community or racial belonging (aswad/Black, Afru-Amriki/Afro-American). The breaking language does not indicate a major ethical question or difficulty in transposing a particular or given word. Rather, I am reading these examples through the breaking language because Ashour herself is breaking with conventions of the Arabic language and creating an alternative soundscape for her readers. Moreover, this break is one that is reproduced in the translation—but in a different way. As the discussion of June Jordan above underlines, words to do with race and color in the English-language context of the United States are never neutral. Words in English, when translated from Arabic—and vice versa—do not represent or convey identical thoughts. This becomes an increasingly complex question when we examine how Ashour uses these concepts together, within the larger narration in more detail below.

Using and Challenging "Race": The Possibilities in Contradiction

Ashour mobilizes race and color markers in ways that can be read as breaking in Arabic in two major ways in *The Journey*. First, Ashour does not describe everyone in the same way—that is, by skin tone/color or race—but rather focuses her attention on people of particular communities who "look like her." They are almost exclusively Puerto Ricans and African Americans. Other people tend not to be described by color, but rather only by other recognizable identity labels (white, Jewish, Iranian, etc.). Second, she refers to people by their color, national, racial, and/or other identity labels much more frequently than is usual today, especially by people of a

similar leftist political orientation. At the time when the novel was translated into English (2018), the continual reference to people by color and/or
national origin feels awkward and at times even sounds "racist" in English.
Because Ashour's goal in *The Journey* is manifestly the opposite of this,
the translation faces a major challenge. How can we render these constant
descriptors? What sort of breaking strategies might or might not convey
the sense of the original but still remain true to the work's politics?

Specific examples that present the challenge of the text include when
the character Radwa, and the author Ashour, refers to the person who
picked her up from the hospital after she had an accident as her "Iranian friend," or when Radwa refers to her supervisor's "Jewish wife." In
the context of *Al-Rihla* as an Arabic-language memoir, this reads straight-
forwardly as a statement of factual identity categories. In these two cases,
moreover, she is stressing the multicultural atmosphere around her and
demonstrating that people who are kind to her belong to many communities, two in particular that might not have been seen in this light in 1970s
Egypt. Because in English, however, it is considered impolite to attach a
national origin, religion, race, or ethnicity when referring to a friend—this
is my Black friend, she is his Puerto Rican wife—translating these directly
means that they will inevitably emphasize something entirely different
than what is meant. This is therefore not a straightforward question of
equivalence and necessitates thinking through some kinds of translational
breaking language in English.

The two examples here—the Iranian friend and Jewish wife—are brief
indications of a larger strategy of identification in the memoir. In most
cases, though perhaps not these two, such descriptions are attached to people who today we would say belong to "communities of color" in the United
States and very often they are contrasted with whiteness.[24] Most often, the
people whom the character Radwa and author Ashour describe in the
memoir share an identity and affiliation with her. This can be read as similar to the kind of relational identities posited by Jarrar, as well as in connection to Therí Pickens's reminders about how African Americans and Arab
Americans have been defined relationally over time. Ashour's descriptions
of people's identity categories in the Arabic language context are meant to

be a positive affirmation for Third World people, later more commonly referred to as people of color in the United States. It is often in her text a not-so-subtle critique of American imperialism and also whiteness.

Ashour's critique is an "insider" critique—offered by a person who identifies as a part of a notional Black/African/Third World community. The examples given often have to do with food and other cultural customs, showing what people have in common[25] and what they do not relate to.[26] At times, these examples are about shared ideas, but at others these identities are shown to be more basic and essential. One prominent example is where Radwa describes the two departments between which her doctorate is cosupervised at the University of Massachusetts and the contrast between them:

> In the English department, I moved around inside whiteness: white faces dominated and even the long corridors were painted in light colors. In the evening, when we would leave the classroom heading for the exit, these corridors were cold, lonely, and depressing despite being heated. Their weak light gave off the pallor of somebody dying.
>
> In contrast, the building in which the Afro-American Studies department was housed was warmer than usual. By the time I'd reach the classrooms on the third floor I would be dripping with sweat. The walls were painted bright colors—green, blue, and orange, even the black shone. In addition to the department, this building also had a daycare for children of students and workers, a special center for Third-World students, and artists' workshops. In this university building it was normal to see little Black and Latino children going up and down the stairs, and it wasn't unusual to hear the sound of a saxophone or drums wafting up from the ground floor where the ateliers were.[27]

This long passage demonstrates how Ashour uses standard, almost cliched, images to depict things as "white" and "of color," in this case depicting white America negatively (cold, lonely, depressing, dying) and Black America positively, as part of the Third World (warm, colorful, noisy, full of children). I cite from this example at length not to show Ashour's reliance on essential identity categories or use of outdated concepts, ideas, and language but instead to suggest that we might understand it as a kind of strategic essentialism, similar to that employed by Jarrar and Abulhawa. In order to unpack and think through what Ashour's text might mean to us in translation in the early twenty-first century, understanding its use of this literary and political strategy is useful.[28]

As briefly mentioned in chapter 4, strategic essentialism has fallen out of favor and has even been disavowed by the theorist generally acknowledged to have coined the term, Gayatri Chakravorty Spivak. The way in which essentialism—the attributing of essences to peoples or groups as something static and unchanging—has been tied to and supported nationalist and xenophobic ideas and movements is one of the main reasons for this. As a conceptual framework to understand the work Ashour is doing through her memoir, thinking about how and why strategic essentialism can be employed and mobilized by authors in solidarity contexts is instructive. Like Susan Abulhawa's use of particular kinds of Palestinian Arabic—like flowery and/or religious language in Mornings in Jenin or Nidali's identification of emotionality as an "Arab" character trait, Ashour's use of essentialist ideas of belonging and identity can be understood as a way to locate and build connections with other people and communities of color, what she referred to as Third World Peoples, and Afro-Americans specifically.

People have used their own identity categories—who they relate to and where they feel comfortable and at home—in strategic ways to build communities, and this was part of the work being done by different groups in the 1970s. Ashour's text is rooted in the notion that such communities can serve as the basis of solidarity and evolve into the work of shared politics. Many people and groups participated and still participate in work that embraces these principles today. Ashour makes use of these ideas as a literary and theoretical intervention when she draws parallels between Arab and Puerto Rican and/or African American communities in a number of ways in her memoir. Her common experiences with friends from Iran and India, moreover, further strengthen rather than undermine these connections. Naming and asserting affiliations through shared identity is not always a straightforward process and can be critiqued and questioned, but also has been a way in which Arab American and women-of-color feminists have formed and formulated literary genealogies in particular.[29]

Neither the repeated mention of people's skin colors and their identity categories, nor her use of strategic essentialism, has posed problems to Ashour's memoir's reception in Arabic—including within progressive or radical Left circles, Third World liberation discourses, or "good politics" around race, belonging, solidarity and/or anti-imperialism. Its incipient reception in English will be determined when the translation has circulated for longer. Whereas Arabic speakers tend not to find the text problematic or uncomfortable in how it represents or names groups and people, the same is not true of what appear to be repeated words and essentialist ideas to English-language readers—particularly university-aged students in the same sorts of left progressive and radical circles and movements in North America.[30] Two further specific examples draw out some of the differences in language and difficulties moving words, ideas, and concepts around race, identity, and belonging. Investigating these in some depth can reveal some of the fault lines around race that are both spoken and unspoken in these contexts and the way in which they might be understood as breaking language.

The first example occurs in chapter 11, the longest chapter in the memoir, when Radwa and Mourid travel from Massachusetts to New York City. They revel in its chaos and how busy it is; they enjoy the diverse communities that form it. As I have argued elsewhere, Ashour uses their visit to Harlem as a teachable moment and contrasts it with the Statue of Liberty in order to emphasize the achievements and struggles of Black Americans culturally and literarily as well as politically.[31] Harlem is often defined as a quintessentially African American location, rich with symbolism in literature. In the section below, I discuss this in more detail in relation to Ashour's translation into Arabic of Langston Hughes's famous poem, "Harlem (2)." Before they arrive in Harlem, Radwa and Mourid are strolling through Washington Square Park and encounter a man playing the drums. In the short scene, Ashour mentions the drummer's race/skin color three times and his national origin once. This is an example of a repetition that does not stand out in Arabic—it simply sounds descriptive. In the English translation, however, this repetition is noticeable and sounds forced. It is clear that Ashour is depicting this man in a positive light and not trying to make his race or color sound strange. In a direct

English translation, however, the effect is awkward. To highlight these features over-racializes him and sounds exaggerated in English. The passage would "sound better" if his color/race was left unmentioned after the first time.

The scene opens, "Steps away at the entrance to the park stood a brown-skinned (asmar) man from the West Indies (al-juzur al-hind al-gharbiya). He was wearing brightly colored, African-print clothes and standing in front of two big barrels, explaining his art to the passersby."[32] In a short two lines, the man calls out to the people he encounters to listen to his music. He calls them brothers and sisters, a racialized use of language in English, as Smitherman has shown,[33] and one also common in spoken Arabic. He tells the passersby that it may look like he is playing on garbage cans, but he can make beautiful music. Ashour then continues on describing him. I have rendered the translation literally, as follows: "The man with the round, Black face (dhu al-wajh al-aswad al-mustadeer) with the sparkling eyes started beating the barrel quickly and powerfully making both rhythmic and irregular beats turn in a beautiful melody. His body swayed back and forth to the sound, as if he himself were a third drum joining the other two to become unified. His perspiring Black face (al-wajh al-aswad al-mudabib) made him all the more powerful and charming."[34]

It is this second part of Ashour's text that puzzled me as a translator and which I altered in the published translation. Rather than render the first sentence, "the man with the round Black face," I used the expression "round-faced Black man," and rather than refer to his "perspiring Black face," I eliminated the word "Black": "The round-faced Black man with the sparkling eyes started beating the barrel quickly and powerfully, making his rhythmic and irregular beats into a beautiful melody. His body swayed back and forth to the sound, as if he himself were a third drum joining the other two. His perspiring face made him all the more powerful and charming."[35]

There are many ways to approach the translation problem posed here, as well as my response to it. The specific decisions about which words in English are used to render those in Arabic, as well as the larger effect of the translation decisions, is one. Another is to think about the role of the translator as interpreter and what constitutes ethical translation practice.

This is all the more complex when read in relation to translation theories, especially trying to join theoretical principles with the actual practice of moving words from one language into another. For example, today it is generally accepted that ethical translation practice should not be overly focused on word-to-word equivalence. Theorists advocate taking units of meaning that convey the spirit of the text ethically. This is in line with thinking about how conceptual categories of race do not always match up word-to-word in different languages. Moreover, in translating between languages with less and more global power, in a particular moment, the focus should be on balancing the concerns of the less powerful languages and cultures with those of the dominant.

The example from Ashour poses multiple ethical questions in relation to positionality of who and what is being translated. Ashour's translational text is portraying Black Americans to an Arab audience in the terms of Third World solidarity in Arabic in the 1970s, in an idiom that makes sense to her Arab readers. She is attempting to show a Black Caribbean man's artistry in a positive light in multicultural New York City. She is translating the terms of Blackness as articulated by this community in a context of claiming Black as beautiful and powerful in what Smitherman has called the "liberation moment" of the 1970s and early 1980s. While Ashour uses words that racialize this person as Black multiple times in her text, as a "break" in standard Arabic use of the time—to reclaim and depict him in a positive light—this does not work in the same way in English translation. My translation of her intervention attempts to invoke breaking language in my own way in order to render this scene that might otherwise sound at best romantic or exotic and at worst racist.

A second example exposes a different angle to think about the issue of origins, race, and ethnicity in a Third World solidarity context. Just as the characters Radwa and Mourid relate to Afro-Americans in the text, they also feel a strong affinity and sameness with Puerto Ricans. This political solidarity is based on shared histories of colonialism and imperialism, and Radwa and Mourid exchange a long dialogue about the colonization of the island and how they relate to Puerto Ricans because of this.[36] They also underline the cultural connections around looks, food, and manners. Thus, Radwa's descriptions of Puerto Rican women being

amply endowed[37] or being noisy in a "Latin way"[38] are meant once again to
be insider comments of shared characteristics, though they do not read as
such in a twenty-first-century English-language context, where Egyptians
and Puerto Ricans are not identified as having a shared ethnic or racial
identity in the United States. Ashour uses these more essentialized, and
what today are racialized, descriptions of Puerto Ricans as a way to deepen
and strengthen community bonds, including the recognition of shared
struggles, especially the liberation of Puerto Rico and Palestine.[39] This
does not translate in the English language context, and breaking language
here suggests a different—perhaps contradictory—range of meaning.

Another example of the character Radwa evincing a deep connection
of recognition with a Puerto Rican woman occurs when she is in an airport and notices a woman who she is sure is Egyptian, more specifically
from Upper Egypt: "In the seat across from me was a stocky woman, with
deep red-brown colored (khamri) skin, like someone from Upper Egypt.
Her face had those particular lines on them from an earlier time. She
had the face of someone who'd labored hard and her hands revealed this
as well. Why did this woman look so Egyptian?"[40] The remark about the
color of her skin—using the adjective "khamri," literally meaning "bur-
gundy" or "the color of red wine"—is relevant because this is partly what
draws the connection, and also because it is repeated below. As she contemplates this Egyptian-looking woman, she then realizes that she is not
in fact Egyptian but Puerto Rican:

> Everything about her told me this—her face, her language, the fullness
> of her hips, and her presence that had labored under American colonial-
> ism. No doubt she was returning to her island. Was it for some occa-
> sion, I wondered? Or to visit her family and country, having saved up
> money for years? The woman got up from her seat. Had they announced
> her flight? She walked relatively slowly, and I closed my eyes and saw
> another woman. Was it the resemblance between them that struck me,
> carried over from an image that lingered in my mind? The woman from
> my memory was around fifty years old, from one of the villages in the
> Delta. She also had that pure, deeply hued red-brown skin and jet-black
> hair, of which you could see only a wisp when it escaped from under the
> tassels on her headscarf. Her eyebrows were perfectly arched, like rising

half-moons; she had dark blue, Arab-style kohl around her eyes and a green tattoo under her lower lip.[41]

This long passage, similar to the description of the drummer in Washington Square Park, is meant to be a positive and complimentary description based in a racialized sameness. The "deep red-brown" color (khamri) of the woman's skin, like the "brown" man in the park with a "round, Black face," is a marker of her beauty and links her directly to a woman from the Egyptian Delta region who Radwa knows.

If we understand this moment as one of self-recognition and sameness—as the many other examples in the text where the character Radwa claims an affiliation to Puerto Ricans, African Americans, Indigenous Peoples, and others—there are nuances here that should not be overlooked. As becomes clear later in the text when Radwa and Mourid attend the Puerto Rican Day Parade in New York City,[42] Ashour defines the colonization of the island to be a crucial example of US imperialism and one that connects this land and its people to struggles throughout the Third World including Egypt and the Arab region. When Ashour directly asserts that this woman has "labored under American colonialism," she links this to bodily signs of Puerto Rico—her face, hips, and skin, as well as her language. This claim is interesting here, especially as the woman from Egypt is also identified as a peasant from a village, complete with a tasseled headscarf and facial tattoo.

Ashour interpellates herself as narrator into a Third World solidarity connection between two peasant working women. Though Ashour defines herself as a Third World subject who fights US imperialism and is committed to the advancement of peoples' struggles, she is not a peasant worker and hails from an entirely different class background and social position. The class-based resonance of this positive—though romanticized, and even exoticized—depiction of two racialized women is important to acknowledge. In translation, the resonance of this moment is even stronger because of how the repetition of the racialized features, especially skin color, resonates awkwardly in English. Because the passages here are long and descriptive, I have not removed or changed the way she depicts these features. The descriptions cushion the awkwardness in translation, though it is not eliminated and the breaks are more visible in the English version. Removing the skin color descriptions completely, I propose, would betray Ashour's purpose in presenting a romantic tone of bonding which is an intended part of the original text. In this way, the passage can be compared to the nostalgically represented scenes of Palestine in *Mornings in Jenin,* which I have above characterized as legible within a framework of strategic essentialism. Ashour's breaking language in Arabic, and in translation, therefore can be read in oblique relation to Abulhawa's breaks and creation of a soundscape, as well as in some of the other works discussed above in *Breaking Broken English.*

The politically committed leftist, "good politics" of Radwa Ashour's *Al-Rihla* in Arabic are connected to her Third World liberation message and her devotion to linking the struggles of people from different locations in resistance to US imperialism. These examples show how the English translation of *The Journey* reveals some of the complications of race, descriptions of color, and other racialized markers that work as "breaking language." Ashour's "good politics" in the break do not always "sound good" in English translation. Breaking language as a concept offers ways to read and interpret this: Ashour's message in inscribing politics through language manifests other kinds of social and/or political breaks. My translation of *The Journey* into English represents these breaking strategies when it can, and at other times creates new ones. The soundscapes created are necessarily extremely divergent, so all the more importance must be placed on thinking in the break. My use of breaking English is a conscious attempt to ethically uphold the messages of Ashour and her text. The break here thus represents the changes when moving from Arabic to English, but also the break in time from the 1970s to 2018, and the ways in which the languages of race and racialization shift in relation to time, place, and context.

Put another way, Ashour's left progressive and radical political position is not invested in a politics of race—as the American contexts of the 1960s/1970s and the twenty-first century both demand. Her conceptualization of peoples and communities in *Al-Rihla* does invoke race insofar as this is important to the people who she is living and working with, but she herself does not use race as an operative category of analysis in her politics. Ashour's descriptions of race in relation to color, and vice versa, are therefore not always easily discernable or identified in a US context. This means there is often a slippage in concepts. One way to explore this further is located in the few moments where Ashour talks about color and race directly to attempt to understand what the operative categories are for her, in Arabic, and attempt to translate these effectively within her larger work.

Half-Black or Half-Blue

There is one particular scene in *The Journey/Al-Rihla* where the question of a politics of race between Egypt, the Arab world, and the United States—as well as Arabic and English—becomes plain. This scene is a memory of a conversation between Radwa and her "elderly friend" and mentor Shirley Graham DuBois when the latter comes to Massachusetts for a visit. Radwa is excited to see her friend and remembers many conversations they had in her flat in Cairo, sitting contemplating the beauty of the Nile through her large picture window.[43] Her friend wants to hear the news from Amherst, particularly of the department named for her late husband at the university, and also to share her news of Cairo: "You left Cairo boiling—the workers in Helwan greeted the New Year with angry demonstrations in Tahrir Square, Qasr al-Nil Bridge, and Bab al-Louq, protesting against the deterioration of the economic situation. They arrested many of the people in the democratic factions, but the movement is ongoing."[44] After sharing the news of the demonstrations and strikes, Shirley goes on to lament Sadat's policies to Radwa, "My assumption was that this man would be an authentic extension of Abdel Nasser. He's half-Black (*nisf aswad*) as you know. I was encouraged by this."[45] Radwa asks herself, "What twisted logic is this, my old friend?" and immediately rejoins, "Half-Black or half-blue (*nisf aswad aw nisf azraq*), color has nothing to do with it."[46] Here Radwa rejects her friend's analysis by transforming her conflation of racial politics with progressive politics—in the assumption that Sadat would follow Nasser's Third World liberation stance because he was "half-Black"—into a comment on color. Her assertion is that unlike her friend she had not assumed that Sadat would have good politics because he was dark-skinned.

Ashour's political analysis, here voiced by the narrator, is explicitly and obviously rooted in an Egyptian context and consciousness, where race and color are not primary bases for political organizing and action. Though Sadat's rural, Nubian origins were recognized, discussed, and seen as important by Egyptians at the time, the way in which this was regarded as a question of "race" differs in Egyptian and US contexts. Because the character Radwa's relationship to US race politics seems to be firmly rooted in a Black American experience, because her relationships with people of this community are consistently described in terms of affiliation, and because this comment by Shirley does not stand out in the racial politics of 1970s United States, this particular scene seems odd in the context of the memoir. Ashour does assume, for example, that Black Americans will have anti-imperialist politics. This seeming inconsistency can be read as a break in the text and translation. It is a translational moment to be explored in both texts because it highlights that Ashour's memoir is not grounded in a politics of race as understood in the United States, and is indeed consistent with her political positions.

This moment between Shirley Graham DuBois and Ashour fits in within the text's larger political concerns and positions, which are not primarily based in or organized around notions of race. She takes her point further with the way she ends this scene and chapter. Immediately following this conversational exchange, Ashour cites W. E. B. DuBois's telegram to the Congress of Black Writers in Paris, where he talks about his persecution for being a communist and specifically links Third World workers' struggles to capitalist exploitation and how Black capital in Africa enslaves Black labor as much as white capital does.[47] Not only does Ashour focus on the exploitation of capital in these reflections, but she also ties them directly to the settler colonialism of the United States. She notes that the name of the hotel Shirley is staying in and where they are having this conversation is the Lord Jeffrey, named for a colonial "hero" who annihilated the Indigenous community of this territory so that there is not, in her words, "even one Indigenous person left."[48]

Today, as they did when Ashour was writing, Indigenous people and Indigenous Peoples still live throughout Turtle Island, in Massachusetts and elsewhere. But her comment reflects her concern with colonialism, settler colonialism as a particular form of this, and their connections to slavery and capitalism. Ashour's unease with Shirley Graham DuBois's race analysis is also one that would not fit well within the political analysis she advances explicitly and implicitly to her Arab readership through the memoir. She invokes W. E. B DuBois's materialist outlook, linking it to settler colonialism to underline her anti-imperial, Third World liberation perspective. The work she does in translating Black America to her readership therefore does not extend to the kinds of narrative that make more sense in a US setting than in the Arab world. Her political commentary on Egypt and its leaders remains rooted in local concerns. Her translation of African American experience remains grounded in the solidarity and resistance of Black Americans with anti-imperial struggles and demonstrating contributions to intellectual work, literature, poetry, and culture.

Is Race Untranslatable?

As the examples above show, words, ideas, and concepts related to race move uneasily and work differently conceptually across contexts, locations, and time periods. Race and notions of racialization therefore can be loaded, and meaningful ideas in one place can have little or no resonance in another. Ella Shohat and Robert Stam have demonstrated some of the complexities of how race and its languages function differently and with different, if at times overlapping, meanings in the United States, France, and Brazil. Their study *Race in Translation* argues that this is true both in spite of and because of the connections between these disparate locations, particularly those engendered by the transatlantic slave trade and its relationship to Indigenous Peoples, Africans, and people of African descent.[49] *Race in Translation* centers the concept of culture wars in order to ask questions like, "What anxieties and hopes, what utopias and dystopias, are provoked by words such as 'race,' 'multiculturalism,' and 'identity politics' in diverse sites?"[50] They question why some concepts have purchase in one location as opposed to others, even if the phenomena being referred to exist in those places—the issue of miscegenation in Brazil, negativity toward communitarianism in France, and so on. Shohat and Stam's work traces the complex ways in which different concepts take root in different contexts across languages, despite and because of the ways they are differently interpellated into the forces that bind them together, including colonialism and the mass expropriation of territory, destruction of Indigenous Peoples and cultures, enslavement of Indigenous people and Africans, and racism throughout the colonized world and in Europe. Their work shows race to be both intelligible and not intelligible in different times and places.

Is race then untranslatable? It can be useful to raise this question both in the context of the 1970s and the debates of that time, and also invoke current discussions about what is and is not "translatable" by literary critics invested in the field of translation studies. June Jordan shows that words are never identical or equivalent, and like Smitherman and Baldwin, shows that even when two languages are mutually intelligible in a general sense, a speaker of one might not understand all the nuances of the other. All of their analyses inflect this concept with the way in which power impacts this. Today's debates within translation studies obliquely reflect some of the same problematics raised by African American literary and linguistic theories of the 1970s and show how they are continued today.[51] Even as we constantly translate words and concepts, some critics have argued that we should embrace a "politics of untranslatability" in order to govern how we read literatures from contexts around the world, as a way to acknowledge their difference.[52] Whether this is meant in the more literal sense of finding "good" or "the right" equivalents for words or concepts between languages, or more figuratively as the impossibility of explaining and interpreting certain concepts, or the even larger problem of being able to develop deep understandings between languages, cultures, communities, and contexts, untranslatability proposes incommensurability and unbridgeable gaps between systems of language and thought.

Many critics have attacked the conceptual difficulties as well as the political problems with this argument and engaged it vigorously. In his scathing but careful critique of Emily Apter's book, for example, Lawrence Venuti charges that the greatest logical flaw in such a proposition is that even as we claim the impossibility of translation, we continue to translate terms, ideas, and concepts.[53] The political problem with untranslatability is that it risks constructing and maintaining essentially "untranslatable" and inherently, ultimately different Others—not a desirable outcome most would argue in terms of moving literary works from Arabic to English. Ashour certainly did not see the ideas, concepts, and words related to Third World liberation and solidarity as "untranslatable." If anything, Ashour's project is to find ways to bridge what seems untranslatable through using Arabic and breaking into it to interpret and write about what she believed in.

Moreover, though she does not discuss it directly in the memoir, the debates around language use, particularly in relation to Black Language in the 1970s United States, are part of the context of Radwa Ashour's Arabic text. She went to the University of Massachusetts in part to study this language in relation to Black American poetics and aesthetics. Thus the debates and discussions that were raging, the contributions of June Jordan, James Baldwin, the earlier works of W. E. B. DuBois, and others are all a part of the atmosphere in which *Al-Rihla* participates. She is reading and writing about African America and participating in the politics of the United States of the 1970s from her own location. Thus Ashour is translating—or as Alim might put it, styleshifting—constantly between Arabic and English, the United States and the Arab world/Egypt to make things intelligible to her audience. And her Black American interlocutors themselves were no doubt styleshifting in speaking to her in an English she would understand.

Thus if we acknowledge that thoughts and feelings, words and concepts are unequal and not identical, does this not mean to some extent we cannot ever translate them, according to Jordan? What solutions can we find for conveying ideas when words are unequal and not identical, especially the difficult and eminently contextual concepts related to race and color? Translation theory today suggests that all translations are interpretations and therefore never free of ideologies, relations of power, and the inequality of systems of social organization. Thus as translators and interpreters we must decide what meanings are and how and why we will translate them as we choose to. In the case of the uneasy movement of ideas around race, color, and identity in Radwa Ashour's memoir from Arabic into English, I made decisions in translating *The Journey* about what I think she meant to say, or how she would have wanted it to sound.

I also crafted a text that was in line with how I thought it should sound to the reader today. This is not an isolated process—in the case of this translation I worked extensively with others and presented many of these words, expressions, passages, and problems to many individuals and groups for discussion and debate, including in classroom settings.[54] I worked extensively in theory and practice with race and gender. In the end, however, as a translator producing a work for publication, I had to make choices about words, expressions, and framings. In this translation, the final decisions were mine.

The responsibilities of the translator are fraught with many difficulties, including linking the theory, politics, and ethics of translation with the words you write down on the page. Deciding to try to use creative, breaking English in a translation that will challenge the reader while rendering the words of the author faithfully is an aspirational project; in other words, easier said than done. The specific challenges of this translation and moving the words of Radwa Ashour into English resonate with Gayatri Chakravorty Spivak's admonition in her often-cited essay, mentioned above, "The Politics of Translation." She says the task of the feminist translator, especially the one based in the West translating the "other" woman, is to locate the "trace of the self" in the other. The idea of locating this trace of the self rhymes well with the project of The Journey itself; it means working through notions of cultural, political, and literary affiliations, building community, and advancing solidarity projects. Spivak further argues that this location of the self in the other must be accompanied by paying close attention to the rhetoricity of the time and place of literary and linguistic contexts, in both the source and target languages—Arabic in Egypt and English in the United States.

This chapter's analyses focus on what Spivak calls "rhetoricity"—specific elements that make languages sound the way that they do, the elements of literary texts that make them literary. What is different and untranslatable—those unequal elements of language that are not exact—are precisely where we have opportunities to think about what is being discussed and manifest. I have presented some of the differences in rhetoricity between Arabic and English through the notion of the breaking language. One way in which the breaks in language manifest other breaks is in how some passages—such as the example of the irrelevance of Anwar Sadat's "Blackness"—seem to contradict Ashour's articulation throughout the text of solidarity based on color. On the one hand, Ashour claims that political solidarity is not based on color, or is at least based on more than color, and politics are something different. It does not matter if Sadat is half-Black or "half-blue" in her words. On the other hand, we see Ashour making political assumptions and connections between people based on an assumed solidarity partly, if not largely, marked by color/race throughout the entire text. The description of the university departments, her immediate recognition of the Puerto Rican woman in the airport, her feelings of ease with her Afro-American friends whom she feels she is "a part of."

One way in which to understand this is that when it comes to the politics of Egypt and the Arab world, Ashour's political analyses and statements are direct, sharp, and sure. She has a keen understanding of the complexities of the Arab context and gives insightful analyses with thoughtful, politically astute commentary about issues like the Six Day War,[55] the death of Umm Kulthum,[56] labor union strikes throughout Egypt,[57] Sadat's policies in the 1973 war,[58] and especially the memoir's final, short chapter,[59] which expresses her cynicism about what is to come in the 1980s. Her Third World solidarity politics are strongly expressed through the book but much less specific. She is elated about the fall of Saigon,[60] evinces solidarity with the massacres of Chileans including Victor Jara,[61] and learns all she can about the American Indian Movement's activism in the United States.[62] These are, however, more general statements of support than they are specifically articulated political positions and encompass a progressive leftist worldview about Third World unity and liberation rather than local political analyses. As becomes clear throughout the text, solidarity of Third World people is a political position, not about race or identity politics, but rather a shared liberation politics of anti-imperialism. As Feldman puts it in his discussion of David Graham DuBois's 1975 historical novel, *And Bid Him Sing* (mentioned above), the Black American characters are frustrated with the, "non transferability of politicized notions of pan-Africanism. African American ideas of blackness just don't translate in Cairo."[63]

The example of how Anwar Sadat's color/race is or is not important, like that of the Puerto Rican woman in the airport or the man playing the drums in Washington Square Park, and the repetition of descriptors of color and race demonstrate Spivak's point about the politics of translation. She argues that the translator must "confront that what seems resistant in the space of English may be reactionary in the space of the original language."[64] What is different here is that the languages are reversed—what is resistant in the space of the original Arabic feels reactionary in the space of the English translation. I faced this issue as the work's translator and debated how to render accurately the work's political messages and concepts, as well as their rhetorics and poetics, so as not to produce what reads as a "reactionary" translation from a memoir that was itself a piece of resistance literature, making an important political, cultural, and literary intervention. The strategies I used include different kinds of breaks in language, including breaking with the original in shifting and omitting words, as well as using closely literal translations in other moments, in order to give what I considered the best possible rendition of the words, expressions, sentences, and passages Ashour produced.

B(l)ack Translations?

The question of translation is also important in *The Journey* because Ashour herself is a translator and includes substantial portions of her own translated work in the memoir. In this section I discuss briefly Ashour's translations of two now-classic, African American literary landmarks: Langston Hughes's poem "Harlem (2)," better known by words taken from its opening line, "A Dream Deferred," and Frederick Douglass's speech, "What, to the American Slave, Is Your Fourth of July?" Her use of these texts within her own text—translated into Arabic for her reading audience—can be seen as homage, in similar ways to other texts read in previous chapters. Her intertextual citation of Hughes and Douglass here can be read as a parallel to Melhem's honoring Amiri Baraka, Jayne Cortez, and Richard Wright. Melhem's works are poems, more specifically kwansabas, so the generic requirements are significantly different, though she does take specific lines and concepts from their works and lives and recasts them. Hammad's poetic homage to June Jordan works similarly. Jarrar's citation of poetry by Darwish in "Lost in Freakin' Yonkers" to punctuate her father's anger is translated into English for her readership and also resonates with what Ashour does here. The main difference between this variety of texts and how they express this homage is generic—Ashour's text is a memoir, and so this is less a literary recasting of words spoken or written and instead a more explicit translation of the works into Arabic for her readership.

Ashour's translations of Hughes and Douglass are some of the most interesting and productive literary engagements with Black America in *The Journey*. They serve a pedagogical, educational purpose within the text—they are translated to convey these works to Ashour's Arabic language readership—and are offered as moments of homage, affirmation, and also literary solidarity. There are other works of poetry mentioned and discussed in the text, T. S. Eliot's *The Waste Land*, for example, but no other works are included in their entirety, like Hughes's, or at such great length, like Douglass's—the translation and discussion of which makes up the entirety of chapter 13. Elsewhere I have compared the translation of *The Waste Land* to the translation of "Harlem (2)," suggesting that she in fact uses Eliot's poem as a contrast to Hughes, to further advance the identification of her Arab readership with the African American poet.[65] This also parallels the contrast between her two departments at the university, the "white" space of the English Department and the "colorful" space of the Afro-American Studies Department.

Radwa Ashour's translations of these two works can be analyzed in relation to the concept of "back translation." This concept encourages us to identify how her strategies of translation can be read as breaking language and how this might function even though the breaks become invisible in the published translation in English, which restores these famous works by Hughes and Douglass to their original English-language form.[66] Another strategy, which would have preserved the translational element of the original Arabic text, would have been to translate Ashour's translation into English. But a second translation of such important texts of African American literary history not only would have sounded and felt awkward, I believed, but also would have been an odd choice in the English-language reception context of twenty-first-century North America, and possibly interpreted as disrespectful to these texts. Back translations are useful for thinking through how Ashour translated these pieces for her readership, however, because they expose some of the dynamics by which race, identity, and questions of "Blackness"—as well as the poetics of Black experience—do and do not translate between Arabic and English.

"Back translation" is generally defined as moving work translated into a language and rendering it anew in its original language. For both Douglass's speech and Hughes's poem, Ashour opts to provide literal translations that privilege equivalence in meaning, content, and context over poetry and form. It is crucial to note here that Ashour herself was a translator and novelist and worked professionally with a number literary genres including poetry. Though she herself was not a published poet, she was one of the translators of her husband Mourid Barghouti's renowned inventory of poetic output. She later also translated poetry by her son Tamim Barghouti into English, some of which was published after her death.[67] We therefore can assume that Ashour was making an aesthetic, poetic, and literary choice informed by her politics in these cases. Should she have wanted to produce works that sounded "more poetic" in Arabic or paid more attention to form, she could have done so. What the back translations of Langston Hughes's poem and Frederick Douglass's speech demonstrate, however, is that her more literal and context-giving translations underline her political vision of Third World unity and solidarity in *The Journey.*

Langston Hughes's poem "Harlem (2)" is best known by its opening line; the powerful alliteration of the letter *d* and leading question means it is often indeed referred to by these words: "What happens to a dream deferred?" Ashour's rendering of this particular line makes the point plainly. A back translation of her Arabic words might read, "What happens to a dream they postpone/put off?" The verb she uses is "ajala," an accurate translation of "defer," which also means to postpone or put off. One thing that makes the rendition of this line so different in English and Arabic is that it has no particular resonance with the noun meaning dream, "hilm," nor would it with other word choices that Ashour might have come up with that also mean dream, like "manam." In such an analysis, it is important to note at the outset that a translation that captures aesthetic and/or linguistic features of a poem might not render these in ways specifically borrowed from the original text—alliteration is not the only way to add an emphasis or layer poetic language into a line. It is not the replication of the words or the strategies that counts. The translator might be able to render the original text's alliteration, for example, in a different line, or find another technique that comes from within the Arabic poetic tradition, such as using multiple words from the same root. The back translation of Hughes's poem shows, however, that Ashour does not make use of these or any other poetic techniques to capture the artistry and skill of the original English poem. All of the lines offer a word-for-word equivalent translation of the poem. The translation is not so literal as to be unpleasant to read. But the artistry of Hughes's punchy, short poem is not captured in Ashour's Arabic translation.

What made Hughes so popular and well known, in English and in translation, was partly what critics have called the rhythm and sway of his lyrical verses.[68] I have argued elsewhere that Ashour does not capture his musicality, rhythm, rhyme, and so on because she is more invested in offering her Arab readers a glimpse into Black American poetry and literature by embedding the ideas and histories of Black people in clear, plain Arabic designed to speak directly to an Arab readership.[69] I also suggest in my analysis of this poem's translation that questions raised by the back translation—because of grammatical features in Arabic like the resumptive pronoun—deepen the poem's questioning of racial justice: Whose dreams are deferred? Who is deferring those dreams?[70] The back translation of this poem shows that Ashour is working with a literal version to convey meaning over aesthetics, content over form. Her concern is to show the conditions of Black Americans—reprised in her translation of Frederick Douglass's speech discussed below. Further, it is relevant that Ashour does not choose to translate any of Hughes's other well-known poems. At the time she was writing his memoir, no collection of Hughes's poetry had yet appeared in Arabic, though not long after a collection named after his well-known poem, "I Too Sing America," did appear in Arabic: *Ana aydan ughani Amreeka*, translated by Samer Abu Hawwash.[71]

This famous poem, for example, is more focused on community, identity, and belonging, whereas "Harlem (2)"—especially in its powerful closing line, "or does it explode?", the explosion referring to the deferred dream—underlines the anger of oppression and what happens to people who are forced to repress their dreams for so long. Ashour advances this message in order for her Arab readership to connect their struggles in the post-1967 period, one in which the dreams of Third World unity were under threat, but whose potential were still so strong.

Frederick Douglass's speech is translated into Arabic and included in *The Journey* in a similar way to Hughes's poem. Unlike Hughes's poem, which is integrated within a chapter and advances the plot of that chapter by introducing Harlem as a neighborhood to Mourid, however, the speech appears in a uniquely crafted chapter. The speech itself makes up the bulk of chapter 13. The inclusion of Douglass's speech as an entire chapter can be read as a strategy of breaking, much as the example above when Jarrar shifts her narrative in *A Map of Home* through a chapter that breaks with the others by being composed of Nidali's compositions. This break in formal structure reemphasizes the other kinds of linguistic and conceptual breaks that Ashour engages in throughout the memoir.

The premise of chapter 13 is that Mourid and Radwa are sitting on a bench in the park on the July Fourth holiday, reading the *New York Times* where the speech was reprinted.[72] Radwa excitedly speaks to Mourid about the speech and she reads long sections of it aloud to him—in Arabic translation. As they read it aloud to each other, she also intersperses her own commentary and he engages her in a conversation. The location of this chapter is significant to it functioning as a break. It comes near the end of the book, when Radwa's time in the United States is finishing, her doctorate is nearly completed, and the memoir itself has already done a great deal of education and preparation for the reader about important literary histories and contributions to the culture of African Americans.[73]

Ashour's citation and translation of Douglass's speech is similar to the Hughes poem in other ways as well. Though she does not transcribe the entire speech word-for-word, she includes a large amount of it. This is one way in which to see that Ashour is most concerned with her Egyptian readership catching the message of the speech and digesting its content, rather than appreciating its literary importance. Her translation does not attempt to convey what Spivak would call the "rhetoricity" of Douglass's speech in any significant way. In fact, as in the Hughes poem, she tends to use literalist translation strategies. The translation's use of interesting linguistic or literary breaks is more connected to her political vision. This might seem an unusual choice for a writer and translator as accomplished as Ashour, but is consistent with her political views.

One translation choice is to render the term "slave," used in the work's title, as "zinji" rather than "abeed." Zinji is the more commonly used, and less derogatory, term for people who are descendants of slaves. Colloquially in Egyptian (and other dialects of) Arabic it also means "Black," but with a different set of connotations. "Abeed" is the harsher term that reads as an epithet, more like what in English is referred to as the "n-word." Using zinji here, therefore, gives the speech a slightly more elevated tone, as Douglass's original text has, while maintaining fidelity to the concept of slavery he evokes. Throughout the text, however, Ashour varies the vocabulary she uses, because she must render the words "Negro," "slave," "bondsman," and "Black," and so changes the vocabulary in some sections to be able to distinguish between them.

Differences in Arabic and English rhetoricity and also the meanings behind a number of words come through in a back translation analysis. For example, the passage where Douglass speaks to white Americans with the exhortation, "My subject then, my fellow citizens, is AMERICAN SLAVERY" does not translate easily or precisely. Arabic does not have a way to render capital letters. Ashour thus uses a grammatical construction of a nominal sentence with a repeated subject, as well as the emphatic particle "Inna" in order to emphasize the rhetorical feel of the sentence. The words she uses to render "my fellow citizens" are also interesting here: she chooses the idiomatic expression "ikhwani al-muwatineen," which carries the same meaning, but uses the word that literally means "brothers" or "brethren" to render "fellow."[74] The impact of this in a speech by a Black man to a white audience excoriating white supremacy and the complicity of white Americans in it is significant. The use of the word "brother" in relation to citizens thus captures the irony intended by "fellow citizens" and makes it sharper.

The rather literal back translation helps to show how Ashour uses different linguistic and translational techniques primarily to teach her Arabic readership about Frederick Douglass. She includes so much of the speech to demonstrate who he was, what he stood for, and his political views, but also his genius and brilliance. Through the inclusion of this speech, she is also able to advance her critique of the United States as a settler colony, built off of the capitalist exploitation of an enslaved labor force. This is a crucially important part of her solidarity-building project. She demonstrates to her Arabic-speaking readership what Black Americans have in common with them. It teaches about the current condition of African Americans as well as their historic conditions through slavery.

Ashour's technique can be read as a break that is a pedagogical intervention: Mourid and Radwa explore this rich historical document together by reading and commenting on it. As in the case of Hughes's poem, this speech once again allows Radwa to teach him what she has been learning about African American art, politics, and poetics. Even though Radwa knows more about this than Mourid, they pour over the words of the speech together, learning and engaging in an active discussion about its contents. The chapter ends with Mourid asking to save the newspaper more than once.[75] They discuss the irony of it being printed on the opposite side of the Declaration of Independence in the paper, and also its relationship to the Emancipation Proclamation in 1863.[76] The chapter ends with Radwa's reflection on her status as a postcolonial subject, where she relates to the world's dispossessed by citing the words of an Indigenous elder who witnessed the massacre at Wounded Knee in 1890.[77]

As these back translations demonstrate, Ashour uses the works of Langston Hughes and Frederick Douglass both as homage and also as an educational intervention. Her breaking with the structure of her chapters, by making one only about Douglass, and into the narrative flow of another chapter by reciting Hughes's poem, is mirrored by her breaking with poetic language in using literal translations. Her translations here thus break language as a pedagogical project based in her politics. This is a similar project to those of other authors, studied in the previous chapters, in which African American literary, cultural, and other figures are referred to for a wide range of different reasons. Above, I briefly compare Ashour's citation of Langston Hughes and Frederick Douglass to Melhem's and Hammad's honoring of Black American literary figures like Amiri Baraka, Jayne Cortez, June Jordan, and Richard Wright. As a pedagogical project, moreover, this move can also be compared to Jarrar's citation of Toni Morrison's *Beloved* and her invocation of Muhammad Ali. The ways in which these textual citations, homage, and pedagogical projects are manifest in *The Journey* as breaks are comparable to, but also different from, these other works. The memoir is a nonfiction form, and *The Journey* is premised upon Ashour recounting her own travels and memories of them. But similar to these other texts, which Ashour's memoir predates, *The Journey* builds and solidifies community links in concrete ways through citing, translating, and teaching about Black America and its literary traditions.

Conclusions: Language, Translation, and the Sounds of Solidarity

The readings of Radwa Ashour's memoir *The Journey* in this chapter explore the difficulties involved in translating words, expressions, and ideas related to race, racism, and solidarity. It investigates these between languages and locations—Arabic and English, the United States and the Arab world—and also between periods of time—the 1970s and the early twenty-first century—and their attendant political cultures. I have shown how concepts and ideas related to race, racialization, and identity are different and also how they change. This chapter uses the literal and metaphorical concept of translation, defining Ashour's text as translational, as a way to reveal breaks in language that manifest other breaks in concepts and ideas. This chapter's readings have also demonstrated how the languages that we have to talk about race are impoverished. The concrete and specific examples analyzing breaks in language and ideas in *The Journey* pose alternative ways of thinking about and expressing race and racism to give insight into building communities and solidarities between communities.

One of the reasons I conclude the detailed readings of literary texts in *Breaking Broken English* with Radwa Ashour's *The Journey* is to suggest how looking at ideas, concepts, and languages through the lens of the 1970s opens new windows onto twenty-first-century thinking. This work was conceived in the 1970s and translated in 2018, so the tensions between languages are not only linguistic but also contextual and generational. This connects *The Journey* to other works explored in this study, particularly how Ashour's exploration of individual and community relationships between Arabs and African Americans can be read dialectically with those in other texts, in their similarities and differences. Her expression of race and color, her political analysis of the importance of these, and her commitment to conveying the histories and stories of African Americans are all informed by the fertile period of building relationships between Arab and Black communities in the United States, the Arab world, and beyond. Ashour's context is Third World solidarity and anti-imperialist struggle, but it is also the time period that was so crucial to the consolidation of Arab American identities and communities. As much of the analysis in this book's other chapters shows, they often went together.

Ashour's text is written in Arabic and orientated toward a different "home" than the other writers analyzed here, all of whom claim the United States at least partly as a home, even if another location—like Palestine—is a home as well. Ashour taps into and analyzes discourses in the United States differently than other authors whose investments and belonging are different. This is important in relation to the Arab American texts because Ashour proposes and promotes a strong alliance and identity with African Americans. Her feelings of alienation and difference in America as an outsider are first overcome with Thelwell, and later only ever truly subside when she is welcomed by and integrated into a community of Black Americans. This prefigures the character of Amal in *Mornings in Jenin*, though she is a more solitary—and fictional—character. Though Nidali's cast of friends in *A Map of Home* is definitively multiracial/ethnic, she also feels comfortable and connected within Black American communities. We see this even more strongly represented by Kinshasa, who is the product of an "interracial" African American-Egyptian partnership. Ashour's bond with the community is how she feels integrated and thus she is able to move among it as "a part of them," making it her home.

These emotional, personal, and cultural links are then the basis for building a deeper engagement and shared political understanding with Black Americans, Puerto Ricans, and other communities of color in the memoir. She builds political solidarity through these links. The analysis of the ways in which breaking language—in Arabic and in translation—advances the message of Ashour's work also reveals her deeper political messages about Black-Arab solidarity and Third World solidarity more generally. Ashour works devotedly for the Palestinian cause in very difficult moments in the United States, in particular the 1973 War. She is very clear about making distinctions about who her comrades are in this struggle and works with Jewish, Arab, and other people in Massachusetts in a solidarity committee, making firm distinctions between Zionism and Jewish religion, ethnicity, and background. She emphasizes shared political agendas and common causes. She gives the example of how Palestinians, other Arabs, Blacks, Puerto Ricans, Jews, and at least one white Trotskyite work together to write a manifesto on behalf of the Palestinian people in the framework of Third World solidarity. She harshly critiques her fellow Arabs who only wish to work with other Arabs and do not see the value in coalition building.[78] Her discussion of this in the book can be read alongside the manifesto itself in English, published in the college newspaper, *The Daily Collegian*,[79] as a way to see the praxis of her community at the time. *The Journey* uses this specific example to advance her discussion of political alliances, but throughout the text the political is always tied to the literary, activism to art and poetry.

Ashour's memoir pushes us to think about the meaning of solidarity in the conclusion to *Breaking Broken English*. Through its translation of ideas, concepts, and literary texts from English into Arabic and back to English again, breaking language offers multiple entry points to contemplate the languages of race. These breaks point up what languages we do and do not have available to talk about race and racialization. They also raise the question of how in our language we can put into practice a solidarity framework that is true to the concepts being articulated, without grossly distorting or changing their meanings, but also not clinging to a literalism that would undermine the authenticity or meaning of the text. Finally, Ashour's writing about anticolonialism and anti-imperialism in the 1970s challenges us to think more profoundly about how we write and think about them today, as well as what kinds of concepts and languages we want to develop for our future.

Conclusions

Breaking to Get Free

Examples of solidarity are inspiring, and rightfully so. Whether political, historical, cultural, literary, or many of these and others at the same time, people working together in shared theory and practice offer us ways to imagine and work to make the world a better place. *Breaking Broken English: Black-Arab Literary Solidarities and the Politics of Language* explores the languages of literatures as a way into telling some of the stories of such shared and collective work over time and place. These histories of solidarity and struggle are often occluded and rarely focus on literary and artistic connections when they are eventually remembered and recorded. One important contribution of this study has been to recover, write, and value the historical and political connections between Arab/Arab American and African American communities in the United States. Emphasizing the presence and development of these connections over time, this book shows the ways in which these intercommunity identities have formed in relation, and at times in opposition, to one another. Bringing these stories to the fore and examining them in critical conversation with one another reflects a commitment to remembering and building on histories and politics of shared struggle in working for social change.

Breaking Broken English makes an important contribution to conversations about solidarity by highlighting some of the less well-known and little-discussed ways that intercommunity connections were and have long been literary, creative, and artistic as well as political; I constantly maintain a focus on how the political and artistic are deeply intertwined. My focus on literature in this book—poetry, fiction, and memoir—is premised on the need to explore these literary languages. Any study with a literary focus can be marginalized as not "really political"—indeed this was Radwa Ashour's fear when she traveled to the United States to study Afro-American poetics. *Breaking Broken English* has argued that the study of the languages of literature itself is invested in and must be deeply tied to a study of power. The use of literary criticism and language theories by Black American intellectuals, theorists, and writers has rarely been used in the study of Arab American literary production and offers new and important lenses with which to read and analyze these works. Putting Arab American texts in conversation with these important theoretical and critical interventions both facilitates the excavation of these longer solidarity histories and provides new ways to read the innovative literary and linguistic practices of these works.

The title *Breaking Broken English* draws attention to the conceptual possibilities of breaking by invoking and engaging wordplay between "breaking" and "broken." It subtly identifies breaking as an active and positive interpretative framework that challenges the idea that language can be broken. In redefining concepts of breaking, we can reimagine what it means to be broken. The analysis throughout the book highlights that breaking is not only a metaphor and a theory, but also a practice. The practice of breaking is analyzed in the book in relation to language, as its central concern, but as the readings of literary texts demonstrate, breaking language manifests many other kinds of breaks. This framework focuses our attention on multiple and expanding meanings and actions that these breaks can imply. To develop the concept of breaking further, my focus on language in *Breaking Broken English* also emphasizes sound, particularly how soundscapes can create home. In the face of oppression, breaking language creates soundscapes of home.

To build this framework, *Breaking Broken English* draws on the important theoretical work on language by Black American scholars and intellectuals, especially June Jordan, James Baldwin, and Geneva Smitherman. Reading Arab and Arab American texts through theoretical lenses built from African American intellectual production opens up ways to understand parallels between these communities' literary output. But this also is a method that enables us to bring out the ways in which languages inscribe resistance, particularly in challenging times for particular individuals and communities. New languages of creative literary expression engender new ways of imagining, conceiving, and promoting action in the face of injustice. The literary works I explore in the preceding chapters are read through the concept of breaking English, revealing how their own creative language manifests different kinds of breaks.

These readings are also shaped by Fred Moten's articulation of how what is perceived of as the "grammatical insufficiency" of people denied equality, marginalized, demonized, and othered by society as lyrical surplus. He suggests that it is within the break that such lyrical surplus is located, and that breaking offers a way to express resistance to oppression both within and not within the culture that oppresses you. His understanding of how music does this expands to literary works and offers ways to read broken English as breaking. Breaking language in literature invokes musical breaks and thus is connected to sound and the soundscapes of texts. These breaks in sound work against old and outmoded histories and are the location of new ways to think and produce knowledge about the world. They remind us of the past and encourage us to recognize it, but also help to shape the future.

This recognition of shared work and struggles that have come before us is not only about recognizing and appreciating them but also about building sustainable connections and action for the future. This leads to larger questions about the meaning and importance of solidarity built and sustained over time and across contexts, pointing to coalition politics as crucial to a larger fight against racism, colonialism, and imperialism. Looking at how this is expressed in the languages of the 1970s, while exposing differences in the languages of the early twenty-first century, is part of this book's pedagogical project. This project of exploring language in *Breaking Broken English* is important because it connects the ways that literary texts imagine solidarity and connections—how they write about community links and bonds—to how they challenge the production of knowledge around Arabs and Arab Americans, especially in relation to race, racialization, and connections to African America. My project throughout this book has been to emphasize generative links in a solidarity context, but this in turn begs the question of what solidarity means in these different texts, contexts, times, and locations. What is the importance in thinking about language and politics in relation to solidarity between these communities? Is it the most useful concept to read these ideas in relation to?

As an exploration of identity, *Breaking Broken English* takes up and contributes to developing liberatory conceptions of language and literature and how the two mutually construct and reinforce each other. A solidarity framework that traces histories through time is important because it emphasizes longer-term social and political visions expressed in these literary works. As Audre Lorde put it in her essay, "Learning from the 60s": "There are no new ideas, just new ways of giving those ideas we cherish breath and power in our own living."[1] Poetry, fiction, and memoirs are creative ways of expressing the world of the past and present, but also of imagining both these and the future. *Breaking Broken English* therefore links the past to the present in order to think about how we can imagine and promote messages of social justice and the fight for liberation in the future. If we take seriously the adage that our freedom as people is bound up in the freedom of other people—and other peoples—this book offers ways of thinking about how we are connected to each other. Through the specific examples of how people link their ideas of liberation to that of others through language in multiple ways, *Breaking Broken English* proposes ways to read literary language as creative expressions of freedom. It asks us to think of breaking free and breaking to get free. For us to get free, we must look back even as we look forward. When we learn from and draw on our shared histories, it is not only to remember, recognize, and honor what others before us did, dreamed, imagined, and fought for, but also how we can dream, imagine, and fight for better futures.

Notes

Bibliography

Index

Notes

Preface

1. John Russell Rickford and Russell John Rickford (*Spoken Soul: The Story of Black English* [New York: Wiley, 2002], 122–24) and Geneva Smitherman (*Talkin and Testifyin: The Language of Black America* [Detroit: Wayne State Univ. Press, 1977], 30–32) both discuss the use of negatives in the grammar of Black English.

2. Geneva Smitherman, *Talkin That Talk: Language, Culture and Education in African America* (New York: Routledge, 2000), 132.

3. Smitherman, *Talkin That Talk.*

4. Smitherman.

5. Smitherman, 156.

6. Smitherman, 155.

Introduction

1. https://policy.m4bl.org/invest-divest/.

2. http://www.blackforpalestine.com/read-the-statement.html.

3. http://www.blackforpalestine.com/1970-black-nyt-statement.html.

4. Audre Lorde, *Sister/Outsider: Essays and Speeches* (Freedom, CA: Crossing Press, 1984), 128.

5. Carol Fadda-Conrey, "Arab American Literature in the Ethnic Borderland: Cultural Intersections in Diana Abu-Jaber's Crescent," *MELUS Journal* 31, no. 4 (2006), 197–205.

6. Carol Fadda-Conrey, *Contemporary Arab American Fiction: Transnational Reconfigurations of Citizenship and Belonging* (New York: NYU Press), 8.

7. Fadda-Conrey, *Contemporary*, 8.

8. Salaita also discusses this term, its replacement paradigm status, and its dynamics in his *Modern Arab American Fiction: A Reader's Guide* (Syracuse: Syracuse Univ. Press, 2011), 125–30. Below I discuss Therí Pickens's critique of this paradigm and her suggestions about working against it.

9. Therí Pickens, *New Body Politics: Narrating Arab and Black Identity in the Contemporary United States* (London: Routledge, 2014), 5.

10. Pickens, *New Body*, 8.

11. Lorde, *Sister*, 119.

12. See, for example, Diana Abu Jaber, *Arabian Jazz* (New York: Norton, 1993); Rabih Alameddine, *Koolaids: The Art of War* (New York: Picador, 1998); Mohja Kahf, *The Girl in the Tangerine Scarf* (New York: Carroll & Graf, 2006); and Alicia Erian, *Towelhead* (New York: Simon & Schuster, 2006), all of which are discussed briefly below, but are not a part of the corpus of works analyzed here.

13. Lorde, *Sister*, 111.

14. Kristian Davis Bailey, "Black-Palestinian Solidarity in the Ferguson-Gaza Era," *American Quarterly* 67, no. 4 (2015): 1019.

15. Davis Bailey, "Black-Palestinian," 1017.

16. http://www.jadaliyya.com/pages/index/21764/roundtable-on-anti-blackness-and-black-palestinian.

17. http://www.jadaliyya.com/pages/index/21764/roundtable-on-anti-blackness-and-black-palestinian. Emphasis in the original.

18. Lubin highlights in particular this group's connections to SNCC (Student Non-Violent Coordinating Committee), Lubin, *Geographies of Liberation: The Making of an Afro-Arab Political Imaginary* (Chapel Hill: Univ. of North Carolina Press, 2014), 129.

19. Capitalization in the original. http://www.blackforpalestine.com/1970-black-nyt-statement.html.

20. http://www.blackforpalestine.com/read-the-statement.html.

21. Capitalization in the original. http://www.blackforpalestine.com/1970-black-nyt-statement.html.

22. http://www.blackforpalestine.com/read-the-statement.html.

23. Lubin, *Geographies*, 157.

24. Therese Saliba, "Resisting Invisibility: Arab Americans in Academia and Activism," in *Arabs in America: Building a New Future*, ed. Michael Suleiman (Philadelphia: Temple Univ. Press, 1999), 304–405.

25. Lubin, *Geographies*, 142.

26. Lubin, 143.

27. Keith P. Feldman, *A Shadow over Palestine: The Imperial Life of Race in America* (Minneapolis: Univ. of Minnesota Press, 2015), vii.

28. Feldman, *Shadow*, 2.

29. These anthologies have been important political and literary projects, offering space to women of color. See Cherríe Moraga and Gloria Anzaldúa, eds., *This Bridge Called My Back: Writings by Radical Women of Color* (Watertown, MA: Persephone, 1981); Gloria Anzaldúa and AnaLouise Keating, eds., *This Bridge We Call Home: Radical Visions for Transformation* (London: Routledge, 2002); and Joanna (now Joe) Kadi, ed.,

Food for Our Grandmothers: Writings by Arab American and Arab Canadian Feminists (Boston: South End Press, 1994). The inclusion of Arab American feminists in the follow-up volume, *This Bridge We Call Home*, contested their inclusion in this space and was undertaken problematically. For a discussion of this and how Zionism shaped the book and the conversations around inclusion and exclusion in the volume, see the chapter by Nada Elia in Rabab Abdulhadi, Nadine Naber, and Evelyne Alsultany, eds., *Arab and Arab American Feminisms: Gender, Violence and Belonging* (Syracuse: Syracuse Univ. Press, 2011).

30. I have drawn together a number of key ideas from Lorde, *Sister*; see especially pp. 110, 122, 138, and 128 for these ideas and political articulations.

31. A recent example of where some of these tensions were manifest is in the Muslim Lives Matter hashtag—some of the problems with it and the pros and cons of using it in the context of #BlackLivesMatter. See Keeanga-Yamahtta Taylor, *From #BlackLivesMatter to Black Liberation* (Chicago: Haymarket, 2016), 186–87, for a discussion. See also Therí A. Pickens, "Modern Family: Circuits of Transmission between Arabs and Blacks," *Comparative Literature* 68, no. 2 (2016): 131–33.

32. Pickens, *New Body*, 9.

33. For example, see Sarah Gualtieri, *Between Arab and White: Race and Ethnicity in the Early Syrian American Diaspora* (Berkeley: Univ. of California Press, 2009); Lisa Suhair Majaj, "Arab-Americans and the Meanings of Race," in *Postcolonial Theory and the United States: Race, Ethnicity, and Literature*, ed. Amritjit Singh and Peter Schmidt (Jackson: Univ. of Mississippi Press, 2000), 320–37; and Helen Samhan, "Not Quite White: Race Classification and the Arab-American Experience," in *Arabs in America: Building a New Future*, ed. Michael Suleiman (Philadelphia: Temple Univ. Press, 1999) and "Politics and Exclusion: The Arab American Experience," *Journal of Palestine Studies* 16, no. 2 (1987): 11–28.

34. Gualtieri, *Between*. See also her "Strange Fruit? Syrian Immigrants, Extralegal Violence and Racial Formation in the United States," in *Race and Arab Americans before and after 9/11*, ed. Amaney Jamal and Nadine Naber, (Syracuse: Syracuse Univ. Press, 2008), 147–69 on the lynching of Arab Americans in the US South for insights into the racial formulations of these groups in relation to each other.

35. Pickens, *New Body*, 5.

36. Gualtieri, *Between* and "Strange Fruit"; Jamal and Naber, *Race and Arab Americans*; Majaj, "Arab-Americans," 320–37; Salaita, *Arab American*; and Samhan, "Not Quite" and "Politics."

37. Pickens, *New Body*, 8.

38. Pickens "Modern."

39. Gualtieri, *Between* and Stan West, "An Afrocentric Look at the Arab Community," *Mizna* 2, no. 3 (2000): 22. For a solidarity-building point of view, see Rabab Abdulhadi, "'White' or Not? Displacement and the Construction of (Racialized and

Gendered) Palestinianness in the United States" (paper presented at the Middle East Studies Association annual meeting, Washington DC, November 24, 2002).

40. West, "Afrocentric," 22.

41. Lorde, *Sister*, 128. "If I participate, knowingly or otherwise, in my sister's oppression and she calls me on it, to answer her with my own only blankets the substance of our exchange with reaction. It wastes energy."

42. Davis Bailey, "Black-Palestinian," 1020.

43. Taylor, *#BlackLivesMatter*, 170–71.

44. Taylor, 162.

45. Taylor, 162.

46. Taylor, 187.

47. Abdulhadi, "Activism and Exile: Palestinianness and the Politics of Solidarity," in *Local Actions: Cultural Activism, Power, and Public Life in America*, ed. Melissa Checker and Maggie Fishman (New York: Columbia Univ. Press, 2005), 238.

48. Abdulhadi, "Activism," 239.

49. Abdulhadi, 239.

50. Abdulhadi, 248.

51. Abdulhadi, 248–49. Emphasis in the original.

52. See, for example, her articulations of this in "Palestinian Resistance and the Indivisibility of Justice," in *With Stones in Our Hands: Writings on Muslims, Racism, and Empire*, ed. Sohail Dautlatzai and Junaid Rana (Minneapolis: Univ. of Minnesota Press, 2018), 56–72. See also her two-part article, "The Spirit of 68 Lives On!: Palestine Advocacy and the Indivisibility of Justice," Mondoweiss, July 14, 2017, http://mondoweiss.net /2017/07/palestine-advocacy-indivisibility, especially the first subtitled, "Palestine Advocacy and the Indivisibility of Justice" (http://mondoweiss.net/2017/07/palestine-advocacy -indivisibility). See also her two pieces on Oscar López, "Marching with Oscar López Rivera: A Long History of Palestinian-Puerto Rican Solidarity," Mondoweiss, June 19, 2017, (http://mondoweiss.net/2017/06/marching-palestinian-solidarity/) and "The Deep Bonds of Palestinian-Puerto Rican Solidarity Were on Display at This Year's NYC Puerto Rican Day Parade," Mondoweiss, June 15, 2017 (http://mondoweiss.net/2017/06/palestinian -solidarity-display/). Her cowritten piece with Dana Olwan also treats this issue, "Shifting Geographies of Knowledge and Power: Palestine and American Studies," *American Quarterly* 67, no 4 (2015): 993–1006.

53. Nadine Naber, "Arab and Black Feminisms: Joint Struggle and Transnational Anti-Imperial Activism," *Departures in Critical Qualitative Research* 5, no. 3 (2016): 121.

54. Naber, "Arab and Black," 123.

55. https://bdsmovement.net/news/call-action-indigenous-and-women-color-feminists.

56. Davis Bailey, "Black-Palestinian," 1017; Abdulhadi, "Black Radicalism, Insurgency in Israel/Palestine and the Idea of Solidarity" (paper presented at the American Studies Association annual meeting, Los Angeles, CA, November 7, 2014). In this context the

research being done by Greg Thomas on connections between George Jackson's and Samih al-Qasim's poetry, discovered with the lists of readings Jackson was doing in prison, is important.

57. Lubin, *Geographies*.

58. Sa'ed Atshan and Darnell L. Moore, "Reciprocal Solidarity: Where the Black and Palestinian Queer Struggles Meet," *Biography* 37, no. 2 (2014): 684.

59. Atshan and Moore, "Reciprocal," 700.

60. Lorde, *Sister*, 111.

61. Pickens, *New Body*, 10.

62. Pickens, 149.

63. Recently the *Feminist Wire* dedicated an issue to June Jordan's poem, and people shared reasons why it was so important to them; see Darnell L. Moore, "The Occupation Stole My Words, June Jordan Helped Me to Find Them," *Feminist Wire*, March 24, 2016, and Therese Saliba, "June Jordan's Songs of Lebanon and Palestine," *Feminist Wire*, March 24, 2016, for examples.

64. Feldman, *Shadow*; Lubin, *Geographies*; Fadda-Conrey, *Contemporary*; Hartman, "'this sweet, sweet music': Jazz, Sam Cooke and Reading Arab American Literary Identities," *MELUS Journal* 31, no. 4 (2006): 145–65; Sirène Harb, "Naming Oppressions, Representing Empowerment: June Jordan's and Suheir Hammad's Poetic Projects," *Feminist Formations* 26, no. 3 (2014): 71–99 and "Between Languages and Selves: Migratory Agency, Fragmentation and Representation in Suheir Hammad's *breaking poems*," *Contemporary Women's Writing* 6, no. 2 (2012): 122–39; Pickens, *New Body*; Dana M. Olwan, "Four Pedagogies of Solidarity in Suheir Hammad's '"First Writing Since,"' in *Muslim Women, Transnational Feminism and the Ethics of Pedagogy: Contested Imaginaries in Post-9/11 Cultural Practice*, ed. Lisa K. Taylor and Jasmine Zine (London: Routledge, 2014), 110–31.

65. Suheir Hammad, *Born Palestinian, Born Black* (New York: Harlem River Press, 1996), x; *Born Palestinian, Born Black & the Gaza Suite* (Brooklyn, NY: UpSet Press, 2010), 12. This is explored in more detail in chapter 1 below.

66. Michelle Hartman, "'Besotted with the Bright Lights of Imperialism'? Arab Subjectivity Constructed Against New York's Many Faces," *Journal of Arabic Literature* 35, no. 3 (2004): 270–96 and "Writing Arabs and Africa(ns) in America: Adonis and Radwa Ashour from Harlem to Lady Liberty," *International Journal of Middle East Studies* 37, no. 3 (2005): 397–420, both deal with the representations of New York in the work of Yusuf Idriss and Adonis. See also Miral Tahawy's *Brooklyn Heights*, trans. Samah Selim (Cairo: American Univ. in Cairo Press, 2012) and Shahla Ujayli's *A Sky So Close*, trans. Michelle Hartman (Northampton, MA: Interlink Publishing, 2018), as well as the epigraph to Jana Elhassan's *The Ninety-Ninth Floor*, trans. Michelle Hartman (Northampton, MA: Interlink Publishing, 2017) for Arabic literary representations of African Americans as politically, intellectually, and culturally inspiring.

67. Two books on the community, one published in 2000 (Nabeel Abraham and Andrew Shyrock, *Arab Detroit: From Margin to Mainstream* [Detroit: Wayne State Univ. Press]), and the other reacting to the events of 2001 (Nabeel Abraham, Sally Howell, and Andrew Shyrock, *Arab Detroit 9/11: Life in the Terror Decade* [Detroit: Wayne State Univ. Press, 2011]), highlight poetic and literary production within their studies of the community. Home to a large, historically rooted Arab American population, Detroit also became the quintessential African American Northern city after reconstruction, in particular in the aftermath of the height of the Black Freedom Struggle in the 1970s. Social inequality, racism, and extreme deprivation culminated in violent confrontations in Detroit, the most famous of which was perhaps the 12th Street Riot of July 1967, when the military was called in by the white governor to quell the uprising.

68. Lisa Suhair Majaj has referred to this as the iconic poem of Arab America, "Arab-American," 330.

69. Fadda-Conrey, *Contemporary*, 33.

70. Lawrence Joseph, "Sand Nigger," in *Curriculum Vitae* (Pittsburgh: Univ. of Pittsburgh Press, 1988), 27–29.

71. Fadda-Conrey, *Contemporary*, 52.

72. Majaj, *Arab American*, 19–21.

73. Pickens, *New Body*, 21. See Salaita's discussion of this term in detail in his *Modern Arab American*, 125–30.

74. Fadda-Conrey, *Contemporary*, 53.

75. Charara in Abraham and Shyrock, *Arab Detroit*, 404; Fadda-Conrey, *Contemporary*, 53.

76. Charara in Abraham and Shyrock, *Arab Detroit*, 404, 412; Fadda-Conrey, *Contemporary*, 53.

77. Kahf, *Girl*, 129.

78. Kahf, 137.

79. Kahf, 95–97.

80. This novel explores both the interracial relationship between an Arab American girl and African American boy, but also the ways in which racism works in that relationship, such as where he calls her "sand nigger" (54). Steven Salaita offers a reading of this in his *Modern Arab American*, 125–30.

81. Abu Jaber, *Arabian Jazz*, 294–96. See also Hartman, "this sweet sweet," which deals with this confrontation and racial identification.

82. Abu Jaber, *Arabian Jazz*, 294. Majaj discusses another short story with a similar idea, "At the Continental Divide," 330. I take this up in relation to *Arabian Jazz* in Hartman, "this sweet sweet." Yousef Awad, "Cartographies of Identities: Resistance, Diaspora, and Trans-cultural Dialogue in the Works of Arab British and Arab American Women Writers" (PhD Diss., Univ. of Manchester, 2011), 98–99, has made a good critique of my argument putting forward that these are stereotyped characters and not a

deep intervention. I would continue to propose that we choose our method of reading to emphasize these connections. I discuss this in more depth below in relation to Randa Jarrar's *A Map of Home* (New York: Penguin, 2009), chapter 4. Pickens discusses Kahf and Alameddine in relation to the Black and Arab American communities being pitted against each other for resources, *New Body*, 6–7.

1. Building a Theory of Language, Poetics, and Politics in the Break

1. See Theresa Perry and Lisa Delpit, eds., *The Real Ebonics Debate: Power, Language, and the Education of African-American Children* (Boston: Beacon, 1998), for a collection of scholars writing on the Ebonics Debate in Oakland, and also H. Samy Alim and Geneva Smitherman, *Articulate While Black: Barack Obama, Language, and Race in the U.S.* (Oxford: Oxford Univ. Press, 2012), for a discussion of Oakland in relation to the earlier debates. See also Smitherman, *Word from the Mother: Language and African Americans* (New York: Routledge, 2006).

2. See for example Larry Neal, "The Black Arts Movement," *The Drama Review: TDR* 12, no. 4 (1968): 28–39; John H. Bracey Jr., Sonia Sanchez, and James Smethurst, *SOS—Calling All Black People: A Black Arts Movement Reader* (Amherst: Univ. of Massachusetts Press, 2014); and Smethurst, *The Black Arts Movement: Literary Nationalism in the 1960s and 1970s* (Chapel Hill: Univ. of North Carolina Press, 2006).

3. Alim and Smitherman go into detail about Obama's speech-giving rhetoric in *Articulate*. For further insights into these issues, see John McWhorter, *Talking Back, Talking Black: Truths about America's Lingua Franca* (New York: Bellevue, 2017) and Smitherman, *Word*.

4. Smitherman, *Talkin That Talk*, 133–34, 143.

5. For more recent in-depth studies see Alim and Smitherman, *Articulate*; McWhorter, *Talking Back*; Imani Perry, *Prophets of the Hood: Politics and Poetics in Hip Hop* (Durham, NC: Duke Univ. Press, 2004); Perry and Delpit, *Real*; Rickford and Rickford, *Spoken Soul*; and Smitherman, *Word*.

6. June Jordan, "White English/Black English: The Politics of Translation (1972)," in *Civil Wars* (New York: Simon & Schuster, 1981), 66. Emphasis in the original.

7. Smitherman, *Talkin and Testifyin*.

8. In her article "What Is Africa to Me? Language, Ideology and African America," *American Speech* 66, no. 2 (1991): 115–32, Smitherman delves into the choice of the community whether or not to adopt the label African American and some of the reasons behind this.

9. For a discussion of the controversy in Oakland in more depth see Perry and Delpit, *Real*. This collection contains a number of studies by different scholars, analysts, and linguists.

10. Smitherman, *Talkin That Talk*, 28.

11. Smitherman, 29.

12. Smitherman, 19.

13. Smitherman, 153–54.

14. Lorde, *Sister*, 111.

15. Smitherman, *Talkin That Talk*, 66; emphasis in the original.

16. Smitherman, 34.

17. There are ample sources of documentation for this. For an exploration of racial formation of Arab Americans from a number of different contexts and approaches, see the collection edited by Amaney Jamal and Nadine Naber, *Race and Arab Americans Before and After 9/11: From Invisible Citizens to Visible Subjects* (Syracuse: Syracuse Univ. Press, 2007).

18. Smitherman, *Talkin That Talk*, 37–38.

19. June Jordan, "Nobody Mean More to Me than You and the Future Life of Willie Jordan," in *On Call: Political Essays* (Boston: South End Press, 1985), 123–39.

20. June Jordan, "Affirmative Acts: Language, Information, and Power," in *Affirmative Acts: Political Essays* (New York: Anchor, 1998), 245–46; "White English."

21. Jordan, "Nobody Mean."

22. Jordan, "White English"; "Nobody Mean."

23. Jordan, "Nobody Mean," 135.

24. Jordan, 136.

25. Jordan, "Affirmative Acts," 245.

26. Jordan, 245.

27. Jordan, 246.

28. Jordan, "White English," 67.

29. Jordan, 71.

30. Jordan, 69.

31. Jordan, 69.

32. James Baldwin, "If Black English Isn't a Language, Then Tell Me What Is," *New York Times*, July 29, 1979, https://www.nytimes.com/books/98/03/29/specials/baldwin-english.html.

33. Baldwin, "If Black."

34. Baldwin, "If Black." Emphasis in the original.

35. Baldwin, "If Black."

36. James Baldwin, "On Language, Race and the Black Writer," in *The Cross of Redemption: Uncollected Writings*, ed. Randall Kenan (New York: Doubleday, 2010), 114–17. Originally published in the *Los Angeles Times*, April 29, 1979.

37. Lorde, *Sister*, 43.

38. John E. Drabinski, "Vernaculars of Home," *Critical Philosophy of Race* 3, no. 2 (2015): 303–26, picks up on this and connects it to other Black thinkers.

39. Henry Louis Gates Jr., "Zora Neale Hurston and the Speakerly Text," in *The Signifying Monkey: A Theory of African-American Literary Criticism* (Oxford: Oxford Univ. Press, 2014), 170–216.

40. Here, see how Geneva Smitherman uses examples from Langston Hughes's iconic character Jesse B. Simple, *Talkin That Talk*, 124–25, and *Talkin and Testifyin*, 32–35.

41. Alice Walker, "Looking for Zora [1975]," in *In Search of Our Mothers' Gardens* (New York: Houghton Mifflin, 1983), 395–411.

42. Alice Walker, *The Color Purple* (New York: Pocket, 1985), 184.

43. Randa Jarrar, *Him, Me, Muhammad Ali* (New York: Sarabande, 2016), 47.

44. There are a few exceptions to this: Mohammed Albakry and Jonathan Siler, "Into the Arab American Borderland: Bilingual Creativity in Randa Jarrar's A Map of Home," *Arab Studies Quarterly* 34, no. 2 (2012): 109–21; Janá Fawwāz Hassan, "Agency and Translational Literature: Ahdaf Soueif's Map of Love," *PMLA* 121, no. 3 (2006): 753–68"; and Sirène Harb, "Between Languages and Selves: Migratory Agency, Fragmentation and Representation in Suheir Hammad's *breaking poems*," *Contemporary Women's Writing* 6, no. 2 (2012): 122–39.

45. See for example Mohammed Abdullah Hussein Muharram's intervention in "The Marginalization of Arabic Fiction in the Postcolonial World and English Curriculum: Slips? Or Orientalism and Racism," *Minnesota Review* 78 (2012): 130–45 and also the important work of Waïl Hassan, "World Literature in the Age of Globalization: Reflections on an Anthology," *College English* 63, no. 1 (2000): 38–47. See also Hassan, "Which Languages?" With few exceptions, works studying literatures in colonial languages from the former colonies studiously ignore or marginalize Arabic. An example is the now classic *The Empire Writes Back: Theory and Practice in Post-Colonial Literatures* (London: Routledge, 1989) by Bill Ashcroft, Gareth Griffith, and Helen Tiffin. See Michelle Hartman, *Native Tongue, Stranger Talk: The Arabic and French Literary Landscapes of Lebanon* (Syracuse: Syracuse Univ. Press, 2014) for a discussion of this work, its contributions, and some of what is lacking for Arab authors in particular, 24–25.

46. Smitherman, *Talkin' That Talk*, 153–54.

47. Fred Moten, *In the Break: The Aesthetics of the Black Radical Tradition* (Minneapolis: Univ. of Minnesota Press, 2003), 38.

48. Moten, *In the Break*, 44.

49. Lorde, *Sister*, 128.

50. Lorde, 122.

51. Lorde, 110.

52. Fadda-Conrey, *Contemporary*; Harb, "Between"; Marwa Helal, "The Vernacular Home," *American Book Review* 34, no. 1 (2012): 5; Pickens, *New Body*, 25–26, 28–29.

53. Carol Fadda-Conrey, "Weaving Poetic Autobiographies: Individual and Community Identities in the Poetry of Mohja Kahf and Suheir Hammad," in *Arab Women's*

Lives Retold: Exploring Identity Through Writing, ed. Nuwar Al-Hassan Golley (Syracuse: Syracuse Univ. Press, 2007), 155–76; Harb, "Naming" and "Transformative Practices and Historical Revision: Suheir Hammad's *Born Palestinian, Born Black*," *Studies in the Humanities* 35, no. 1 (2008): 34–49; Michelle Hartman, "A Debke Beat Funky as PE's Riff: Hip Hop Poetry and Politics in Suheir Hammad's *Born Palestinian, Born Black*," *Black Arts Quarterly* 7, no. 1 (2002): 6–8; Marcy Jane Knopf-Newman, "Broken Ground," *Journal of Palestine Studies* 39, no. 4 (2010): 263–64; Sunaina Maira, "'We A'int Missing'": Palestinian Hip Hop—A Transnational Youth Movement," *New Centennial Review* 8, no. 2 (2008): 161–92; Tony Medina and Louis Reyes Rivera, eds., *Bum Rush the Page: A Def Poetry Jam* (New York: Three Rivers Press, 2001); Kenza Oumlil, "'Talking Back': The Poetry of Suheir Hammad," *Feminist Media Studies* 13, no. 5 (2013): 850–59.

54. Kevin Coval, Quraysh Ali Lansana, and Nate Marshall, *The BreakBeat Poets: New American Poetry in the Age of Hip-Hop* (Chicago: Haymarket, 2015).

55. Coval et al., *The BreakBeats*, xvii.

56. Coval et al., xvii.

57. Pickens, *New Body*, 28–29. See also, Zoe Anglesey, ed., *Listen Up!: Spoken Word Poetry* (New York: Ballantine, 1999).

58. Suheir Hammad, "first writing since," in *September 11, 2001: Feminist Perspectives*, ed. Susan Hawthorne and Bronwyn Winter (Melbourne: Spinifex, 2002), 4–9.

59. The most important work on the relationship between Hammad and Jordan has been done by critic Sirène Harb. See her "Naming Oppressions." In the introduction above I mention others who have pointed out these connections.

60. It is notable that one of June Jordan's major projects, founded in 1991, and developed from her teaching poetry at the University of California at Berkeley, is still surviving today, "Poetry for the People."

61. June Jordan, "Moving towards Home," in *Living Room: New Poems, 1980–1984* (New York: Thunder's Mouth Press, 1985), 134. The collection, *Living Room*, in which this poem appears, is dedicated to "the children of Atlanta and the children of Lebanon," and it is important that those children of Lebanon include Palestinians. It is also worth noting here in a chapter on the poetry of homage, that June Jordan dedicates a poem to Arab American poet Etel Adnan in this collection as well. For more on connections between Adnan and African American art, see Hartman, "this sweet sweet," in which I discuss her poem "Beirut-Hell Express."

62. Hammad, *Born Palestinian, Born Black*, 1996, xi; *Born Palestinian, Born Black*, 2010, 13.

63. Hammad, *Born Palestinian, Born Black*, 1996, ix; *Born Palestinian, Born Black*, 2010, 11.

64. Hammad, *Born Palestinian, Born Black*, 1996, x; *Born Palestinian, Born Black*, 2010, 12.

65. Hammad, *Born Palestinian, Born Black*, 1996, ix; *Born Palestinian, Born Black*, 2010, 11.

66. Harb, "Naming Oppressions," 90. This argument is also important to Pickens's analysis in *New Body*, see for example 25–26.

67. Lorde, *Sister*, 138.

68. Hammad, *Born Palestinian, Born Black*, 1996, xi; *Born Palestinian, Born Black*, 2010, 13.

69. It is worth noting in this context that many in her community did not appreciate her poetry when she was just beginning, in particular because of her use of vulgar language. Also, the ways she affiliated to African Americans offended respectability politics and challenged who to align with in Arab American communities.

70. Other Arabs and Arab Americans—including D. H. Melhem and Radwa Ashour, discussed in chapters 2 and 5 respectively—have longstanding, stated, and celebrated connections with Black communities and Black figures, and have expressed feeling at home in these locations as well. Melhem and Ashour forged their bonds in the height of the political climate of the 1970s, when the Black Panther Party and other movements of Third World solidarity were at their peak. They do not, however, use Black Language in their work, nor do other later poets, like Saladin Ahmed, who is a contemporary of Suheir Hammad.

71. For an analysis of the contradictory and paradoxical position of Black Language as reviled in the mainstream but contributing to mainstream culture, see McWhorter, *Talking Back*, which asserts this language is a "lingua franca" in the United States. See also Alim and Smitherman, *Articulate*, for a contemporary analysis of this language, related to the rise of Barack Obama and his election as president.

72. Hammad, *Born Palestinian, Born Black*, 2010, 16.

73. Helal, "The Vernacular," 5. This is also relevant to the argument by Cariello, "Pervasive," 10–25, that Hammad refuses translation in order to advance a new cultural politics.

74. Helal, "The Vernacular," 5.

75. Harb, "Between."

76. Smitherman, *Talkin and Testifyin*, 273.

77. Jordan, "Affirmative Acts," 69. See also Rickford and Rickford, *Spoken Soul*, 114–16, who also connect Black Language to Russian, Hungarian, and Swahili in a similar way. For a longer discussion of copula absence also see H. Samy Alim, *You Know My Steez: An Ethnographic and Sociolinguistic Study of Styleshifting in a Black American Speech Community* (Durham, NC: Duke Univ. Press, 2004).

78. Jordan, "Affirmative Acts," 69.

79. Suheir Hammad, *breaking poems* (New York: Cypher Books, 2008), 25.

80. Hammad, *breaking*, 25.

81. Hammad, 30.

82. Hammad, 30.

83. Hammad, 35.

84. Hammad, 35

85. Smitherman identifies the linguistic processes in which negative words with positive meanings have come into Black English from West African language origins and moved into the language of earliest enslaved people in Americas. They exist in Black English as calques of words carried over, *Talkin and Testifyin*, 44–45; she also discusses these uses as a process of semantic inversion in *Talkin That Talk*, 280–82.

86. Hammad, *breaking*, 61.

87. For example, see "break (layla bye)," which refers to "om kolthom, fairuz, nina, ana spinning" in Hammad, *breaking*, 31.

88. rosalind hampton and I use this poem and others from Hammad, as well as a collection of material from Rastafarian language, in our "Toward Language and Resistance: A Breaking Manifesto," in *Manifestos for World Thought*, ed. Lucian Stone and Jason Bahbak Mohaghegh (London: Rowman and Littlefield, 2017), 115–28.

89. Hammad, *breaking*, 16.

90. This is not the only allusion to or invocation of June Jordan in this collection; for example, in "break (still)" Hammad alludes directly to the collection in which "Moving towards Home" was published, *Living Room*: "the first civil war is there / and always happening / in june's living room" (Hammad, *breaking*, 18).

91. Hammad, *breaking*, 51.

92. Pickens, *New Body*, 26.

2. Homage as a Politics of Solidarity

1. Hayan Charara, *Inclined to Speak: An Anthology of Contemporary Arab American Poetry* (Fayetteville: Arkansas Univ. Press, 2008); Gregory Orfalea and Sharif Elmusa, eds., *Grape Leaves: A Century of Arab American Poetry* (Northampton, MA: Interlink, 2000).

2. Munir Akash and Khaled Mattawa, eds., *Post-Gibran: Anthology of New Arab American Writing* (Syracuse: Syracuse Univ. Press, 1999); Pauline Kaldas and Khaled Mattawa, eds., *Dinarzad's Children: An Anthology of Contemporary Arab American Fiction* (Fayetteville, AK: Univ. of Arkansas Press, 2009).

3. Rabab Abdulhadi, Nadine Naber, and Evelyne Alsultany, eds., *Arab and Arab American Feminisms: Gender, Violence and Belonging* (Syracuse: Syracuse Univ. Press, 2011); Joanna (Joe) Kadi, ed., *Food for Our Grandmothers: Writings by Arab American and Arab Canadian Feminists* (Boston: South End Press, 1994); Abraham and Shyrock, *Arab Detroit*; Abraham et al., *Arab Detroit 9/11*.

4. Kadi's *Food for our Grandmothers* has played an important role in this, as has the anthology cited above, edited by Abdulhadi, Alsultany, and Naber. Critical work, like

Harb's analyses linking Hammad and June Jordan, as discussed in the previous chapter, are crucial in making these connections visible.

5. Lorde, *Sister*, 119, 128.

6. Lorde, 142.

7. Fadda-Conrey, *Contemporary*, 193n52. It should be remarked here that she was active in the same period as Radwa Ashour, whose work is discussed in depth in chapter 5 below.

8. D. H. Melhem, *Notes on 94th Street* (New York: Poet's Press, 1972), back cover.

9. Here I will cite from the more recent edition of these poems (D. H. Melham, *New York Poems* [Syracuse Univ. Press, 2005]).

10. Philip Metres, "Introduction to Focus: Arab American Literature after 9/11," *American Book Review* 34, no. 1 (2012): 3. Metres does not take her connections with Black Americans any further than this though and leaves his comments there.

11. D. H. Melhem, *Gwendolyn Brooks: Poetry and the Heroic Voice* (Lexington: Univ. Press of Kentucky, 1988), viii.

12. Melhem, vii.

13. On her website, there is a slideshow put together by her children after her death, part of which chronicles her literary engagements throughout her life, and this shows her deep commitment to Black art.

14. http://www.alwanforthearts.org/event/121. Melhem discusses how she attended his class at the New School for Social Research in 1977, "Art and Marxism"; see below for more discussion of this.

15. Melhem, *New York*, 79–80 and 83–84. Emphasis in the original.

16. Melhem, 79–80.

17. Melhem, 74 and 75. Capital letters in the original. For more on the Catonsville Nine, see *The Trial of the Catonsville Nine* by Daniel Berrigan.

18. Melhem, *New York*, 73.

19. Melhem, 77. Lower case in the original.

20. Premilla Nadasen, *Welfare Warriors: The Welfare Rights Movement in the United States* (New York: Routledge, 2005), 47, 51.

21. Nadasen, *Welfare Warriors*, 25.

22. Nadasen, *Welfare Warriors* and Felicia Ann Kombluh, *The Battle for Welfare Rights: Politics and Poverty in Modern America* (Philadelphia: Univ. of Pennsylvania Press, 2007).

23. Melhem, *New York*, 77.

24. Melhem, 77.

25. Melhem, 77.

26. Melhem, 81–82.

27. Lubin, *Geographies*.

28. Lubin, 113; see all of chapter 4 for more details: "The Black Panthers and the PLO: The Politics of Intercommunalism," 111–41.

29. Brian Shih and Yohuru Williams, eds., *The Black Panthers: Portraits from an Unfinished Revolution* (New York: Nation Books, 2016,) 76.

30. Shih and Williams, *The Black Panthers*, 74.

31. Jane Rhodes, *Framing the Black Panther Party: The Spectacular Rise of a Black Power Icon* (Champaign: Univ. of Illinois Press, 2017).

32. It is perhaps relevant that Eldridge Cleaver's widely read and circulated memoir, *Soul on Ice*, had already been published at the time.

33. This also prefigures Suheir Hammad's later conceptualization and definition of Blackness, in her *Born Palestinian, Born Black*, cited and discussed in the chapter above (*Born Palestinian, Born Black*, 1996, x; *Born Palestinian, Born Black*, 2010, 12).

34. Melhem, *New York*, 81.

35. Melhem, 81.

36. The symbol was chosen before the BPP formulated—its predecessor in voter registration efforts led by SNCC in Alabama chose it, and it was later adopted as the symbol. On the power of its imagery see Stokely Carmichael's speech in 1966 Berkeley, California (Catherine Ellis and Stephen Smith, *Say it Plain: A Century of Great African American Speeches* [London: New Press, 2005], 55–73): "We chose for the emblem a black panther—a *beautiful* animal—which symbolizes the strength and dignity of black people. An animal that never strikes until he is backed so far into the wall that he's got nothing to do but spring out. And when he springs he does not stop" (71).

37. Melhem, *New York*, 81.

38. Melhem, 82.

39. The poem itself is placed in her collection between one written for the Catonsville Nine protesting the Vietnam War and an even harsher one that condemns the white media's lies, "CORRECTION, PLEASE."

40. The other two are called "Mostly Political" and "Wars."

41. D. H. Melhem, *Heroism in the New Black Poetry: Introductions and Interviews* (Lexington: Univ. Press of Kentucky, 2015).

42. D. H. Melhem, *Art and Politics/Politics and Art* (Syracuse: Syracuse Univ. Press, 2010), 6.

43. Melhem, *Art and Politics*, 3

44. Melhem, 3.

45. Melhem, 3.

46. It is perhaps relevant to note here that the ending of the original book was changed at the time it was published. Wright's work was gaining in popularity and was one of the few works by a Black author to have achieved the status of being chosen for the national book club, therefore he complied with this group's insistence that the second

half of the book as it was originally not be published. It has since been published and is included in newer editions.

47. Richard Wright, *Black Boy* (New York: Harper Perennial, 1945), 285 (emphasis in the original); D. H. Melhem, *Country: An Organic Poem* (Merrick, NY: Cross Cultural Communications, 1998), 83.

48. Cherríe Moraga and Gloria Anzaldúa, eds., *This Bridge Called My Back: Writings by Radical Women of Color* (Watertown, MA: Persephone, 1981) and Lorde, *Sister.*

49. For Amiri Baraka, in Melhem, *Art and Politics*, 4, for Jayne Cortez, Melhem, *Art and Politics*, 5.

50. For a collection of essays on Jayne Cortez, see Laura Hinton, ed., *Jayne Cortez, Adrienne Rich, and the Feminist Superhero: Voice, Vision, Politics, and Performance in U.S. Contemporary Women's Poetics* (London: Rowman and Littlefield, 2016).

51. As cited above (chapter 1, note 85), Smitherman discusses the use of semantic inversion in Black Language and how this has predecessors in West African languages. She discusses some well-known examples: "bad" meaning "good," "cool" meaning "good" and also a synonym for "hot"; see Smitherman, *Talkin That Talk*, 280–82.

52. http://movingpoems.com/poet/jayne-cortez/ and https://www.youtube.com/watch?v=6h0qYZTXaiI.

53. Melhem, *Art and Politics*, 5.

54. Melhem, 3.

55. Melhem, 4.

56. Melhem, 4.

57. Angela Davis, "Prison Memoirs," *Village Voice*, October 10, 1974, https://news.google.com/newspapers?nid=KEtq3P1Vf8oC&dat=19741010&printsec=frontpage&hl=en, 8, 10, 11, 14, 40, 41.

58. Melhem, *Art and Politics*, 6.

59. Melhem, 6.

60. The dream of Langston Hughes is also important to Radwa Ashour, who translates the iconic poem into Arabic in her memoir, *The Journey*, discussed in chapter 5 below.

61. Melhem, *Art and Politics*, 1.

62. Lorde, *Sister*, 128.

63. http://www.metrotimes.com/detroit/meet-author-saladin-ahmed/Content?oid=2199800.

64. Abraham and Shyrock, *Arab Detroit*, 317–18.

65. Abraham and Shyrock, 319–20.

66. He is now a well-known science fiction/fantasy writer whose series is titled *Throne of the Crescent Moon.*

67. Based in Dearborn, it ran from 1999 to 2001, when it was closed because of lack of advertising revenue after the 2001 attacks.

68. *Callaloo* 32, no. 4 (Fall 2009): 1232–34.

69. Abraham and Shyrock, *Arab Detroit*, 319.

70. Abraham and Shyrock, 319.

71. Abraham and Shyrock, 320.

72. It is composed in a formally difficult iambic tetrameter.

73. See essays by David K. Kirby, "Countee Cullen's 'Heritage': A Black Waste Land," *South Atlantic Bulletin* 36, no. 4 (1971): 14–20, https://www.jstor.org/stable/3196596, and Phillips, "What Is Africa?"

74. Kirby, "Countee Cullen."

75. Smitherman, "What is Africa?," 115.

76. Edited by Gregory Orfalea and Sharif Elmusa.

77. Saladin Ahmed, "Poem for Countee Cullen," in *Post-Gibran: Anthology of New Arab American Writing*, ed. Munir Akash and Khaled Mattawa (Syracuse: Syracuse Univ. Press, 1999), 255.

78. Ahmed, 255.

79. Ahmed, 256.

80. Ahmed, 256.

81. https://www.poets.org/poetsorg/poem/jamyla-bolden-ferguson-missouri.

82. For some of Naomi Shihab Nye's extensive poetic publications, see the bibliography. She has published many collections and her poems are reprinted extensively.

83. Susan Muaddi-Darraj, ed., *Scheherazade's Legacy: Arab and Arab American Women's Voices on Writing* (Westport, CT: Praeger, 2004), 3.

84. Naomi Shihab Nye, "Cross That Line," *Mizna* 1, no. 2 (1999): 10.

85. Naomi Shihab Nye, "Long Overdue," in *Post-Gibran: Anthology of New Arab American Writing*, ed. Munir Akash and Khaled Mattawa (Syracuse: Syracuse Univ. Press, 1999), 127–32. The African American friend who is depicted here says to the narrator when she experiences racism: "now you know a little more what it feels like to be black."

86. https://arablit.org/2016/08/02/talking-forever-a-poem-by-naomi-shihab-nye-for-dareen-tatour. The Tatour case is discussed in particular because of the way the translation was manipulated. Nye wrote an earlier poem for another young Palestinian woman, Ibtisam Bozieh, that has many similarities; see "For the 500th Dead Palestinian, Ibtisam Bozieh," in *19 Varieties of Gazelle: Poems of the Middle East* (New York: Greenwillow Books, 1994), 53–54.

87. https://www.washingtonpost.com/posteverything/wp/2014/08/28/on-growing-up-in-ferguson-and-gaza/?utm_term=.9ea215d5f520.

88. www.poets.org.

89. The poem can be heard read by the poet on the website http://poets.org/poetsorg/poem/jamyla-bolden-ferguson-missouri.

90. Coval et al., *The BreakBeats*, 309, 320, 329.

91. Pickens, *New Body*, 5.

3. Palestine, or a Language as Home

1. It is important to note here that Susan Abulhawa felt uncomfortable about the title chosen for her piece by the editors and says she feels like it sounds like appropriation. She discusses this in the comments to the article, which are posted below it: https://electronicintifada.net/comment/15271#comment-15271.

2. Susan Abulhawa, "The Palestinian Struggle is a Black Struggle," Electronic Intifada, June 11, 2013, https://electronicintifada.net/content/palestinian-struggle-black -struggle/12530.

3. Lorde, *Sister*, 122, 128, 142.

4. Susan Abulhawa, "Confronting Anti-Black Racism in the Arab World," Al Jazeera, July 7, 2013, http://www.aljazeera.com/indepth/opinion/2013/06/201362472519107286 .html.

5. Susan Abulhawa, *Mornings in Jenin* (New York: Bloomsbury, 2010), 165.

6. Smitherman, *Talkin That Talk*, 66.

7. Smitherman, 37–38.

8. This is once again consistent with the thought of many Black feminists; see Audre Lorde, "Man Child" in *Sister*, 72–80.

9. Abulhawa, *Mornings*, xi

10. Abulhawa, 324.

11. Marcy Jane Knopf-Newman, "Review: *Mornings in Jenin*," *Journal of Palestine Studies* 39, no. 4 (2010): 83–84, https://bodyontheline.files.wordpress.com/2011/11/jps3904 _06_recent-books_8.pdf; see also Knopf-Newman, *The Politics of Teaching Palestine to Americans* (New York: Palgrave-Macmillan, 2001).

12. Bashir Abu-Manneh, *The Palestinian Novel: From 1948 to the Present* (Cambridge: Cambridge Univ. Press, 2016), 71–95.

13. Abulhawa, *Mornings*, 260–61.

14. Ghassan Kanafani, "Returning to Haifa," in *Palestine's Children: Returning to Haifa and Other Stories*, trans. Barbara Harlow and Karen E. Riley (Boulder, CO: Three Continents Press, 2000), 157.

15. Abulhawa, *Mornings*, 256–57. These scenes are discussed in detail below, in particular how the Arabic language is used as haunting sounds to punctuate the English-language narrative.

16. Abulhawa, *Mornings*, 167. This is discussed in more detail, as are the other chapter titles, below. See also Marta Cariello, "The Pervasive Borderland: Anglophone Arab Poetry and Polyglossia," in *Cultures and Languages International Conference Proceedings Two* (El-Jadida, Morocco: Chouaib Dukkali Univ., 2012), 21, for analysis.

17. Abulhawa, *Mornings*, 172.

18. Abulhawa, 175.

19. Abulhawa, 175.

20. Abulhawa, 175.

21. The protagonist Mohammad in Rabih Alameddine's *Koolaids: The Art of War* (New York: Picador, 1998) relates differently to his Black best friend than he does other white gay men in the United States. The character Jemorah in Diana Abu Jaber's *Arabian Jazz* eventually claims belonging as Black after being harassed for her father being "no better than a Negro." *The Girl in the Tangerine Scarf*, by Mohja Kahf, explores friendships between Arab American characters and their African American friends and coreligionists, including anti-Black racism in the Muslim Arab American community.

22. Pickens, *New Body*, 8.

23. Abulhawa, *Mornings*, 177–78.

24. A metaphor for people who would be legally or socially considered Black and who chose or were forced to be white in society, this is referred to in the United States especially—and elsewhere—as "passing."

25. Lorde, *Sister*, 111, 128.

26. Rabab Abdulhadi, "'White' or Not? Displacement and the Construction of (Racialized and Gendered) Palestinianness in the United States," (paper presented at the Middle East Studies Association annual meeting, Washington DC, November 24, 2002).

27. Abulhawa, *Mornings*, 176.

28. See Hartman, "this sweet, sweet," for an analysis of Black American music as thematized in Arab American literary works. See also Hartman, "Grandmothers, Grape Leaves, and Kahlil Gibran: Writing Race in Anthologies of Arab American Literature," in *Race and Arab Americans Before and After 9/11: From Invisible Citizens to Visible Subjects*, ed. Amaney Jamal and Nadine Naber (Syracuse: Syracuse Univ. Press, 2007), 170–203, on how racialized understandings of Arab Americans are asserted relationally with Black Americans through shared "ethnic" rhythm, p. 163.

29. Abulhawa, *Mornings*, 176.

30. Abulhawa, 177.

31. Abulhawa, 178.

32. Abulhawa, 72.

33. Abulhawa, 245.

34. Abulhawa, 179.

35. Abulhawa, 195.

36. Abulhawa, 289.

37. Abulhawa, 322.

38. Smitherman, *Talkin and Testifyin*, 57. See also, Smitherman, *Word*, 24, 43. In his essay, "'What's in a Name?': Some Meanings of Blackness," Gates explores the connections the change in names for the community and the ways in which naming has been thematized literarily from Baldwin's *Nobody Knows my Name*, to Morrison's *Beloved*, and beyond, situating these within community discussions on self-naming practices (Henry

Louis Gates Jr., *Loose Canons: Notes on the Culture Wars* [Oxford: Oxford Univ. Press, 1992], 131–51). For discussion of slavery and naming in *Beloved*, see p. 146.

39. Abulhawa, *Mornings*, 327–30.

40. Jordan, "White English," 66.

41. Abulhawa, *Mornings*, 33.

42. The essay "Man Child" in Audre Lorde, *Sister*, 72–80, is an example of the complexity of theorizing the role of men and boys in a feminist, Lesbian movement that is grounded in recognizing the lived experiences of racial and other difference/s. In it she explores the limits of separatism, especially for Black women and interracial families and also the specific challenges of raising a son to be a Black man "who will not be destroyed but, nor settle for, those corruptions called *power*" (74).

43. Abulhawa, *Mornings*, 37.

44. Abulhawa, 38.

45. Abulhawa, 277.

46. Smitherman, *Talkin and Testifyin*, 57.

47. Abulhawa, *Mornings*, 321.

48. In her use of such expressions, along with extensive discussions and other techniques, Susan Abulhawa resembles a writer like Evelyne Bustros, who encodes extensive messages about gender roles and the liberation of women, as well as challenging class-divides and French colonial domination of Lebanon, through her experiments with language using unidiomatic translations of Arabic expressions (Hartman, *Native Tongue*, 91–94 and 100–103).

49. Abulhawa, *Mornings*, 185.

50. Abulhawa, 185.

51. In the introduction to his edited collection, *Black Literature and Literary Theory* (London: Routledge, 2016), Henry Louis Gates Jr. asserts that call-and-response, also referred to by the more formal term antiphony, is "central to Black art" (*Black Literature*, n.p.) and identifies the technique as a way for the Black community to find assurance in the communal voice of the people. He also emphasizes this in a number of other locations in his work (*Loose Canons*, 33) and together with Jennifer Burton has edited a reader on key debates in African American Studies titled *Call and Response: Key Debates in African American Studies* (New York: Norton, 2008), underlining its role as the quintessential African American art form. For a discussion of the origins and use of call-and-response in speech, see Smitherman, *Talkin and Testifyin*, 104–18 and also *talking that talk*, 352. For a book on how the technique is used in African American literature see John F. Callahan, *In the African-American Grain: Call-and-Response in Twentieth-Century Black Fiction* (Chicago: Univ. of Illinois Press, 1989). Another important analysis is Imani Perry's discussion in *Prophets*, in which she builds on the linguistic analysis of Smitherman to isolate a specifically African American aesthetics and poetics in this musical art form. Alim devotes a section to call-and-response in hip-hop language in *You Know My Steez*.

52. Maggie Sale, "Call and Response as Critical Method: African-American Oral Traditions and *Beloved*," *African American Review* 2, no. 1 (1992): 41–42.

53. Abulhawa, *Mornings*, 169–70.

54. For a longer discussion of how such a technique can have a political and social meaning, see also Hartman, *Native Tongue*, 91–94 and 100–103. For a discussion of how "chokran" is different than the French word "merci" (thank you) in Leïla Barakat's *Sous les vignes du pays Druze*, see Hartman, *Native Tongue*, 249–51.

55. Abulhawa, *Mornings*, 214.

56. Dima Ayoub ("Translatability in Contemporary Arab Women's Literature," PhD diss., McGill Univ., 2015, 101–3) highlights when such expressions do and do not evoke religion per se, through a comparison of the glossaries offered by Andrea Rugh and Ahdaf Soueif. She also discusses Apter's suggestion to think about Islamophobia in the translation of "Allah," and the analysis of Emily Jacir's artistic interventions around this question (Emily Apter, *Against World Literature: On the Politics of Untranslatability* [London: Verso, 2014], 9). Roger Allen also gestures to this problem in his article reflecting on a career as a translator in "The Happy Traitor: Tales of Translation," *Comparative Literature Studies* 47, no. 4 (2010): 479.

57. See Marilyn Booth, "On Translation and Madness," *Translation Review* 65, no. 1 (2003): 47–53; Hartman, "Dreams Deferred, Translated: Radwa Ashour and Langston Hughes," *CLINA* 2, no. 1 (2016): 65; and Hartman, "'My Tale's Too Long to Tell:' The Locust and the Bird between South Lebanon and New York City," *Journal of Arabic Literature* 46: nos. 2–3 (2015): 179–80. This latter essay grapples with the question of extreme domestication in some depth in the case of a Lebanese women's novel/memoir. On this issue, see also Shamma's study of *1001 Nights* (Tarek Shamma, *Translation and the Manipulation of Difference: Arabic Literature in Nineteenth-Century England* [London: Routledge, 2014]), which shows that these terms do not apply in the case of the time and context of this work.

58. Gayatri Chakravorty Spivak, *In Other Worlds: Essays in Cultural Politics* (London: Routledge, 2006 [1987]). Later, in *Other Asias* (Oxford: Blackwell, 2008), Spivak disavows the concept, particularly for how it has been misused and manipulated by nationalist feminists, 260.

59. Abulhawa, *Mornings*, 129.

60. Abulhawa, 328.

61. Abulhawa, 327–30.

62. Ayoub, *Translatability*, 97–103.

63. Abulhawa, *Mornings*, 327.

64. Abulhawa, 329.

65. Abulhawa, 327.

66. Abulhawa, 327. Emphasis in the original.

67. Abulhawa, 64, 77, 81, 82, 87 (twice), 95, 122 (twice), 128, 151 (twice), 285, and 307.

68. Abulhawa, 87.

69. Abulhawa, 95.

70. Abulhawa, 151.

71. Abulhawa, xvii–ix.

72. Abulhawa, 208.

73. Abulhawa, 80, 99, 277.

74. Knopf-Newman, "Review: *Mornings.*"

75. Robin Yassin-Kassab, "Review: *Mornings in Jenin*, by Susan Abulhawa," *Sunday Times*, February 8, 2010.

76. Abulhawa, *Mornings*, 136.

77. Pickens, *New Body*, 18–39.

78. Vani Natarajan and Hannah Mermelstein ("Knowledge, Access and Resistance: A Conversation on Librarians and Archivists to Palestine," in *Informed Agitation: Library and Information Skills in Social Justice Movements and Beyond*, ed. Melissa Monroe [Sacramento: Library Juice Press, 2014]), 247–61, http://librarianswithpalestine.org /publications/informed-agitation-chapter/) provide an extensive discussion on the Librarians and Archivists with Palestine (LAP) delegation to Palestine that conceived of the successful One Book, Many Communities reading group project that is held yearly, and was inaugurated with *Mornings in Jenin*. See the LAP website for more details about the project: https://librarianswithpalestine.org/campaigns-2/onebookcampaign/.

79. Abulhawa has continued to build her successful literary career ever since, and has published a second novel, *Between Water and Sky*, an equally poignant and haunting tale of "reverse immigration" in which an American girl of Palestinian origin travels back to Palestine as an adult. Many of the same ideas and themes are brought out, in a very different and compelling story, building political solidarity with South Africa, also firmly centering its story around the liberation of Palestine and a politics of emancipation.

4. Stories to Pass On

1. Jarrar, *Him, Me*, 47.

2. Gates, *Loose Canons*, 143.

3. Gates, 91–92. Gates singles out Morrison, Alice Walker, and Toni Cade Bambara, as well as Gloria Naylor and Rita Dove, as Black women having an impact on the American literary scene, ensuring that Black women's studies emerged from common terrains of Black Studies and Women's Studies in unprecedented ways.

4. Gates, *Loose Canons*, 146.

5. See in particular Sirène Harb's analysis of how Hammad's poetry draws attention to a lineage of women poets and claims a feminist literary history of women of color through their connections, "Naming." See also her "Transformative."

6. Jarrar, *Him, Me*, 44.

7. Randa Jarrar's short story, "Lost in Freakin' Yonkers," was also published in the first edition of *Dinarzad's Children*, which appeared in 2004 (see pp. 327–39). It contains slightly different details, including a different author. In the earlier version, the books were by Egyptian feminist Latifa al-Zayyat, also a well-known feminist author, but of an earlier generation and a different resonance than Khalifeh, whose works deal with the colonization of Palestine and dispossession of the Palestinians from women's perspectives, rather than being set in the period of early Egyptian independence.

8. Jarrar, *Him, Me*, 40,

9. Jarrar, 41.

10. Jarrar explores this idea at length in her novel *A Map of Home* (New York: Penguin, 2009), discussed below.

11. Jarrar, *Him, Me*, 40.

12. Jarrar, 39. This is prefigured in *A Map of Home* by the character Nidali's date to her junior prom, "Juman, the fly black junior" (Jarrar, *A Map*, 279). For a discussion, see below.

13. Smitherman, *Talkin That Talk*, 19.

14. Jarrar, *Him, Me*, 44.

15. Jarrar, 47.

16. Jarrar, 45.

17. Jarrar, 45.

18. Jarrar, 50.

19. Jarrar, 49.

20. Jarrar, 51.

21. Jarrar, 51.

22. Critics have focused on the narrative voice and tone, especially its humor. See Marta Cariello, "Coming of Age in the Solitude of the Lost Land: Randa Jarrar's *A Map of Home*," *Hawwa: Journal of Women in the Middle East and the Islamic World* 12, nos. 2–3 (2014): 268–88; Nancy El Gendy, "Trickster Humour in Randa Jarrar's *A Map of Home*: Negotiating Arab American Muslim Female Sexuality," *Women: A Cultural Review* 27, no. 1 (2016): 1–19; and Salaita, *Modern Arab American*.

23. See for example, Cariello, "Coming of Age"; El Gendy, "Trickster"; Fadda-Conrey, *Arab American*, 133–37; Salaita, *Modern Arab American*.

24. Albakry and Siler, "Into the Arab American," 120.

25. Smitherman, *Talkin That Talk*, 153–54.

26. Here Carol Fadda-Conrey's analysis of movement, geography, and transnationalism are helpful in understanding some of the textual dynamics, *Contemporary*.

27. Unlike Abulhawa's novel, however, *A Map of Home* does not include paratextual devices that cushion and present these experimentations with English. There is no family tree, list of resources, chapter outline, and, most importantly, glossary in *A Map of Home*.

28. Jordan, "White English," 66.

29. Jarrar, *A Map*, 3. Capitals in the original.

30. Jarrar, 5.

31. Jarrar, 6.

32. Jarrar, 7.

33. Jarrar, 6.

34. Jarrar, 8. This recalls the later cover song by Will Smith about him and his son.

35. Albakry and Siler, "Into the Arab American," 114.

36. It is important that this is not absent totally in the Arab world, but fades and is of less importance. See, for example, the discussion of her friend who is Sudanese; Jarrar, *A Map*, 110 and 141. This is also important to connect to chapter 5 below and the different discourses of race in Arabic, in the Arab world, in the case of Radwa Ashour.

37. Jarrar, *A Map*, 6.

38. Jarrar, 6.

39. As mentioned above, Randa Jarrar's short story "Lost in Freakin' Yonkers" was also published in the first edition of the anthology *Dinarzad's Children* in 2004.

40. Diana Jadallah, "Review: *A Map of Home* by Randa Jarrar," *Arab Studies Quarterly* 32, no. 2 (2010): 111–12.

41. Jarrar, *A Map*, 6.

42. Jarrar, 258. Emphasis in the original.

43. For a more comprehensive discussion of her conflicted relationship with her father, see Marta Bosch-Vilarrubias, "New Arab Masculinities: A Feminist Approach to Arab American Men in Post 9/11 Literature Written by Women," In *Masculinity and Literary Studies: Intersections and New Directions*, ed. Joseph M. Armengol, Marta Bosch Vilarrubias, Àngels Carabí, and Teresa Requena (London: Routledge, 2017), 66–76. Also on the father being depicted as grotesque in order to break stereotypes, see Cariello, "Coming of Age," 273.

44. Jarrar, *A Map*, 58–59.

45. This is the grammatical feature in which no verb "to be" is expressed in the present tense. It is discussed in chapters 1–3 above.

46. Jordan, "White English," 66.

47. Smitherman, *Talkin That Talk*, 66. Emphasis in the original.

48. The way she refers to her Sudanese friend in Kuwait, for example, is marked by difference in color, not by differences coded as racialized in the same way as in the States, Jarrar, *A Map*, 110, 141. A longer discussion of race and color follows below in chapter 5.

49. Fadda-Conrey, *Contemporary*, 137.

50. Fadda-Conrey, 137.

51. Jarrar, *A Map*, 221.

52. Jarrar, 233.

53. Jarrar, 226.

54. Jarrar, 225.

55. This argument is followed up below in the case of Radwa Ashour's depiction of essentialized features of groups of color in the United States: Black Americans, Puerto Ricans, and Arabs. See also Cariello, "Coming of Age," for arguments about how exaggeration is used in Jarrar to both invoke and challenge stereotypes. Cariello's argument also recalls the work of Mireille Rosello on "declining" stereotypes—invoking the double meaning of decline as both a declension like a verb declension and refusing them through this. See Mireille Rosello, *Declining the Stereotype: Ethnicity and Representation in French Cultures* (Hanover, NH: Univ. Press of New England, 1998).

56. For a definition of "race thinking" in relation to constructions and depictions of Muslims in particular culturalist arguments, see Sherene Razack, *Casting Out: The Eviction of Muslims from Western Law and Politics* (Toronto: Univ. of Toronto Press, 2007). Dana M. Olwan's work on honor crimes is also helpful. See her "Gendered Violence, Cultural Otherness, and Honour Crimes in Canadian National Logics," *Canadian Journal of Sociology* 38, no. 4 (2013): 533–55.

57. Jarrar, *A Map*, 273.

58. Jarrar, 273.

59. Jarrar, 273.

60. Recalling the teachers at my school who humiliated children for speaking their home language at school and not mastering white English (see the preface) leads us to think about how much racialized classroom experiences of students are linked and the ways in which it is not merely one or another group that experiences racialized intimidation and humiliation by teachers. See also the experience recalled by Suheir Hammad, whose teacher doubted she'd read Tolstoy (Danny Simmons, *Def Poetry Jam on Broadway . . . and More: The Choice Collection* [New York: Atria, 2003], 189).

61. For explication of and challenges to such culturalist arguments, see Dana Olwan, Sherene Razack, Sunera Thobani, and also Lila Abu Lughod. The discourse around so-called honor crimes is particularly important in this context and the construction of domestic violence as gender-based violence as fundamentally different.

62. Jarrar, *A Map*, 279.

63. Jarrar, 245.

64. The conclusion (chapter 13) of David Roediger's *Colored White: Transcending the Racial Past* (Berkeley: Univ. of California Press, 2002) has a long discussion of musical appropriation, crossing over, and passing by whites and non-Black people of color in relation to Black music, 212–40.

65. Abu Jaber, *Arabian Jazz*, 294. See the discussion in chapter 1 and my "this sweet, sweet."

66. Yousef Awad has critiqued this argument on the basis that the engagements between the communities are too superficial to be a meaningful intervention and that the family disavows its connections to African Americans in other ways. See "Cartographies of Identities: Resistance, Diaspora, and Trans-cultural Dialogue in the Works of

Arab British and Arab American Women Writers," PhD diss., Univ. of Manchester, 2011, 98–99. For a fuller discussion of racial identification in *Arabian Jazz*, see his discussion on pp. 97–101. My discussion of these issues is the topic of my article "this sweet, sweet."

67. Jarrar, *A Map*, 247.

68. Lorde, *Sister*, 111.

69. Recent scholarship discusses international hip-hop culture extensively. Among others, see for example Su'ad Abdul Khabeer, *Muslim Cool: Race, Religion, and Hip Hop in the United States* (New York: NYU Press, 2016); Hisham Aidi, *Rebel Music: Race, Empire, and the New Muslim Youth Culture* (New York: Vintage, 2014); and Samy Alim, *Roc the Mic Right: The Language of Hip Hop Culture* (London: Routledge, 2006) and *You Know My Steez*. On links to politics and internationalism specifically, see Sohail Daulatzai, *Black Star, Crescent Moon: The Muslim International and Black Freedom beyond America* (Minneapolis: Univ. of Minnesota Press, 2012), 89–136.

70. Jarrar, *A Map*, 254.

71. Jarrar, 254.

72. It is no accident that this scene of conflict but also fascination played out between Nidali and her father parallels and mirrors the real-life drama over the lawsuits brought against Jay-Z for using this particular sample. Jay-Z won the suit eventually, but it is deeply imbricated in notions of cultural propriety in addition to property, and differences in musical tastes across generations, as well as traditions. See for example, Jared Malsin, "Legal Battle over Jay-Z's Sampling on Big Pimpin' Comes to Head After Eight Years," *Guardian*, April 5, 2015, https://www.theguardian.com/music/2015/apr/05/legal-battle-over-jay-zs-sampling-on-big-pimpin-comes-to-head-after-eight-years and Alyssa Klein, "Jay-Z's Egyptian Legal Troubles Over Big Pimpin Sample," April 7, 2015, *Okay Africa*, http://www.okayafrica.com/news/jay-z-big-pimpin-khosara-khosara-egyptian-song-case-heads-to-trial/.

73. Jarrar, *A Map*, 254.

74. Jarrar, 254.

75. Jarrar, 254.

76. Jarrar, 255.

77. Jarrar, 263.

78. Jarrar, 263.

79. Jarrar, 263.

80. Hammad, *Born Palestinian, Born Black*, 1996, x; Hammad, *Born Palestinian, Born Black*, 2010, 12. Spacing in the original. For a discussion of this see chapter 1, above.

81. This will be reprised in chapter 5 below in relation to Radwa Ashour's discussion of how she feels at home with African Americans in Amherst, but alienated by the rest of American society and the majority of white Americans she meets there.

82. On the racial prerequisite cases, see Gualtieri, "Strange Fruit" and *Between*; Samhan, "Not Quite White"; and Majaj, "Arab-Americans."

83. Jarrar, A Map, 166–67.

84. Jarrar, 167.

85. Jarrar, Him, Me, 142.

86. Jarrar, 142.

87. Jarrar, 139.

88. Jarrar, 139.

89. For some examples see Macollvie Jean-François, "Protests at King Tut Exhibit: 'He's Back, He's Black,'" Wenatchee World, December 20, 2005, http://www.wenatchee world.com/news/2005/dec/20/protests-at-king-tut-exhibit-hes-back-hes-black/ and American Renaissance, "Outraged Black Activists Protest That King Tut Has Been Whitewashed," June 16, 2005, https://www.amren.com/news/2005/06/outraged_black. For a good analysis of the earlier King Tut exhibition and its racial politics in the United States, including how this is connected to Middle East policy see Melani McAlister, "The Common Heritage of Mankind: Race, Nation, and Masculinity in the King Tut Exhibition," Representations 54 (1996): 80–103. See also her book Epic Encounters: Culture, Media, and US Interests in the Middle East (Berkeley: Univ. of California Press, 2005), particularly the chapter titled "King Tut, Commodity Nationalism, and the Politics of Oil 1973–1979," 125–54. This chapter discusses the racial identification of Tut as Black and the cultural politics of the 1970s in some detail.

90. In the same collection (Him, Me, Muhammad Ali) one other character, Anna, shares the same heritage—an Egyptian mother and a Black American father—in the story "Building Girls" (21), where the racial politics are not dissected and engaged in in as much detail. I am not aware of any other fictional characters in works by Arab American authors who share this background.

91. Jarrar, Him, Me, 143.

92. Jarrar, 144.

93. Jarrar's use of Muhammad Ali as a figure, therefore, echoes other literary representations by Arab writers; see, for example, my article, "Writing Arabs and Africa(ns)."

94. Jarrar, Him, Me, 159.

95. Jarrar, 159.

96. Jarrar, 160.

97. Jarrar, 142–43.

5. "The Most Pressing Causes of Our Times"

1. Radwa Ashour, "Eyewitness, Scribe and Storyteller: My Experience as a Novelist," Massachusetts Review 41, no.1 (2000): 85–92.

2. Radwa Ashour, Al-Rihla: Ayyam taliba misriyya fi Amrika (Beirut: Adab, 1983), 175; Radwa Ashour, The Journey: An Egyptian Woman Student's Memoirs in America, trans. Michelle Hartman (Northampton, MA: Interlink, 2018), 144–45. For other accounts

of this scene, as well as others that occur in the memoir, see also Mourid Barghouti's memoir *I Saw Ramallah*, trans. Ahdaf Soueif (New York: Anchor, 2003).

3. Marina Warner, "Radwa Ashour: Obituary," *Guardian*, December 8, 2014, https://www.theguardian.com/books/2014/dec/08/radwa-ashour.

4. Ashour, *Al-Rihla*, 7, *The Journey*, 6. Michelle Hartman, "Introduction to *The Journey* by Radwa Ashour," *Comparative American Studies* 13, no. 4 (2015): 211.

5. Ashour, *The Journey*.

6. Hassan, "Agency," 754.

7. Ashour, *Al-Rihla*, 170, *The Journey*, 139.

8. For a good study of these issues, see Ella Shohat and Robert Stam, *Race in Translation: Culture Wars around the Postcolonial Atlantic* (New York: NYU Press, 2012).

9. Jordan, "White English," 66

10. See works on language in the hip-hop nation, including Alim, *You Know My Steez* and *Roc the Mic* and Imani Perry, *Prophets*, and in mainstream contexts, Alim and Smitherman, *Articulate* and McWhorter, *Talking Back*.

11. Smitherman, *Talkin and Testifyin*, 41; also see discussion on pp. 39–42.

12. Smitherman, *Talkin That Talk*, 41–66.

13. Ashour, *Al-Rihla*, 163, *The Journey*, 133.

14. Ashour, *Al-Rihla*, 168, *The Journey*, 139.

15. Ashour, *Al-Rihla*, 99, *The Journey*, 80. For the original, see W. E. B. DuBois, "To the Congress of Ecrivains et Artistes Noirs," *Presence Africaine: Cultural Journal of the Negro World* 8-9-10 (1956): 390.

16. Ashour, *Al-Rihla*, 25. The translation of the word slave as "abeed" occurs on the following pages: 25, 26, 73, 97, 99, and 101.

17. Ashour, *Al-Rihla*, 133, *The Journey*, 110.

18. Ashour, *Al-Rihla*, 133, *The Journey*, 110.

19. On her distinction between Jews and Zionists, see Ashour, *Al-Rihla*, 31–32, 101–2, *The Journey*, 23–24, 83.

20. For examples of this see Ashour, *Al-Rihla*, 24, 39, 50, 51, 62, 73, 101–3, 136, 138, 146.

21. Ashour, *Al-Rihla*, 10, *The Journey*, 6.

22. See the argument for foreignized translation by Lawrence Venuti in his classic, "Hijacking Translation: How Comp Lit Continues to Suppress Translated Texts," *boundary 2* 43, no. 2 (2016): 179–204. These arguments have been taken up by many scholars of Arabic-English translation theory. See Booth, "Translation and Madness," Hartman, *Native Tongue*, and Kahf, "Packaging 'Huda'" for examples.

23. Ashour, *Al-Rihla*, 152, *The Journey*, 124. Elsewhere I have discussed the way in which Ashour uses the expression "kannana minhum" to render "as if we were a part of them" using an Arabic expression that implies belonging very strongly. See Hartman,

"Writing Arabs and Africa(ns)," 407. For more examples about belonging in the community, see Ashour, *Al-Rihla*, 6, 39, 50–51, 62, 73, 136, 138, 142, 147.

24. Two studies that explore this in depth are the now classic *How Jews Became White Folks: And What that Says About Race in America* (New Brunswick: Rutgers Univ. Press, 2002) by Karen Brodkin and the more recent work on Iranian racialization in the United States by Neda Maghbouleh, *The Limits of Whiteness: Iranian Americans and the Everyday Politics of Race* (Palo Alto: Stanford Univ. Press, 2017).

25. On how people shared food, for example, see Ashour, *Al-Rihla*, 66–67, *The Journey*, 53–54.

26. On being alienated at streaking parties, see Ashour, *Al-Rihla*, 74–75, *The Journey*, 60–61.

27. Ashour, *Al-Rihla*, 43, *The Journey*, 33.

28. For a long meditation on strategic essentialism, including how Spivak both coined the term and later disavowed it, see Sangeeta Ray, "Reading Woman, Reading Essence, Whither Gender?" in *Gayatri Chakravorty Spivak: In Other Words* (Sussex: Wiley-Blackwell, 2009), 107–38. See also the discussion of Jarrar and Abulhawa above.

29. On how anthologies build identity, a critique of essentialist identity categories, and strategic essentialism see my critique in "Grandmothers, Grape Leaves, and Kahlil Gibran." Carol Fadda-Conrey's notion of affiliation between Arab Americans and other people of color can be seen in this framework, *Arab American*. See also Harb, "Naming Oppressions."

30. In the course of translating this novel, I have presented it to dozens of groups of students, researchers, and others in different contexts, gauging their reactions. This generalization is almost universally true. I have had only one English speaker in all of these presentations not identify this as at least "awkward."

31. Hartman, "Writing Arabs and Africa(ns)."

32. Ashour, *Al-Rihla*, 138, *The Journey*, 113–14.

33. Smitherman, *Talkin and Testifyin*, 57. See also Gates, *Loose Canons*, 131–51.

34. Ashour, *Al-Rihla*, 139, *The Journey*, 114.

35. Ashour, *Al-Rihla*, 139, *The Journey*, 114.

36. Ashour, *Al-Rihla*, 148–49, *The Journey*, 121.

37. Ashour, *Al-Rihla*, 147, *The Journey*, 120.

38. Ashour, *Al-Rihla*, 65, *The Journey*, 53.

39. The long history of Palestinian-Puerto Rican solidarity has been begun to be documented by scholarship; see Sara Awartani, "In Solidarity: Palestine in the Puerto Rican Political Imaginary," *Radical History Review* 128 (2017): 199–222 and Abdulhadi, "The Deep Bonds" and "Marching." The latter two pieces are written on the occasion of the Puerto Rican Day Parade 2017, where a significant delegation of Palestinians marched and supported the marshal, political prisoner Oscar López Rivera.

40. Ashour, *Al-Rihla*, 50, *The Journey*, 41.

41. Ashour, *Al-Rihla*, 51, *The Journey*, 41–42.

42. Ashour, *Al-Rihla*, 148–49, *The Journey*, 120–21.

43. Ashour, *Al-Rihla*, 97, *The Journey*, 79.

44. Ashour, *Al-Rihla*, 98, *The Journey*, 79.

45. Ashour, *Al-Rihla*, 98, *The Journey*, 79.

46. Ashour, *Al-Rihla*, 98, *The Journey*, 79.

47. Ashour, *Al-Rihla*, 99, *The Journey*, 80; DuBois, "To the Congress," 390.

48. Ashour, *Al-Rihla*, 100, *The Journey*, 81.

49. Shohat and Stam, *Race in Translation*.

50. Shohat and Stam, xiv.

51. Alim and Smitherman, *Articulate* and McWhorter, *Talking Back*.

52. For example, see Apter's *Against World Literature*. Critics of Arabic literature have engaged this concept in a number of productive and evocative ways. For example, see Stephen Sheehi's "Untranslatability, Discomfort, Ideology: Should We Teach Arabic Literature?" in *Teaching Modern Arabic Literature in Translation*, ed. Michelle Hartman (New York: MLA, 2018), 41–61, which asks not how but *if* we should teach Arabic literature in translation in the United States today.

53. Venuti, "Hijacking Translation."

54. I would here like to acknowledge only some of the people with whom I worked extensively on this text and its translation in discussion over time: Ghiwa AbiHaidar, Dima Ayoub, Yasmine Nachabe Taan, Ralph Haddad, rosalind hampton, Amanda Hartman, Rabab Abdulhadi, Rula Jurdi, among others.

55. Ashour, *Al-Rihla*, 6, 83, *The Journey* 1, 87.

56. Ashour, *Al-Rihla*, 120–22, *The Journey*, 99–100.

57. Ashour, *Al-Rihla*, 119, *The Journey*, 99.

58. Ashour, *Al-Rihla*, 62–63, *The Journey*, 50–51.

59. Ashour, *Al-Rihla*, 173–75, *The Journey*, 143–45.

60. Ashour, *Al-Rihla*, 114–15, *The Journey*, 99–95.

61. Ashour, *Al-Rihla*, 83, 110, *The Journey*, 66–67, 91.

62. Ashour, *Al-Rihla*, 109, *The Journey*, 90.

63. Keith P. Feldman, "Towards an Afro-Arab Diasporic Culture: The Translational Practices of David Graham Du Bois," *Alif: Journal of Comparative Poetics* (2011): 152.

64. Gayatri Chakravorty Spivak, "The Politics of Translation," in *Outside in the Teaching Machine* (London: Routledge, 1993), 188.

65. Hartman, "Reading Arabs and Africa(ns)" and "Dreams," 68–69.

66. In fact, in the final published translation of *The Journey*, the text by Douglass is restored to its original form in English, but Hughes's famous poem had to be omitted and only referred to by one line because of copyright protection. See my translator's note in *The Journey*, 147–49.

67. See her translations in Mourid Barghouti, *Midnight and Other Poems* (London: Arc, 2008) and Tamim Barghouti, *In Jerusalem and Other Poems* (Northampton, MA: Interlink, 2017).

68. See Vera M. Kutzinski's book on his verse and his translation into several languages, *The Worlds of Langston Hughes: Modernism and Translation in the Americas* (Ithaca: Cornell Univ. Press, 2013).

69. Hartman, "Dreams," 71.

70. Hartman, 72-73.

71. Langston Hughes, *Ana aydan ughani Amrika*, trans. Samir Abu Hawwash (Fribourg: Kamel, 2009).

72. The speech was printed in the *New York Times* on that day and is available in the archives; see Frederick Douglass, "What, to the American Slave, Is Your Fourth of July?," *New York Times*, July 4, 1975, http://www.nytimes.com/1975/07/04/archives/1852-what-to -the-american-slave-is-your-4th-of-july.html?_r=0.

73. It is perhaps important to note that Ashour does not include his imprecations to Black Americans to master Standard English in the excerpts included. This point in Douglass's speech is expanded upon by Rickford and Rickford, *Spoken Soul*, 227, and relevant to the larger issues I am discussing throughout *Breaking Broken English*.

74. Ashour, *Al-Rihla*, 164, *The Journey*, 134.

75. Ashour, *Al-Rihla*, 164, 168, *The Journey*, 134, 137.

76. Ashour, *Al-Rihla*, 167, *The Journey*, 135. An interesting back-translation note is that the Emancipation Proclamation is translated into an expression in Arabic that would more literally be rendered "Declaration of Freeing the Slaves."

77. Ashour, *Al-Rihla*, 169, *The Journey*, 137–38.

78. Ashour, *Al-Rihla*, 30–31, *The Journey*, 22–23.

79. See Third World Students in Solidarity with Arab Brothers and Sisters, "Third World People Must Work for the Liberation of Palestine," *The Daily Collegian*, October 26, 1973, 3.

Conclusions

1. Lorde, *Sister*, 134.

Bibliography

Literary Texts

Abulhawa, Susan. *Mornings in Jenin.* New York: Bloomsbury, 2010.

Ahmed, Saladin. "Poem for Countee Cullen." In *Post-Gibran: Anthology of New Arab American Writing,* edited by Munir Akash and Khaled Mattawa, 255–57. Syracuse: Syracuse Univ. Press, 1999.

Ashour, Radwa. *Al-Rihla: Ayyam taliba misriyya fi Amrika.* Beirut: Adab, 1983.

———. *The Journey: An Egyptian Woman Student's Memoirs in America.* Translated by Michelle Hartman. Northampton, MA: Interlink, 2018.

Hammad, Suheir. *Born Palestinian, Born Black.* New York: Harlem River Press, 1996.

———. *Born Palestinian, Born Black & the Gaza Suite.* Brooklyn, New York: UpSet Press, 2010.

———. *breaking poems.* New York: Cypher Books, 2008.

———. "first writing since." In *September 11, 2001: Feminist Perspectives,* edited by Susan Hawthorne and Bronwyn Winter, 4–9. Melbourne: Spinifex, 2002.

Jarrar, Randa. *Him, Me, Muhammad Ali.* New York: Sarabande, 2016.

———. *A Map of Home.* New York: Penguin, 2009.

Melhem, D. H. *Art and Politics/Politics and Art.* Syracuse: Syracuse Univ. Press, 2010.

———. *New York Poems.* Syracuse: Syracuse Univ. Press, 2005.

———. *Notes on 94th Street.* New York: Poet's Press, 1972.

Nye, Naomi Shihab. "To Jamyla Bolden of Ferguson, Missouri." In *Voices in the Air: Poems for Listeners.* New York: Greenwillow, 2018. https://www.poets.org/poetsorg/poem/jamyla-bolden-ferguson-missouri; https://soundcloud.com/poets-org/naomi-shihab-nye-to-jamyla-bolden-of-ferguson-missouri.

Works Cited

Abdulhadi, Rabab. "Activism and Exile: Palestinianness and the Politics of Solidarity." In *Local Actions: Cultural Activism, Power, and Public Life in America*, edited by Melissa Checker and Maggie Fishman, 231–54. New York: Columbia Univ. Press, 2005.

———. "Black Radicalism, Insurgency in Israel/Palestine and the Idea of Solidarity." Paper presented at the American Studies Association annual meeting, Los Angeles, CA, November 7, 2014.

———. "The Deep Bonds of Palestinian-Puerto Rican Solidarity Were on Display at This Year's NYC Puerto Rican Day Parade." Mondoweiss, June 15, 2017. http://mondoweiss.net/2017/06/palestinian-solidarity-display/.

———. "Marching with Oscar López Rivera: A Long History of Palestinian-Puerto Rican Solidarity." Mondoweiss, June 19, 2017. http://mondoweiss.net/2017/06/marching-palestinian-solidarity/.

———. "Palestinian Resistance and the Indivisibility of Justice." In *With Stones in Our Hands: Writings on Muslims, Racism, and Empire*, edited by Sohail Dautlatzai and Junaid Rana, 56–72. Minneapolis: Univ. of Minnesota Press, 2018.

———. "Roundtable on Anti-Blackness." *Jadaliyya*, June 3, 2015. http://www.jadaliyya.com/pages/index/21764/roundtable-on-anti-blackness-and-black-palestinian.

———. "The Spirit of 68 Lives On!: Palestine Advocacy and the Indivisibility of Justice." Mondoweiss, July 14, 2017. http://mondoweiss.net/2017/07/palestine-advocacy-indivisibility.

———. "'White' or Not? Displacement and the Construction of (Racialized and Gendered) Palestinianness in the United States." Paper presented at the Middle East Studies Association annual meeting, Washington DC, November 24, 2002.

———. "Zionism as Racism and the Network of Lies." Mondoweiss, July 21, 2017. http://mondoweiss.net/2017/07/spirit-zionism-network/.

Abdulhadi, Rabab, Nadine Naber, and Evelyne Alsultany, eds. *Arab and Arab American Feminisms: Gender, Violence and Belonging*. Syracuse: Syracuse Univ. Press, 2011.

Abdulhadi, Rabab, and Dana Olwan. "Shifting Geographies of Knowledge and Power: Palestine and American Studies." *American Quarterly* 67, no 4 (2015): 993–1006.

Abdul Khabeer, Su'ad. *Muslim Cool: Race, Religion, and Hip Hop in the United States*. New York: NYU Press, 2016.

Abraham, Nabeel, Sally Howell, and Andrew Shyrock, eds. *Arab Detroit 9/11: Life in the Terror Decade*. Detroit: Wayne State Univ. Press, 2011.

Abraham, Nabeel, and Andrew Shyrock, eds. *Arab Detroit: From Margin to Mainstream*. Detroit: Wayne State Univ. Press, 2000.

Abu Jaber, Diana. *Arabian Jazz*. New York: Norton, 1993.

Abukhater, Jalal. "Black People against Zionism, Black People against Apartheid." Electronic Intifada, March, 6, 2012. https://electronicintifada.net/blogs/jalal -abukhater/black-people-against-zionism-black-people-against-apartheid.

Abulhawa, Susan. "Confronting Anti-Black Racism in the Arab World." Al Jazeera, July 7, 2013. http://www.aljazeera.com/indepth/opinion/2013/06/2013 62472519107286.html.

———. "The Palestinian Struggle is a Black Struggle." Electronic Intifada, June 11, 2013. https://electronicintifada.net/content/palestinian-struggle-black -struggle/12530.

Abu-Lughod, Lila. *Do Muslim Women Need Saving?* Cambridge: Harvard Univ. Press, 2013.

Abu-Manneh, Bashir. *The Palestinian Novel: From 1948 to the Present*. Cambridge: Cambridge Univ. Press, 2016.

Abu-Shomar, Ayman M. "Diasporic Reconciliations of Politics, Love and Trauma: Susan Abulhawa's Quest for Identity in *Mornings in Jenin*." *Advances in Language and Literary Studies* 6, no. 2 (2015): 127–36.

Adnan, Etel. "Beirut-Hell Express." In *Grape Leaves: A Century of Arab American Poetry*, edited by Gregory Orfalea and Sharif Elmusa, 87–99. Northampton, MA: Interlink, 2000.

AFP. "Outraged Black Activists Protest That King Tut Has Been Whitewashed." American Renaissance, June 16, 2005. https://www.amren.com/news/2005 /06/outraged_black/.

Ahmed, Leila. *A Border Passage: From Cairo to America, A Woman's Journey*. New York: Penguin, 2012.

Ahmed, Saladin. *Throne of the Crescent Moon*. New York: DAW Books, 2012.

Aidi, Hisham. *Rebel Music: Race, Empire, and the New Muslim Youth Culture*. New York: Vintage, 2014.

Akash, Munir, and Khaled Mattawa, eds. *Post-Gibran: Anthology of New Arab American Writing*. Syracuse: Syracuse Univ. Press, 1999.

Alameddine, Rabih. *Koolaids: The Art of War*. New York: Picador, 1998.

Albakry, Mohammed, and Jonathan Siler. "Into the Arab American Borderland: Bilingual Creativity in Randa Jarrar's *A Map of Home*." *Arab Studies Quarterly* 34, no. 2 (2012): 109–21.

Alim, H. Samy. *Roc the Mic Right: The Language of Hip Hop Culture*. London: Routledge, 2006.

———. *You Know My Steez: An Ethnographic and Sociolinguistic Study of Style-shifting in a Black American Speech Community*. Durham, NC: Duke Univ. Press, 2004.

Alim, H. Samy, and Geneva Smitherman. *Articulate While Black: Barack Obama, Language, and Race in the U.S.* Oxford: Oxford Univ. Press, 2012.

Allen, Roger. "The Happy Traitor: Tales of Translation." *Comparative Literature Studies* 47, no. 4 (2010): 472–86.

Al-Ma'amari, Abdulrahman, Noraini Md Yusof, and Ravichandran Vengadasamy. "Strangers in My Home: The Quest for Identity in *Mornings in Jenin*." *Procedia-Social and Behavioral Sciences* 118 (2014): 29–36.

Anglesey, Zoe, ed. *Listen Up!: Spoken Word Poetry*. New York: Ballantine, 1999.

Antoon, Sinan. "Why Speaking Arabic in America Feels like a Crime." *Guardian*, April 19, 2016. http://www.theguardian.com/commentisfree/2016/apr/19/why-speaking-arabic-america-feels-like-crime.

Anzaldúa, Gloria, and AnaLouise Keating, eds. *This Bridge We Call Home: Radical Visions for Transformation*. London: Routledge, 2002.

Apter, Emily. *Against World Literature: On the Politics of Untranslatability*. London: Verso, 2014.

Ashcroft, Bill, Gareth Griffith, and Helen Tiffin. *The Empire Writes Back: Theory and Practice in Post-colonial Literatures*. London: Routledge, 1989.

Ashour, Radwa. *Athqal min Radwa*. Cairo: Dar Al-Shorouq, 2013.

———. *Atyaf*. Cairo: Dar al-Hilal, 1999.

———. "Eyewitness, Scribe and Storyteller: My Experience as a Novelist." *Massachusetts Review* 41, no.1 (2000): 85–92.

———. "My Experience with Writing." In *The View from Within: Writers and Critics on Contemporary Arabic Literature*, edited by Ferial Ghazoul and Barbara Harlow, 27–33. Cairo: American Univ. in Cairo Press, 1994.

———. "The Search for a Black Poetics: A Study of Afro-American Critical Writing." PhD diss., Univ. of Massachusetts–Amherst, 1975.

———. *Siraaj*. Cairo: Dar al-Hilal, 1992.

———. *Siraaj: An Arab Tale*. Translated by Barbara Romaine. Austin: Univ. of Texas Press, 2007.

————. *Specters*. Translated by Barbara Romaine. Northampton, MA: Interlink, 2010.

Atshan, Sa'ed, and Darnell L. Moore. "Reciprocal Solidarity: Where the Black and Palestinian Queer Struggles Meet." *Biography* 37, no. 2 (2014): 680–705.

Awad, Yousef. "Cartographies of Identities: Resistance, Diaspora, and Transcultural Dialogue in the Works of Arab British and Arab American Women Writers." PhD diss., Univ. of Manchester, 2011.

Awartani, Sara. "In Solidarity: Palestine in the Puerto Rican Political Imaginary." *Radical History Review* 128 (2017): 199–222.

Ayoub, Dima. "Translatability in Contemporary Arab Women's Literature." PhD diss., McGill Univ., 2015.

Baldwin, James. "Black English: A Dishonest Argument." In *The Cross of Redemption: Uncollected Writings*, edited by Randall Kenan, 125–30. New York: Doubleday, 2010.

————. "If Black English Isn't a Language, Then Tell Me What Is." *New York Times*, July 29, 1979. https://www.nytimes.com/books/98/03/29/specials/baldwin-english.html.

————. "On Language, Race and the Black Writer." In *The Cross of Redemption: Uncollected Writings*, edited by Randall Kenan, 114–17. New York: Doubleday, 2010. Originally published in the *Los Angeles Times*, April 29, 1979.

Barghouti, Mourid. *I Saw Ramallah*. Translated by Ahdaf Soueif. New York: Anchor, 2003.

————. *Midnight and Other Poems*. Translated by Radwa Ashour. London: Arc, 2008.

Barghouti, Tamim. *In Jerusalem and Other Poems*. Translated by Radwa Ashour. Northampton, MA: Interlink, 2017.

Barrows-Friedman, Nora. "'I Wasn't Prepared for the White Supremacy': Dream Hampton on her Visit to Palestine." Electronic Intifada, February 4, 2014. https://electronicintifada.net/blogs/nora-barrows-friedman/i-wasnt-prepared-white-supremacy-dream-hampton-her-visit-palestine.

Bayoumi, Moustafa. *How Does It Feel to Be a Problem? Being Young and Arab in America*. New York: Penguin, 2009.

Booth, Marilyn. "On Translation and Madness." *Translation Review* 65, no. 1 (2003): 47–53.

Bosch Vilarrubias, Marta. "New Arab Masculinities: A Feminist Approach to Arab American Men in Post 9/11 Literature Written by Women." In *Masculinity and Literary Studies: Intersections and New Directions*, edited by Joseph M. Armengol, Marta Bosch Vilarrubias, Àngels Carabí, and Teresa Requena, 66–76. London: Routledge, 2017.

Bracey, John H., Jr., Sonia Sanchez, and James Smethurst. *SOS—Calling All Black People: A Black Arts Movement Reader*. Amherst: Univ. of Massachusetts Press, 2014.

Brenner, Lenni, and Matthew Quest. *Black Liberation and Palestine Solidarity*. Atlanta: On our Own Authority! Publishing, 2013.

Brodkin, Karen. *How Jews Became White Folks: And What That Says About Race in America*. New Brunswick, NJ: Rutgers Univ. Press, 2002.

Callahan, John F. *In the African-American Grain: Call-and-Response in Twentieth-Century Black Fiction*. Champaign: Univ. of Illinois Press, 1989.

Cariello, Marta. "Coming of Age in the Solitude of the Lost Land: Randa Jarrar's *A Map of Home*." *Hawwa: Journal of Women in the Middle East and the Islamic World* 12, no. 2–3 (2014): 268–88.

———. "The Pervasive Borderland: Anglophone Arab Poetry and Polyglossia." In *Cultures and Languages International Conference Proceedings Two*, 10–24. El-Jadida, Morocco: Chouaib Dukkali Univ., 2012.

Charara, Hayan. *Inclined to Speak: An Anthology of Contemporary Arab American Poetry*. Fayetteville: Arkansas Univ. Press, 2008.

Cleaver, Eldridge. *Soul on Ice*. San Francisco: Ramparts Press, 1968.

Coval, Kevin, Quraysh Ali Lansana, and Nate Marshall, eds. *The BreakBeat Poets: New American Poetry in the Age of Hip-Hop*. Chicago: Haymarket, 2015.

Daulatzai, Sohail. *Black Star, Crescent Moon: The Muslim International and Black Freedom beyond America*. Minneapolis: Univ. of Minnesota Press, 2012.

Davis, Angela. *Freedom Is a Constant Struggle: Ferguson, Palestine and the Foundation of a Movement*. Chicago: Haymarket, 2016.

———. "Prison Memoirs." *Village Voice*, October 10, 1974. https://news.google.com/newspapers?nid=KEtq3P1Vf8oC&dat=19741010&printsec=frontpage&hl=en.

Davis Bailey, Kristian. "Black-Palestinian Solidarity in the Ferguson-Gaza Era." *American Quarterly* 67, no. 4 (2015): 1017–26.

———. "The Ferguson/Palestine Connection." *Ebony*, August 19, 2014. http://www.ebony.com/news-views/the-fergusonpalestine-connection-403#axzz3Fgljw369.

Davis, Kimberly Chabot. "White Book Clubs and African American Literature: The Promise and Limitations of Cross-Racial Empathy." *Literature Interpretation Theory* 19, no. 2 (2008): 155–86.

Douglass, Frederick. "What, to the American Slave, Is Your Fourth of July?" *New York Times*, July 4, 1975. http://www.nytimes.com/1975/07/04/archives/1852-what-to-the-american-slave-is-your-4th-of-july.html?_r=0.

Drabinski, John E. "Vernaculars of Home." *Critical Philosophy of Race* 3, no. 2 (2015): 303–26.

DuBois, David Graham. *And Bid Him Sing*. Oakland, CA: Ramparts, 1975.

DuBois, W. E. B. "To the Congress of Ecrivains et Artistes Noirs." *Presence Africaine: Cultural Journal of the Negro World* 8-9-10 (1956): 390.

Dworkin, Ira. "Radwa Ashour, African American Criticism, and the Production of Modern Arabic Literature." *Cambridge Journal of Postcolonial Literary Inquiry* 5, no. 1 (2018): 1–19.

Edwards, Brent Hayes. *The Practice of Diaspora: Literature, Translation and the Rise of Black Internationalism*. Cambridge: Harvard Univ. Press, 2003.

El Gendy, Nancy. "Trickster Humour in Randa Jarrar's *A Map of Home*: Negotiating Arab American Muslim Female Sexuality." *Women: A Cultural Review* 27, no. 1 (2016): 1–19.

Elhassan, Jana Fawwaz. *The Ninety-Ninth Floor*. Translated by Michelle Hartman. Northampton, MA: Interlink Books, 2017.

Elia, Nada. "The Burden of Representation: When Palestinians Speak Out." In *Arab and Arab American Feminisms: Gender, Violence, and Belonging*, edited by Rabab Abdulhadi, Evelyn Alsultany, and Nadine Naber, 141–58. Syracuse: Syracuse Univ. Press, 2011.

Ellis, Catherine, and Stephen Smith. *Say it Plain: A Century of Great African American Speeches*. London: New Press, 2005.

Erian, Alicia. *Towelhead*. New York: Simon & Schuster, 2006.

Fadda-Conrey, Carol. "Arab American Literature in the Ethnic Borderland: Cultural Intersections in Diana Abu-Jaber's *Crescent*." *MELUS Journal* 31, no. 4 (2006): 197–205.

———. *Contemporary Arab American Fiction: Transnational Reconfigurations of Citizenship and Belonging*. New York: NYU Press, 2014.

———. "Weaving Poetic Autobiographies: Individual and Community Identities in the Poetry of Mohja Kahf and Suheir Hammad." In *Arab Women's Lives Retold: Exploring Identity through Writing*, edited by Nuwar Al-Hassan Golley, 155–76. Syracuse: Syracuse Univ. Press, 2007.

Farr, Cecilia Konchar. *Reading Oprah: How Oprah's Book Club Changed the Way America Reads*. Binghamton: SUNY Press, 2005.

Feldman, Keith P. *A Shadow over Palestine: The Imperial Life of Race in America*. Minneapolis: Univ. of Minnesota Press, 2015.

———. "Towards an Afro-Arab Diasporic Culture: The Translational Practices of David Graham Du Bois." *Alif: Journal of Comparative Poetics* (2011): 152–72.

Gana, Nouri, ed. *The Edinburgh Companion to the Arab Novel in English: The Politics of Anglo Arab and Arab American Literature and Culture*. Oxford: Oxford Univ. Press, 2013.

Gates, Henry Louis, Jr. *Loose Canons: Notes on the Culture Wars*. Oxford: Oxford Univ. Press, 1992.

———. "Zora Neale Hurston and the Speakerly Text." In *The Signifying Monkey: A Theory of African-American Literary Criticism*, 170–216. Oxford: Oxford Univ. Press, 2014.

Gates, Henry Louis, Jr., ed. *Black Literature and Literary Theory*. London: Routledge, 2016.

Gates, Henry Louis, Jr., and Jennifer Burton, eds. *Call and Response: Key Debates in African American Studies*. New York: Norton, 2008.

Gohar, Siddik. "Exile and Revolt: Arab and Afro-American Poets in Dialogue." In *Creativity in Exile*, edited by Michael Hanne, 181–95. Amsterdam: Rodopoi, 2004.

Gualtieri, Sarah. *Between Arab and White: Race and Ethnicity in the Early Syrian American Diaspora*. Berkeley: Univ. of California Press, 2009.

———. "Strange Fruit? Syrian Immigrants, Extralegal Violence and Racial Formation in the United States." In *Race and Arab Americans before and after 9/11*, edited by Amaney Jamal and Nadine Naber, 147–69. Syracuse: Syracuse Univ. Press, 2008.

Gurel, Perin. "Transnational Feminism, Islam, and the Other Woman: How to Teach." *Radical Teacher* 86, no. 1 (2009): 66–70.

hampton, rosalind, and Michelle Hartman. "Toward Language and Resistance: A Breaking Manifesto." In *Manifestos for World Thought*, edited by Lucian Stone and Jason Bahbak Mohaghegh, 115–28. London: Rowman and Littlefield, 2017.

Harb, Sirène. "Between Languages and Selves: Migratory Agency, Fragmentation and Representation in Suheir Hammad's *breaking poems*." *Contemporary Women's Writing* 6, no. 2 (2012): 122–39.

———. "Naming Oppressions, Representing Empowerment: June Jordan's and Suheir Hammad's Poetic Projects." *Feminist Formations* 26, no. 3 (2014): 71–99.

———. "Transformative Practices and Historical Revision: Suheir Hammad's *Born Palestinian, Born Black*." *Studies in the Humanities* 35, no. 1 (2008): 34–49.

Hartman, Michelle. "'Besotted with the Bright Lights of Imperialism'? Arab Subjectivity Constructed against New York's Many Faces." *Journal of Arabic Literature* 35, no. 3 (2004): 270–96.

———. "A Debke Beat Funky as PE's Riff: Hip Hop Poetry and Politics in Suheir Hammad's *Born Palestinian, Born Black*." *Black Arts Quarterly* 7, no. 1 (2002): 6–8.

———. "Dreams Deferred, Translated: Radwa Ashour and Langston Hughes." *CLINA* 2, no. 1 (2016).

———. "Grandmothers, Grape Leaves, and Kahlil Gibran: Writing Race in Anthologies of Arab American Literature." In Jamal and Naber, *Race and Arab Americans*, 170–203.

———. "Introduction to *The Journey* by Radwa Ashour." *Comparative American Studies* 13, no. 4 (2015): 209–19.

———. "'My Tale's Too Long to Tell:' *The Locust and the Bird* between South Lebanon and New York City." *Journal of Arabic Literature* 46, nos. 2–3 (2015): 168–92.

———. *Native Tongue, Stranger Talk: The Arabic and French Literary Landscapes of Lebanon.* Syracuse: Syracuse Univ. Press, 2014.

———. "'this sweet, sweet music': Jazz, Sam Cooke and Reading Arab American Literary Identities." *MELUS Journal* 31, no. 4 (2006): 145–65.

———. "Writing Arabs and Africa(ns) in America: Adonis and Radwa Ashour from Harlem to Lady Liberty." *International Journal of Middle East Studies* 37, no. 3 (2005): 397–420.

Hassan, Waïl S. "Agency and Translational Literature: Ahdaf Soueif's *Map of Love*." *PMLA* 121, no. 3 (2006): 753–68.

———. *Immigrant Narratives: Orientalism and Cultural Translation in Arab American and Arab British Literature.* Oxford: Oxford Univ. Press, 2011.

———. "Which Languages?" *Comparative Literature* 65, no. 1 (2013): 5–14.

———. "World Literature in the Age of Globalization: Reflections on an Anthology." *College English* 63, no. 1 (2000): 38–47.

Helal, Marwa. "The Vernacular Home." *American Book Review* 34, no. 1 (2012): 5.

Hinton, Laura, ed. *Jayne Cortez, Adrienne Rich, and the Feminist Superhero: Voice, Vision, Politics, and Performance in U.S. Contemporary Women's Poetics.* London: Rowman and Littlefield, 2016.

Hughes, Langston. *Ana aydan ughani Amrika.* Translated by Samir Abu Hawwash. Fribourg: Kamel, 2009.

——. "Harlem (2)." In *The Collected Works of Langston Hughes: Volume Three, Poetry 1951–1967,* edited by Arnold Rampersad. Columbia: Univ. of Missouri Press, 2001.

Hurston, Zora Neale. *Their Eyes Were Watching God.* New York: Harper Perennial, 2006.

Jadallah, Dina. "Review: *A Map of Home* by Randa Jarrar." *Arab Studies Quarterly* 32, no. 2 (2010): 109–13.

Jamal, Amaney, and Nadine Naber, eds. *Race and Arab Americans Before and After 9/11: From Invisible Citizens to Visible Subjects.* Syracuse: Syracuse Univ. Press, 2007.

Jean-François, Macollvie. "Protests at King Tut Exhibit: He's Back, He's Black." *Wenatchee World,* December 20, 2005. http://www.wenatcheeworld.com/news/2005/dec/20/protests-at-king-tut-exhibit-hes-back-hes-black/.

Jordan, June. "Affirmative Acts: Language, Information, and Power." In *Affirmative Acts: Political Essays,* 240–56. New York: Anchor, 1998.

——. "Moving towards Home." In *Living Room: New Poems, 1980–1984,* 132–34. New York: Thunder's Mouth Press, 1985.

——. "Nobody Mean More to Me Than You and the Future Life of Willie Jordan." In *On Call: Political Essays,* 123–39. Boston: South End Press, 1985.

——. "White English/Black English: The Politics of Translation (1972)." In *Civil Wars,* 59–73. New York: Simon & Schuster, 1981.

Joseph, Lawrence. "Sand Nigger." In *Curriculum Vitae,* 27–29. Pittsburgh: Univ. of Pittsburgh Press, 1988.

Kadi, Joanna (Joe), ed. *Food for Our Grandmothers: Writings by Arab American and Arab Canadian Feminists.* Boston: South End Press, 1994.

Kahf, Mohja. *The Girl in the Tangerine Scarf.* New York: Carroll & Graf, 2006.

——. "Packaging 'Huda': Sha'rawi's Memoirs in the United States Reception Environment." In *Going Global: The Transnational Reception of Third World Women Writers,* edited by Amal Amireh and Lisa Suhair Majaj, 148–72. New York: Garland, 2000.

Kaldas, Pauline, and Khaled Mattawa, eds. *Dinarzad's Children: An Anthology of Contemporary Arab American Fiction*. Fayetteville: Univ. of Arkansas Press, 2005.

Kanafani, Ghassan. "Returning to Haifa." In *Palestine's Children: Returning to Haifa and Other Stories*, 149–96. Translated by Barbara Harlow and Karen E. Riley. Boulder, CO: Three Continents Press, 2000.

Kane, Alex. "The Growing Ties Between #Blacklivesmatter and Palestine." Mondoweiss, January 26, 2015. http://mondoweiss.net/2015/01/between-blacklives matter-palestine/.

Kirby, David K. "Countee Cullen's 'Heritage': A Black Waste Land." *South Atlantic Bulletin* 36, no. 4 (1971): 14–20. https://www.jstor.org/stable/3196596.

Klein, Alyssa. "Jay-Z's Egyptian Legal Troubles over Big Pimpin Sample." Okay Africa, April 7, 2015. http://www.okayafrica.com/news/jay-z-big-pimpin-khosara -khosara-egyptian-song-case-heads-to-trial/.

Knopf-Newman, Marcy Jane. "Broken Ground." *Journal of Palestine Studies* 39, no. 4 (2010): 263–64.

———. *The Politics of Teaching Palestine to Americans*. New York: Palgrave-Macmillan, 2001.

———. "Review: *Mornings in Jenin*." *Journal of Palestine Studies* 39, no. 4 (2010): 83–84. https://bodyontheline.files.wordpress.com/2011/11/jps3904_06_recent -books_8.pdf.

Kombluh, Felicia Ann. *The Battle for Welfare Rights: Politics and Poverty in Modern America*. Philadelphia: Univ. of Pennsylvania Press, 2007.

Kulbaga, Theresa A. "Pleasurable Pedagogies: *Reading Lolita in Tehran* and the Rhetoric of Empathy." *College English* 70, no. 5 (2008): 506–21.

Kutzinski, Vera M. *The Worlds of Langston Hughes: Modernism and Translation in the Americas*. Ithaca: Cornell Univ. Press, 2013.

Lomax, Michael. "Countee Cullen: A Key to the Puzzle." In *Harlem Renaissance Re-examined: A Revised and Expanded Edition*, edited by Victor A. Kramer and Robert A. Russ. Troy, NY: Whitston, 1997.

Long, Elizabeth. *Book Clubs: Women and the Uses of Reading in Everyday Life*. Chicago: Univ. of Chicago Press, 2003.

Lorde, Audre. *Sister/Outsider: Essays and Speeches*. Freedom, CA: Crossing Press, 1984.

Lubin, Alex. "'Fear of an Arab Planet': The Sounds and Rhythms of Afro-Arab Internationalism." *Journal of Transnational American Studies* 5, no. 1 (2013).

———. *Geographies of Liberation: The Making of an Afro-Arab Political Imaginary*. Chapel Hill: Univ. of North Carolina Press, 2014.

Maghbouleh, Neda. *The Limits of Whiteness: Iranian Americans and the Everyday Politics of Race*. Palo Alto: Stanford Univ. Press, 2017.

Maira, Sunaina. "We A'int Missing": Palestinian Hip Hop—A Transnational Youth Movement. *The New Centennial Review* 8, no. 2 (2008): 161–92

Majaj, Lisa Suhair. "Arab-Americans and the Meanings of Race." In *Postcolonial Theory and the United States: Race, Ethnicity, and Literature*, edited by Amritjit Singh and Peter Schmidt, 320–37. Jackson: Univ. of Mississippi Press, 2000.

Maleh, Layla, ed. *Arab Voices in the Diaspora: Critical Perspectives on Anglophone Arab Literature*. Amsterdam: Rodopi, 2009.

Malsin, Jared. "Legal Battle over Jay-Z's Sampling on Big Pimpin' Comes to Head After Eight Years." *Guardian*, April 5, 2015. https://www.theguardian.com/music/2015/apr/05/legal-battle-over-jay-zs-sampling-on-big-pimpin-comes-to-head-after-eight-years.

McAlister, Melani. "The Common Heritage of Mankind: Race, Nation, and Masculinity in the King Tut Exhibition." *Representations* 54 (1996): 80–103.

———. *Epic Encounters: Culture, Media, and US Interests in the Middle East*. Berkeley: Univ. of California Press, 2005.

McWhorter, John. *Talking Back, Talking Black: Truths about America's Lingua Franca*. New York: Bellevue, 2017.

Medeiros, Paulo de. "'Poetry Shall Not Serve': Poetry and Political Resistance." *eLyra: Revista da Rede Internacional Lyracompoetics* 1, no. 1 (2013).

Medina, Tony, and Louis Reyes Rivera, eds. *Bum Rush the Page: A Def Poetry Jam*. New York: Three Rivers Press, 2001.

Melhem, D. H. *Country: An Organic Poem*. Merrick, NY: Cross Cultural Communications, 1998.

———. "Dudley Randall: A Humanist View." *Black American Literature Forum* 17, no. 4 (1983): 157.

———. *Gwendolyn Brooks: Poetry and the Heroic Voice*. Lexington: Univ. Press of Kentucky, 1988.

———. *Heroism in the New Black Poetry: Introductions and Interviews*. Lexington: Univ. Press of Kentucky, 2015.

———. "A MELUS Profile and Interview: Jayne Cortez." *MELUS Journal* 21, no. 1 (1996): 71–79.

———. *Rest in Love*. New York: Dovetail, 1975.

————. "Revolution: The Constancy of Change: An Interview with Amiri Baraka." *Black American Literature Forum* 16, no. 3 (1982): 87.

————. "Sonia Sanchez: Will and Spirit." *MELUS Journal* 12, no. 3 (1985): 73–98.

Metres, Philip. "Introduction to Focus: Arab American Literature after 9/11." *American Book Review* 34, no. 1 (2012): 3–4.

Moore, Darnell. "The Occupation Stole my Words, June Jordan Helped me to Find Them." *The Feminist Wire*, March 24, 2016, originally March 1, 2012. http://www.thefeministwire.com/2016/03/june-jordan-and-israeli-occupation/.

Moraga, Cherríe, and Gloria Anzaldúa, eds. *This Bridge Called My Back: Writings by Radical Women of Color*. Watertown, MA: Persephone, 1981.

Morrison, Toni. *Beloved*. New York: Knopf, 1987.

Morsy, Soheir. "Beyond the Honorary 'White' Classification of Egyptians: Societal Identity in Historical Context." In *Race*, edited by Steven Gregory and Roger Sanjek, 175–98. New Brunswick, NJ: Rutgers Univ. Press, 1994.

Moten, Fred. *In the Break: The Aesthetics of the Black Radical Tradition*. Minneapolis: Univ. of Minnesota Press, 2003.

Muaddi-Darraj, Susan, ed. *Scheherazade's Legacy: Arab and Arab American Women's Voices on Writing*. Westport, CT: Praeger, 2004.

Muharram, Mohammed Abdullah Hussein. "The Marginalization of Arabic Fiction in the Postcolonial World and English Curriculum: Slips? Or Orientalism and Racism." *Minnesota Review* 78 (2012): 130–45.

Naber, Nadine Christine. *Arab Americans: Gender, Cultural Politics and Activism*. New York: NYU Press, 2012.

————. "Arab and Black Feminisms: Joint Struggle and Transnational Anti-Imperial Activism." *Departures in Critical Qualitative Research* 5, no. 3 (2016): 116–25.

————. "The U.S. and Israel make Connections for US: Anti-Imperialism and Black-Palestinian Solidarity." *Critical Ethnic Studies Association Journal* 3, no. 2 (2016): 15. http://www.kzoo.edu/praxis/anti-imperialism-and-black-palestinian-solidarity/#_ednref7.

Nadasen, Premilla. *Welfare Warriors: The Welfare Rights Movement in the United States*. New York: Routledge, 2005.

Natarajan, Vani, and Hannah Mermelstein. "Knowledge, Access and Resistance: A Conversation on Librarians and Archivists to Palestine." In *Informed Agitation: Library and Information Skills in Social Justice Movements and Beyond*, edited by Melissa Monroe, 247–61. Sacramento, CA: Library Juice Press,

2014. Accessed June 23, 2017. http://librarianswithpalestine.org/publications /informed-agitation-chapter/.

Neal, Larry. "The Black Arts Movement." *Drama Review: TDR* 12, no. 4 (1968): 28–39.

Nye, Naomi Shihab. "Always Talking: A Poem for Dareen Tatour." *Arabic Literature and Translation*, August 2, 2016. https://arablit.org/2016/08/02/talking -forever-a-poem-by-naomi-shihab-nye-for-dareen-tatour/.

———. "Cross that Line." *Mizna* 1, no. 2 (1999): 10.

———. "For the 500th Dead Palestinian, Ibtisam Bozieh." In *19 Varieties of Gazelle: Poems of the Middle East*, 53–54. New York: Greenwillow Books, 1994.

———. "Long Overdue." In Akash and Mattawa, *Post-Gibran*, 127–32.

———. "On Growing up in Ferguson and Palestine." *Washington Post*, August 28, 2014. https://www.washingtonpost.com/posteverything/wp/2014/08/28/on -growing-up-in-ferguson-and-gaza/.

Olwan, Dana M. "Four Pedagogies of Solidarity in Suheir Hammad's 'First Writing Since.'" In *Muslim Women, Transnational Feminism and the Ethics of Pedagogy: Contested Imaginaries in Post-9/11 Cultural Practice*, edited by Lisa K. Taylor and Jasmine Zine, 110–31. London: Routledge, 2014.

———. "Gendered Violence, Cultural Otherness, and Honour Crimes in Canadian National Logics." *Canadian Journal of Sociology* 38, no. 4 (2013): 533–55.

Orfalea, Gregory, and Sharif Elmusa, eds. *Grape Leaves: A Century of Arab American Poetry*. Northampton, MA: Interlink, 2000.

Oumlil, Kenza. "'Talking Back': The Poetry of Suheir Hammad." *Feminist Media Studies* 13, no. 5 (2013): 850–59.

Perry, Imani. *Prophets of the Hood: Politics and Poetics in Hip Hop*. Durham: Duke Univ. Press, 2004.

Perry, Theresa, and Lisa Delpit, eds. *The Real Ebonics Debate: Power, Language, and the Education of African-American Children*. Boston: Beacon, 1998.

Phillips, Caryl. "What Is Africa to Me Now?" *Research in African Literatures* 46, no. 4 (2015): 10–14.

Pickens, Therí A. "Modern Family: Circuits of Transmission between Arabs and Blacks." *Comparative Literature* 68, no. 2 (2016): 130–40.

———. *New Body Politics: Narrating Arab and Black Identity in the Contemporary United States*. London: Routledge, 2014.

Ray, Sangeeta. "Reading Woman, Reading Essence, Whither Gender?" In *Gayatri Chakravorty Spivak: In Other Words*, 107–38. Sussex: Wiley-Blackwell, 2009.

Razack, Sherene. *Casting Out: The Eviction of Muslims from Western Law and Politics*. Toronto: Univ. of Toronto Press, 2007.

Rhodes, Jane. *Framing the Black Panther Party: The Spectacular Rise of a Black Power Icon*. Champaign: Univ. of Illinois Press, 2017.

Rickford, John Russell, and Russell John Rickford. *Spoken Soul: The Story of Black English*. New York: Wiley, 2002.

Roediger, David. *Colored White: Transcending the Racial Past*. Berkeley: Univ. of California Press, 2002.

Rose, Tricia. *Black Noise: Rap Music and Black Culture in Contemporary America*. Middletown, CT: Wesleyan Univ. Press, 1994.

Rosello, Mireille. *Declining the Stereotype: Ethnicity and Representation in French Cultures*. Hanover, NH: Univ. Press of New England, 1998.

Sabry, Somaya Sami. *Arab-American Women's Writing and Performance: Orientalism, Race, and the Idea of The Arabian Nights*. New York: Tauris, 2011.

Salaita, Steven. *Arab American Literary Fictions, Cultures, and Politics*. New York: Palgrave Macmillan, 2007.

———. *The Holy Land in Transit: Colonialism and the Quest for Canaan*. Syracuse: Syracuse Univ. Press, 2006.

———. *Inter/Nationalism: Decolonizing Native America and Palestine*. Minneapolis: Univ. of Minnesota Press, 2016.

———. *Modern Arab American Fiction: A Reader's Guide*. Syracuse: Syracuse Univ. Press, 2011.

Sale, Maggie. "Call and Response as Critical Method: African-American Oral Traditions and *Beloved*." *African American Review* 2, no. 1 (1992): 41–50.

Saliba, Therese. "June Jordan's Songs of Lebanon and Palestine." *The Feminist Wire*, March 24, 2016. http://www.thefeministwire.com/2016/03/june-jordans-songs-of-palestine/.

———. "Resisting Invisibility: Arab Americans in Academia and Activism." In *Arabs in America: Building a New Future*, edited by Michael Suleiman, 304–19. Philadelphia: Temple Univ. Press, 1999.

Samhan, Helen. "Not Quite White: Race Classification and the Arab-American Experience." In *Arabs in America: Building a New Future*, edited by Michael Suleiman, 209–26. Philadelphia: Temple Univ. Press, 1999.

———. "Politics and Exclusion: The Arab American Experience." *Journal of Palestine Studies* 16, no. 2 (1987): 11–28.

Sarnou, Dalal. "Narratives of Arab Anglophone Women and the Articulation of a Major Discourse in a Minor Literature." *International Studies: Interdisciplinary Political and Cultural Journal* 16, no. 1 (2014): 65–81.

Schotten, Heike. "Analysis: Racism and Rhetoric from Ferguson to Palestine." Ma'an News Agency, January 22, 2015. http://www.maannews.com/Content.aspx?id=755659.

Seidel, Timothy. "'Occupied Territory is Occupied Territory': James Baldwin, Palestine and the Possibilities of Third World Solidarity." *Third World Quarterly* 37, no. 9 (2016): 1644–60.

Shalal-Esa, Andrea. "Arab-American Writers Identify with Communities of Color." *Al Jadid* 9, no. 43 (2003): 24–26.

Shamma, Tarek. *Translation and the Manipulation of Difference: Arabic Literature in Nineteenth-Century England.* London: Routledge, 2014.

Sheehi, Stephen. "Untranslatability, Discomfort, Ideology: Should We Teach Arabic Literature?" In *Teaching Modern Arabic Literature in Translation*, edited by Michelle Hartman, 41–61. New York: MLA, 2018.

Shih, Brian, and Yohuru Williams, eds. *The Black Panthers: Portraits from an Unfinished Revolution.* New York: Nation Books, 2016.

Shohat, Ella, and Robert Stam. *Race in Translation: Culture Wars around the Postcolonial Atlantic.* New York: NYU Press, 2012.

Simmons. Danny. *Def Poetry Jam on Broadway . . . and More: The Choice Collection.* New York: Atria, 2003.

Smethurst, James. *The Black Arts Movement: Literary Nationalism in the 1960s and 1970s.* Chapel Hill: Univ. of North Carolina Press, 2006.

Smitherman, Geneva. *Talkin and Testifyin: The Language of Black America.* Detroit: Wayne State Univ. Press, 1977.

———. *Talkin That Talk: Language, Culture and Education in African America.* New York: Routledge, 2000.

———. "What Is Africa to Me?": Language, Ideology and "African American." *American Speech* 66, no. 2 (1991): 115–32.

———. *Word from the Mother: Language and African Americans.* New York: Routledge, 2006.

Spivak, Gayatri Chakravorty. *In Other Worlds: Essays in Cultural Politics.* London: Routledge, 2006 [1987].

———. *Other Asias.* Oxford: Blackwell, 2008.

———. "The Politics of Translation." In *Outside in the Teaching Machine*, 179–200. London: Routledge, 1993.

Tahawy, Miral al-. *Brooklyn Heights*. Translated by Samah Selim. Cairo: American Univ. in Cairo Press, 2012.

Tahtawi, Rifa'a Rafi' al-. *An Imam in Paris: Al-Tahtawi's Visit to France 1826–1831*. Translated by Daniel Newman. London: Saqi, 2011.

Taylor, Keeanga-Yamahtta. *From #BlackLivesMatter to Black Liberation*. Chicago: Haymarket, 2016.

Third World Students in Solidarity with Arab Brothers and Sisters. "Third World People Must Work for the Liberation of Palestine." *The Daily Collegian*, October 26, 1973, 3.

Thobani, Sunera. *Exalted Subjects: The Making of Race and Nation in Canada*. Toronto: Univ. of Toronto Press, 2007.

Thomas, Greg. "Blame it on the Sun: George Jackson and the Poetry of Palestinian Resistance." *Comparative American Studies* 13, no. 4 (2015): 236–53.

Ujayli, Shahla. *A Sky So Close to Us*. Translated by Michelle Hartman. Northampton, MA: Interlink, 2018.

Venuti, Lawrence. "Hijacking Translation: How Comp Lit Continues to Suppress Translated Texts." *boundary 2* 43, no. 2 (2016): 179–204.

———. *The Translator's Invisibility: A History of Translation*. London: Routledge, 2005.

Walker, Alice. *The Color Purple*. New York: Pocket, 1985.

———. "Looking for Zora [1975]." In *In Search of Our Mothers' Gardens*, 395–411. New York: Houghton Mifflin, 1983.

Warner, Marina. "Radwa Ashour: Obituary." *Guardian*, December 8, 2014. https://www.theguardian.com/books/2014/dec/08/radwa-ashour.

West, Stan. "An Afrocentric Look at the Arab Community." *Mizna* 2, no. 3 (2000): 20–22.

Wright, Richard. *Black Boy*. New York: Harper Perennial, 1945.

Yassin-Kassab, Robin. "Review: *Mornings in Jenin*, by Susan Abulhawa," *Sunday Times*, February 8, 2010.

Index

Arabian Jazz, 31, 128, 146, 186, 187, 246n12
Arabic language, 30, 73–76, 128–33, 152, 212, 251n16; grammar shared with Black language, 66–72; marginalized in postcolonial studies, 253n45; mixing with English, 51, 53–56, 59, 64–65, 97, 133–53, 155, 162–82; speaking in United States, 43, 34–35; as spoken language, 110, 159; spoken Palestinian, 63, 118–20, 133–53, 155; translation of, into English, 218, 221, 226–27, 229–38, 259n60, 263n48, 271n73, 274n76
Arabica, 103
Arab Women's Solidarity Association, 22
Arafat, Yasser, 88
Ashcroft, Bill, 64, 253n45
Ashour, Radwa, 7, 11, 198, 199–238, 267n36, 271n23; Black America/n solidarity and, 26–27, 35–36, 240, 255n70, 268n55, 269n81, 274n73
Atshan, Sa'ed, 23–24, 102
Australia, 194; Aboriginal Australians, 88, 195, 197
Awad, Yousef, 250–251n81, 268n66
AWSA (Arab Women's Solidarity Association), 22
Ayoub, Dima, 264n56

Bab al-Louq, 222
back translation. *See* translation, back
Baldwin, James, 15, 43, 79, 119, 147, 226, 240, 262n38; Black English, 38, 41, 50, 143, 225; breaking English, 47–48, 49, 53, 120, 136, 306; Zionism, 13–14
Baltimore, 8
Bambara, Toni Cade, 265n3

Baraka, Amiri, 33, 83–84, 113, 114, 236; in Melhem's poetry, 92, 94, 97–99, 229
Barakat, Deah, 19
Barakat, Leïla, 264n54
Barghouti, Mourid, 199, 231, 271n2, 274n67
Barghouti, Tamim, 231, 274n67
Bayoumi, Moustafa, 25
BDS movement, 5, 23
Beastie Boys, 185
Bedouin, 107–8
Beirut, 60, 141, 142, 151, 187, 201
Beloved, 50, 146, 153, 156–57, 162, 164, 167, 236, 262n38
Berrigan, Daniel, 85
Big Pimpin', 188–89, 269n72
bilingualism, 64–65, 167, 178; English-Arabic, 64
Bir Zeit University, 20
Bird, Joan, 99
Bizmarkie, 85
Black Arts Movement, 38, 57, 84, 95, 99, 251n2; in relation to literary reclamation, 44, 49, 92, 97
Black English. *See* Black Language
Black feminism. *See* feminisms, Black
Black4Palestine, 1, 10, 20, 23, 202
Black Freedom Struggle, 44, 90, 95, 250n67
Black Language, 57, 163, 165, 177, 190, 255n77, 259n51; Ebonics debate, 38–50; interaction with Arabic language, 97, 110, 204, 226, 255n70; use of, in Suheir Hammad, 56, 59, 64–66, 67, 69–70; use of, in Susan Abulhawa, 119, 120, 128, 137, 143, 146, 153
Black Lives Matter, 1, 19–20, 111, 113, 119, 247n31

Michelle Hartman is professor of Arabic literature and director of the Institute of Islamic Studies at McGill University. Her research focuses on language use in literature by Arab authors. Her previous book, *Native Tongue, Stranger Talk: The Arabic and French Literary Landscapes of Lebanon*, was also published by Syracuse University Press. Her edited volume, *Teaching Modern Arabic Literature in Translation*, was recently issued by the MLA. She is also a literary translator from Arabic and French to English. Her most recent works include Radwa Ashour's *The Journey* and Shahla Ujayli's *A Sky So Close to Us*, both published by Interlink Books.